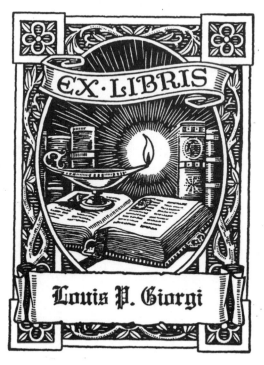

FRANCIS OF ASSISI

FRANCIS
of
ASSISI

John
Holland Smith

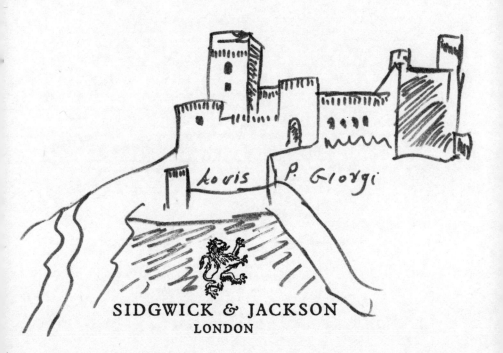

SIDGWICK & JACKSON
LONDON

First published in Great Britain in 1972
by Sidgwick and Jackson Limited
Copyright © 1972 John Holland Smith

For A.C.C.

ISBN 0 283 97894 5

Printed in Great Britain by
William Clowes & Sons, Limited
London, Beccles and Colchester
for Sidgwick and Jackson Limited
1 Tavistock Chambers, Bloomsbury Way
London WC1A 2SG

Contents

Illustrations

The plates are by courtesy of the Mansell Collection, Popperfoto, the Mary Evans Picture Library, and *Réalités*

I

Italy 1198

'My brothers: praise God who created you, and dressed you with feathers, and gave you wings to fly with, and endowed you with the pureness of the air, and gives you the food you need.'

Saint Francis's preaching to the birds has been one of the favourite subjects for the Christian artist since Giotto painted the first cycle of scenes from the saint's legend in the Upper Church of Assisi. The story is capable of touching even those rationally convinced that if Francis ever did preach to the birds, the birds did not sit and listen, for all that the legends assure us that they did, and the brothers at the Carcere, a hermitage near to Assisi, still show pilgrims the tree where this miracle of avine endurance occurred.

Why the persistent legends – and why, after seven hundred and fifty years, the pilgrims? For still they come to this once-quiet corner of provincial Umbria, between the mountains and the plain of the Tiber, as they have come daily through all the centuries to see where the Poor Man of Assisi taught, and perhaps worked miracles, and is buried.

Why?

Not because the birds listened to his preaching. To be remembered so long, and by so many, a man has to have more to offer than a tongue eloquent enough to charm the birds off the trees or a sinner into church. If Francis had been simply another medieval miracle-worker, another scourge of the popes and thorn in the side of bad barons and worse bishops, the modern world would never have heard of him. The truth lies deeper, in his hard character, and the abrasion of that character on his times. The legends show very little of this real Francis, and the well-known portraits even less; to find him, one must put aside the awestruck birds and even the awestruck crowds of his later years, and see him in his world as that world really was. The portrait that then emerges is to some extent an unexpected one, but it is much more human and credible than that the Lives and the frescoes propose for our reverence. Its significance for our own times, if it has one – and the feeling that it has seems still to be widely current – must be left to the reader's own evaluation.

In the Middle Ages Assisi, a hill-town crowning a south-western spur from Mount Subasio, was the natural northern outpost of the Duchy of Spoleto, a broad valley ringed with hills, whose wealth lay in the rich agricultural lands between Assisi and the city of Spoleto itself at its southern end. The nearest towns to Assisi of any consequence were Foligno to the south, in the heart of the Duchy, and the 'foreign' city of Perugia bordering Papal Tuscany, a few miles to the north-west, beyond the Tiber.

At high summer in the year 1198, when Francis of Assisi was between seventeen and eighteen years of age, a German knight named Conrad of Urslingen rode proudly through the stubble-fields of Spoleto, saying a reluctant farewell to the vineyards and olive groves, the monasteries and hill villages that he had ruled so heavily for twenty years past. At Narni, a few days later, he was to kneel in submission before the legates of the Lord Pope Innocent III and surrender into their hands the fief he had once received as a reward for valour from his sworn liege-lord, the late Christian of Buch, Archbishop of Mainz and commanding general in Italy to the Emperor Frederick Barbarossa: the Duke of Spoleto would kneel to the representatives of the Servant of the Servants of God. These were humiliating days for every German in Italy.

As the Duke rode away, on his duchy's northern border the fortress of Assisi burned fiercely, while under a blood-red banner proclaiming 'Liberty' men were already tearing stones from its keep to build a wall around their city.

It is impossible to catch the whole spirit of an age, or even a year, in a single, simple image. But the picture of the knightly Duke Conrad riding to surrender his lands and people to the pope's political commissioners in 1198 reflects much of the truth

about the world in which John Bernardone, Saint Francis of
Assisi, came to maturity. He must have stood with his adolescent
contemporaries and watched the duke's men evacuate the *rocca*,
and he may well have been one of the gang who sacked it in the
name of freedom. Certainly the knightly ideal embodied for him
throughout his childhood by the Duke of Spoleto and the nobles
of his train coloured his thinking till the day he died, and Pope
Innocent's demonstrated ability to give orders to dukes as well
as to clergymen made a deep impression on him. Although few
political events exerted an overt influence on the day-to-day
course of his life, the whole of his story is nevertheless coloured
by the political and religious problems of his times.

For a century and a half, ever since the descendants of Tancred
of Hauteville had conquered southern Italy, there had been four
major contenders for power in the peninsula: the Normans, a
dying force by the 1190s except in Sicily; the Lombards of the
north and centre, dreaming of the independence they believed
their cities had enjoyed four centuries earlier when a Lombard
king had worn Milan's Iron Crown; the Germans, convinced that
their emperor was entitled to rule all Italy as the successor to
Otto the Great and so ultimately of Charlemagne; and the papacy,
certain always that it was destined to control the world, and
temporarily anxious then to govern central Italy and prevent a
union between the Germans of the north and those of the south.

The geography of the duchy of Spoleto made it a crucial area
in this struggle. It lay across the main route from Rome to
Ravenna, and close to the main roads from Rome to northern
Italy. Racially, its population was very mixed, but its sympathies
were with the Lombards and their dreams of independence. The
popes had long claimed but rarely held it. It had come into the
hands of Conrad of Urslingen after a long and bloody war,
sparked off by a revolt of the Lombard cities against the policies
of the Emperor Frederick Barbarossa, who in 1159 had responded
to a demand by Pope Alexander III for a return of some nine
central Italian fiefs to the papacy by electing an antipope and
appointing his own bishops.

One of Barbarossa's appointees had been 'Archbishop' Christian
of Buch. He was a better soldier than he was churchman, and
Frederick had named him commander in the fight to regain the
rebel Lombard cities. Among the best captains serving under him

had been Conrad of Urslingen. City by city, the Germans had reconquered Lombardy. The duchy of Spoleto, with the cities of Assisi, Foligno, and Spoleto itself, had fallen in 1174, about eight years before Francis's birth, and Archbishop Christian had given it as a fief to Conrad in recognition of his courage in the field.

But the war was not yet over. In May 1176 the Lombards had smashed a German army led by the Emperor Frederick himself, at the Battle of Legnano, and at this point Pope Alexander III had intervened, arranging a peace conference at Anagni to cobble together a treaty legalizing the position of the irregular bishops and bringing tranquillity to Italy. One of the four imperial delegates at Anagni was Archbishop Christian, and partly because of his loyalty to those who had served him well during the war – he was determined that such men as Conrad should not be forced to surrender what they had won – it took eighteen months to settle the peace terms. Even then, the Lombards rejected the settlement, not making their peace with the Empire till the signature of the Peace of Constance in 1183. One of the provisions finally agreed at Anagni was, as Christian had insisted, that the pope should recognize the rights of German lords granted Lombard holdings, so Conrad of Urslingen was confirmed in his Italian fief, and German-paid troops made themselves at home in the *rocca* at Assisi, while the *majores* of the city, those few families with claims to nobility there, sought accommodations with the conqueror which would preserve their towered palaces and fortunes in land for a few more generations. It was not precisely what the Lombards had hoped for when they had risen in the name of Italian freedom.

Assisi now became a frontier post in the fullest sense. Perugia, its nearest neighbour, was in papal hands. The garrison of the *rocca* was not concerned with anything except preserving the duke's interests. As long as those interests were not threatened, and rents were regularly paid both in kind and service, it did not matter to the soldiers whether Assisians and Perugians squabbled or not. They did quarrel, for like many neighbouring Italian cities, their towns were deadly rivals. In the long run, to both Assisians and Perugians, the provisions of the Treaty of Anagni and the Peace of Constance were excuses for prolonging their differences, as indeed any other imaginable settlement would also have been.

One of the provisions of the Peace of Constance insisted on by the pope's legates was that the cities of the former Lombard League should be permitted to elect consuls responsible for local affairs from among their middle-class, the *minores*. Whatever Duke Conrad's private feelings about such interference by the lower-born natives in the mystique of government, he was careful to implement this clause in the treaty. Assisi's archives show that he approved the election of the city's two first *consules* within months of the agreement's ratification. Nevertheless, for the next fourteen years Assisi's real business, the constant watch on the fords of the Tiber and the important river-crossing at Saint John's Bridge on the road to Perugia, was carried on from the *rocca* under neither the *consules* nor the *majores* of Assisi, but Duke Conrad's Germans.

The compromise reached under the treaty outlived all its signatories. Officially, the papacy and the empire were at peace throughout Francis's boyhood, and it suited both pope and emperor that their local commanders should enforce tranquil conditions throughout turbulent Italy. Both were too preoccupied with events in the Near East to want trouble nearer home – though the Italians often gave it to them. Islamic armies were massing against the Norman Kingdom of Jerusalem, and in 1187 the Holy City fell to the forces of Saladin, after the most resounding defeat Christian arms had suffered for centuries, at the Battle of the Horns of Hattin. By 1189 all that remained in Christian hands of what had been won in the first crusade were the ports of Jaffa, Acre, Tyre, and Antioch. It was clear to the reigning pope, Clement III, that something had to be done quickly, if anything was to be saved at all. He preached a crusade so successfully that he was soon able to send a dispatch to Constantinople announcing that all the cities of Italy and also five kings from the rest of Europe and the Emperor Frederick himself had all sworn to fight for the cross.

Barbarossa was over seventy, but while the kings of England and France were hesitating over accepting the Truce of God proposed to them by Clement's legates, he set off at the head of a German army to reconquer the Holy Land, only to drown in a bizarre accident while trying to ford the River Aleph on the frontiers of Syria. As soon as his death was known, the Lombard cities of Italy revolted against the Germans.

Barbarossa's son and elected successor, Henry VI, felt bound

by none of his father's oaths. He had spent years intriguing and
fighting for power in Italy, and was heir to the throne of Sicily by
his marriage to Constance, the daughter of its Norman King
William III. He had no intention of throwing all this away for the
sake of an eastern adventure, the outcome of which he could not
foresee. In 1191, he swept through the levies of the Lombard
cities as though they had not existed, and was crowned as King
of the Romans at Rome by Clement III's successor, Pope Celestine III.

Only Naples and Sicily stood out against him. He left an army
to besiege Naples, and himself forced a landing in Sicily, but met
strong Norman opposition there, under a rival heir to the throne,
Prince Tancred, and his son-in-law Walter III of Brienne.
Ominous rumblings of revolt from northern Europe compelled
his return to Germany before he could achieve much more than
a quarrel with the pope, who as usual was trying to play middle-
man between the Normans and the Germans, the banker who in
the long run could not lose.

Throughout the Lombard states, this renewed tension between
the pope and the emperor served as an excuse for re-opening old
arguments; and on their frontiers rival cities such as Assisi and
Perugia squared up to one another again while Henry and
Celestine played diplomatic chess with the future of Europe.

According to the town records of Perugia, that city felt strong
enough in 1194 to ignore the threat of papal sanctions and attack
Assisi, driving Duke Conrad's garrison out of the *rocca* and
sacking the soldiers' quarters. There is no other record of this
skirmish, and in the context of European events it was obviously
insignificant. Duke Conrad appears not even to have mounted a
punitive expedition. There was a risk, though probably a remote
one, that such an expedition would have brought him to war
with papal Tuscany, and for the time being at least none of the
principals wanted war in central Italy. He left it to the elected
consuls of Assisi to make the peace and demand compensation.

That same year, having confirmed his authority in Germany
with his sword, the Emperor Henry returned to Sicily, and was
crowned King of that island in Palermo, so closing the German
ring around the pope and holding him in check.

The next three years were relatively peaceful, though filled with
the hatred of those French-born lords of the south like Walter of

Brienne to whom a German victory meant dispossession, and loss of revenues and power. In fact, peace survived only because neither the pope nor the emperor could see a move that must be decisively advantageous for his side. Then the situation changed dramatically. On 28 September 1197, Henry VI died at Messina, leaving as his designated heir his three-year-old son by Princess Constance, Prince Frederick of Sicily, who was later to be known as 'the Wonder of the World'.

In those Norman lands, where the hereditary principle was already firmly established, no one doubted that Frederick should be the next king, no one, that is, except those (including his mother) so fiercely opposed to German domination that they would rather be ruled by a Norman usurper than by a true but part-German prince.

In the German world, however, although Henry's nomination of his son as his successor carried weight, blood was not as important as the ability to meet the practical demands of the immediate situation. The empire needed an adult ruler, capable of making and enforcing decisions. Unfortunately, the electors were not unanimous as to who that adult should be. They concurred only in rejecting the infant prince as their new ruler, though they confirmed his title to Sicily and approved the late emperor's choice of his brother, the prince's uncle Philip of Swabia, as his guardian there.

On 8 May 1198, this same Philip was himself elected emperor, but on 9 June the Rhineland princes held a counter-election and nominated Otto of Brunswick, a Guelph, to rule them. Civil war in Germany was inevitable.

Meanwhile, a few months after the death of Henry VI, on 8 January 1198, Pope Celestine III had died at Rome, and within hours of the cardinals assembling to elect his successor, power in the church had passed into the most capable hands ever to wield it, the hands of the youngest cardinal at the conclave, Cardinal-Deacon Lothario di Segni, the mighty Pope Innocent III.

Lothario di Segni is a key-figure in the history of the Franciscan movement. His somewhat cold sympathy with Francis's ideals later decided the issue between the Order's survival or dissolution. From his descent and upbringing, it is remarkable that he found within himself any understanding of Francis, the son of a merchant from provincial Assisi. The child of Count Trasimond of

Segni and a Roman lady named Clarina Scotta, he was kin to most of the ancient Roman nobility. He had been educated first at Rome; then at the recently-founded Universities of Paris and Bologna, where he had studied theology and law. Returning to Rome in the mid-eighties, he had been ordained subdeacon by Pope Gregory VIII in 1187, the year Jerusalem fell to Saladin, and that same year had found himself nephew to a pope when Gregory died and Clarina's brother Paul was elected as Clement III. The new pope had lost no time in promoting his sister's son, making him Cardinal-Deacon of Saints Serguis and Bacchus, a post he filled until his own election as pope some eight years later, at the age of thirty-seven.

As a Cardinal-Deacon, he had lived quietly, making a reputation for himself as a writer, a preacher, and an ascetic, apparently content to play a minimal role in the conflict between Popes Clement and Celestine on the one hand and the increasingly independent and nationalistic kings of Europe on the other. But very soon after his election, Europe began to realize that it had a pope with inflexible ideas about his position. God had set him over the church, and he intended to rule it, and through it, the world.

His tutor at Bologna, the famous canon lawyer Hugaccio, had taught him that 'whatever God can do, the pope can do' and he had learned that lesson well. Only three and a half months after his election, he wrote to the Archbishop of Montreale in Sicily, 'by virtue of this power [over the other Apostles] which Peter received from the Lord, the Holy Roman Church, instituted and founded by the Blessed Peter at the Lord Jesus Christ's command, has received authority over all the churches'. By October of that same year, he had further extended his claims on behalf of himself and the church, in his notorious analogy of the sun and moon:

> The creator of the universe established two great luminaries in the firmament of heaven, the greater to rule the day, the lesser the night. In the same way he appointed two great dignities within the firmament of the universal church. . . . These dignities are the authority of the pontificate and that of royalty. Moreover, the moon derives her light from the sun; and is actually inferior to the sun in both size and quality, position

and effect. In the same way, royal power derives its dignity from the pontiff's authority.

Whether he would have dared to speak so if there had been only one German emperor, or would have succeeded in maintaining his claim had he made it, is still a matter of controversy. It has sometimes been claimed that he asserted his 'total plenitude of power' (*totum plenitudo potestatis*) only over those lands to which the Holy See claimed legal title; this may be literally true, but from time to time the papacy laid claim to most of the known world, and Innocent everywhere acted as though he were what he called himself, God's viceroy and regent in the world, the *Vicarius Christi*.

Among the first to learn how implacably the new pope meant to fight for God's rights were the two most devoted servants of the late Emperor Henry VI then holding land in Italy, the Imperial Seneschal, Markward of Anweiler, the Marquis of Ancona and Duke of Ravenna, and Conrad of Urslingen, the Duke of Spoleto.

To take Spoleto, Ancona, and Ravenna would give the pope the advantage not only of ridding Italy of these two supporters of the Hohenstauffen, but also of splitting German forces in Italy, giving him control of all roads between north and south. Taking advantage of the confused situation in Germany, Innocent advanced papal armies to the frontiers of the states loyal to him in central Italy, and waited. Both Markward and Conrad had seen enough fighting to know when an exposed position becomes untenable. Markward sent to the pope what he claimed was Henry VI's deathbed testament, in which he apparently bequeathed to the Holy See all it claimed in Italy from coast to coast, and reminded the German dukes that they held their lands as fiefs from the pope. It also named the pope as heir to the kingdom of Sicily, if Prince Frederick should die without issue. Whether or not this document was authentic is not known; only fragmentary quotations from it survive. Even if it was genuine, it did not soften the pope's resolve. Papal legates excommunicated Markward. The cities of the former papal states of Romagna and the March of Ancona forthwith repudiated their allegiance to him and their German nobility, and declared for the pope. Markward bowed to the inevitable, withdrawing southwards into the former

Norman territories of Calabria and Apulia, leaving the lesser lords either to follow him or to make what peace they could with the pope.

So by July 1198, Conrad of Urslingen found himself in an unenviable situation. Already in the six months since Innocent's election, he had tried offering men, money, and even – from a distance – fealty to the church, but Innocent would accept only his personal submission to appointed legates. Thus the situation was reached with which this chapter began: Conrad rode sadly through his holdings and on to Narni, and there surrendered his lands into the hands of two of Innocent's cardinals. The pope appointed Cardinal Gregorio Crescenzi as Cardinal-Rector of Spoleto, and Conrad of Urslingen rode north, to join Philip of Swabia in Germany and plot revenge.

It was while Duke Conrad was riding to Narni that the men of Assisi sacked the *rocca* and, determined to try and hold what they had against all comers, built walls around their city. Their independence was short-lived. Assisi's history was necessarily governed by that of Spoleto to the south and Perugia to the northwest. After Duke Conrad's submission, the officials with whom its newly-elected consuls dealt tended to be Roman or 'Italian' ecclesiastics, rather than German knights or clerks: the change was not, probably, as important on the day-to-day level as it has sometimes been made to appear. Once Cardinal-Rector Crescenzi had assumed authority, the Assisians bowed to him.

Much more important was the fact that the rebellion triggered off by the change of overlord was accompanied by civil conflict within Assisi itself, as it was also in many other Lombard towns. The *minores* of Assisi, the 'lesser men' led by the merchants, rose against those with pretensions to aristocratic blood and hereditary rights, the *boni homines*, the *majores*. Houses were burned and the towers guarding aristocratic property were pulled down. The quarter of the *majores* was largely reduced to rubble. A few of the *boni homines* were killed, but most fled to Perugia, where they formed a faction-in-exile powerful enough four years later to provoke a renewal of warfare between that city and their home town.

Francis of Assisi was born in 1181 or 1182, shortly before the signature of the Peace of Constance. The news of the fall of

Jerusalem must have been one of his earliest memories, and the
fact that he himself took a knight's role in the levy of Assisi a few
years after Duke Conrad was expelled from Spoleto shows that
his father must have been prominent in the revolt of the *minores*
in 1198. No boy could have been left untouched by so exciting a
background. Francis certainly was not. When later he himself
bore arms, it was not with any great success, and not for very
long. But he dreamed of a military career, and even after the
dream had faded still thought in crusading and military terms.
The crusaders' cross was his personal sign: he 'made his mark'
with it over, for instance, some cloth he took from his father's
stock to sell for the poor,* and on his first religious habit, the
labourer's smock he wore after renouncing his father's world.
Later in life, he mounted a personal crusade to save the holy
places by converting the Mahommedan sultan with the only
weapon he knew he could sometimes successfully wield, his per-
suasive tongue. He fought for his Lady, poverty. For decades, the
two ideals of the knight and the sovereign pope – the one representing freedom and glory sought through self-discipline and
dedication, the other self-identification with the glory of God and
the aims of the church – were paramount influences in his thinking and actions. Most men found it impossible to reconcile them.
Christian knights were not generally renowned for their Christianity, even when they wore the crusader's cross and were loyal
to it after their fashion. But in his own unique way, Francis did
succeed in bringing together the best from chivalry and from the
church, and perhaps even more surprisingly, in re-expressing it in
terms acceptable to the outcasts of the towns and the soil-bound
labourers and semi-free peasants of the countryside, whose stories
about *il Poverello* struggling to be hermit and knight, cleric,
labourer, and crusader all at the same time, are those by which he
is universally remembered.

Significantly, he never succeeded in identifying himself with the
rising merchant class from which he came, and this despite the
fact that he called his brothers by the name of that class, the
minores. He attracted men from trade to the pursuit of perfection,
but he found no place for proprietorship and acquisitiveness in

---

* I Celano 1, 8; i.e. Thomas of Celano, *Legenda Prima*, 1, 8.

his Order. His rejection of his father's world was total. And this was a pity, for it was with his father's business world that much of the future of Europe lay.

2

John the son of
Peter Bernardone

In the year 1550, deliberately setting out to denigrate the memory of Francis of Assisi, Grafton published in London under the title *Alcoran of the Barefoote Friers* (an English version of the continental *Liber Conformitatem*),* a collection of legends about the saint which the reformers judged either blasphemous or laughable. On the reverse of the title page, in the form of an excerpt from one of the offices of the Roman Catholic church, there appeared the words:

> *Versicle:* Frances is in heaven.
> *Answer:* Who dowsteth that?
> *Anthem:* Al the world.

The reformers' problem was that even as late as 1550, when Franciscans had been making a public spectacle of their disagreements for over two hundred years, very few people did in fact doubt that Francis was in heaven. He was, and for many still is, the ideal Christian. The pre-reformation church had declared him a saint in heaven at the ceremonies of his canonization only two years after his death in October 1226. And for the more romantic and credulous there were many stories like the sworn statement of one of his companions to Thomas of Celano who

---

* A Lutheran satire on Bartholemew of Pisa's *De conformitate vitae beati Francisci ad vitam domini Jesu,* written to demonstrate how closely Francis's life paralleled Christ's, and approved by the General Chapter of the Franciscans in 1399.

composed his *Legenda Prima* (the *First Life of Saint Francis*)*
at the direct command of Pope Gregory IX only two years or so
after Francis died:

> One of his brothers and followers, a man of no small reputation,
> but one whose name I consider it best to conceal, as he does
> not wish to be glorified by such fame while he still lives in the
> flesh, saw the soul of the holy father ascend straight to heaven
> over many waters. It was like a star, but in a certain respect as
> large as the moon, while it had something of the sun's bright-
> ness, and was carried up on a small white cloud.

Thomas's story of the anonymous brother's vision of the holy
father's soul shooting up to heaven like a comet may not reveal
much about the true character of Francis himself, but it does show
the reverence in which his memory was held, and uncovers something of the beliefs and attitudes of those closest to him, beliefs
which must have been coloured by their long and intimate
association with him.

Francis and his associates were men of the Christian Middle
Ages: the point is so obvious that it is easy to overlook its immense
significance. To the brothers who watched him die, heaven was
'up there', beyond 'the waters' of the 'firmament'. Souls stood on
clouds to reach it. The anonymous brother had a vision, and to
Thomas of Celano that vision was as worthy of permanent record
as any other part of Francis's life story. In fact, in the contemporary view it was more worthy of inclusion in this *First Life*
than many other happenings, because it proved how holy
Francis was: he went straight to heaven. Thomas and his contemporaries were devoted to Francis and to God. They really believed in salvation and damnation. Their lives were haunted by
the Four Last Things of theology: death, judgement, heaven,
and hell. They had devoted themselves to Francis and to God in
order to come as safely as possible through the vale of tears, called
this world, and reach heaven by the most direct route available.
The *Life* Thomas wrote at the pope's command is not really the

* The most readily available translations include: P. Hermann, *The First
and Second Life of St Francis*, The Franciscan Herald Press, Chicago,
1963; and N. J. Paterson, *The First Life* in *Early Franciscan Classics*,
St Anthony Guild Press, 1962.

biography of a man named Francis, but the story of Francis's soul and its progress towards God.

Thomas fulfilled his commission well, but his omissions seem unfortunate today. He has so little to say about the circumstances of Francis's daily life. He names his father only by accident, and his blood-brothers not at all. He tells us that as a young man he was extravagant, but not what he paid for his cloaks or his boots. He records that he could sing in French, but not where he had learned that language or why. Franciscans have always gloried in how close Francis came to reproducing in his own life the pattern of the life of Christ; we could wish that Thomas's and the other early lives and legends were not so good an imitation of the gospels of the New Testament, omitting everything that has no obvious spiritual value. All too soon the 'Saint Francis Manufacturing Company' was to take over, not only adding new pious tales to the 'gospel' of Saint Francis, but also fabricating facts to make good the deficiencies from the human interest point of view in the more nearly contemporary records.

All that chapter 1 of the *First Life* records of the circumstances of Francis's birth and childhood is that: 'There was once a man of the city of Assisi, which stands on the edge of the valley of Spoleto, whose name was Francis. From his earliest years, his parents brought him up without discipline, following the foolish standards of the world. He imitated their deplorable way of life for so long that he became even more worldly and loose-living than they were.'

In chapter 53, Francis calls himself the son of Pietro Bernardone: 'When [urged to it by Francis] a brother did, albeit unwillingly, call him a boor, a hired man, a worthless creature, Francis . . . would reply, "The Lord bless you: you have told the exact truth: it is fitting that the son of Peter Bernardone should hear such things".'

A Franciscan living at Erfurt in Germany a quarter of a century after Francis's death fixed the year of his birth as 1182, and the date 1181–82 seems to be confirmed by thirteenth-century chronicles which speak of his dying in his forty-fifth year, in 1226. Yet such was his immaturity at the time of his conversion from his parents' foolish standards, about the year 1205 or 1206, that it seems incredible that he was already then about twenty-five.

His father, Pietro Bernardone, was a cloth merchant. His

mother's name was Giovanna; nothing more is certainly known about her. Despite the frequent claims of later times that the family was noble, no evidence of this exists. There is no justification for presenting Francis's family as anything more grand than an average unit in the new middle classes on which Europe's prosperity was slowly becoming ever more dependent. All that is really known about it was summed up long ago by the careful author of the *Anonymous Life of Saint Francis* now at Brussels: 'There was once a man worthy of respect in the town of Assisi, called Francis, whose father was Pietro Bernardone of the same town, who had a wife Giovanna by name.'

The origin of the surname Bernardone is uncertain. Surnames were only just coming into use in twelfth-century Italy and the grounds on which they were adopted are not well understood. 'Bernardone' may mean 'son of Bernard', or that the family had moved to Assisi from a place near to, or owned by, a monastery of St Bernard. No one knows.

In many later accounts of Francis's family, Giovanna is called *la pica*, or even *di Pica*, as though she had been noble. In the form *di Pica*, the later Middle Ages took her name to mean 'of Picardy' and held it to prove that she was at least the daughter of a knight. This story was still being embroidered upon as late as the year 1703, when a certain Father Frassen claimed to have proved that Giovanna di Pica was related to a Provençal family named Bourlemont, and so was a woman of Picardy, which explained why her son spoke French. In fact, Picardy seems to have acquired its name only in the thirteenth century, the reference being to the skill with which its soldiers wielded their unhandy long pikes, and *la pica* was not a surname as we know it, but a nickname. It meant 'the magpie', and suggests that Giovanna was a loud-mouthed, acquisitive woman, with an eye for a glittering effect.

Research into Assisi's town records has shown that Assisians were free with such nicknames in the twelfth and thirteenth centuries: those culled from the archives include *la rossa*, 'the red', *la Spoletina*, 'her from Spoleto', *la sfacciata*, 'the saucy one', and *la torta*, 'the tart' or 'the pudding'.*

---

* Cf. G. Abate, *Storia e legenda intorna alla nascita di S.F.A.*, in *Miscellanea Francescana* 48, pp. 515ff., and 49, pp. 123ff, and pp. 350ff.

According to a story related by the Anonymous Chronicler of Brussels* and apparently current at Assisi only a few years after Francis's death:

Giovanna was a woman devout above the ordinary; she had visited the holy sepulchre, the place of the Blessed Archangel Michael,† the houses of the Apostles [in Rome], and daily made efforts to visit other shrines. And she begged the Lord most earnestly in her prayers to give her a son, but always asked that things might be accomplished as was well-pleasing to God. So then she conceived a child. And when she realized that she was near her time, she happened to be alone. And she began to grow faint because of her labour-pains. And she could not give birth to her child on her own. And suddenly there flooded into her mind a recollection of the childbearing of the glorious Virgin, and the humble place in which the Lord had been born. So she followed that pattern, going down into their own stable, where the cows and donkeys were led in, and there, by His Benevolent Will, she gave birth to her son in the middle of them, with very little pain.

So to the devout, Giovanna became the second Mary, and her son was the new Christ from the moment of his birth. To Thomas of Celano, however, when he wrote his *Second Life*, some twenty years after the first, Giovanna was the second Saint Elizabeth, the mother of the second John the Baptist, the herald of Christ, the saint for whom 'John, the son of Peter Bernardone' was named.‡

It is not known whether the story of Francis's birth in a stable was current at Assisi during Giovanna's lifetime. If it was fabricated later, it is of only passing interest, as another example of how Francis's followers were willing to adjust the facts to prove his Christ-likeness. But if it is in any sense true, or if Giovanna herself invented it, it gives an interesting glimpse of the sort of

---

* *Vita S. Francisci Anonyma Bruxellensis*, MS. II. 2326, in the Royal Library at Brussels.

† Monte Gargano, in south-east Italy, where the Archangel had appeared to a local bishop centuries earlier. It had become the favourite place of pilgrimage after Jerusalem, Rome, and St James at Compostella.

‡ II Celano 1, 1, 3.

woman Francis's mother was. Combine it with the implications
of her nickname, and add Thomas of Celano's black-and-white
snapshot of a dissolute woman, bringing up her son 'in accordance with the foolish standards of the world', and she emerges as
a very lively figure indeed – one worthy to join the women in
Chaucer's pilgrim-train to Canterbury a century later; a bustling,
sharp-tongued, inquisitive woman, fond of good living though
she was always in and out of church, artful enough to cajole her
middle-class husband into giving her the money she needed to
visit the kingdom of Jerusalem, where Christ had lived and died,
the miraculous cave where Saint Michael had appeared in A.D. 493,
and Rome, where the pope lived and Saints Peter and Paul were
buried; chattering all the time, until one day she found herself
alone, about to have her first baby, and very much afraid. So for
her own comfort, she re-enacted the birth of Christ, performing
(though she did not realize it) a piece of sympathetic magic more
potent – because she believed vividly in Christ and his Mother –
than the ancient practice of untying every knot in the house to
unknot the womb.

Admittedly, this story of Francis's birth may be wholly untrue.
But if it is true, or if during his childhood Giovanna convinced
herself that it was true, and told it to him as the truth, its influence upon his future thinking about himself, and so ultimately
upon the form of rule he drew up for the lesser brothers, may have
been very profound indeed.

Where exactly in Assisi the Bernardone house and stable stood
is a question hotly disputed at Assisi and among scholars,*
especially those scholars with a religious or financial interest in
the matter, for the two most probable sites belong to different
branches of the Franciscan Order, and it is naturally a matter of
prestige and profit to them to be able to claim the original and
authentic birthplace. Both these sites lie in the quarter now called
Santa Chiara, to the east of the Piazza del Comune. The most
convincing arguments have been made in support of the claims
of the tiny Oratorio di San Francesco Piccolino, in the modern
Vicolo di San Antonio, over the door of which is the inscription
in Latin: '+This oratory was the stable for ox and ass in which

---

* Cf. Englebert, S. Francis of Assisi, appendix (pp. 407ff), Franciscan
Herald Press, 1965.

was born St Francis, the Mirror of the World + '. This inscription has been authoritatively dated on palaeological grounds in the mid-fourteenth century; a hundred years earlier, the house of which the stable-oratory formed part certainly belonged to the Bernardone family: it was included in a list of properties divided between Piccardo and Giovanetto, the saint's nephews, on the death of their father, Angelo Bernardone 'della Picca'. In 1281–82, the archives record, Piccardo erected a commemorative arch over the door, to mark the centenary of his uncle's birth. Traces of an ancient flat arch can still be seen over the pointed arch of the oratory's present doorway. The later history of this property is fairly well documented, and if no claims were advanced for other sites this oratory, now the property of the Conventual Friars, would probably find general acceptance as the birthplace.*

The legends say that during Francis's infancy Giovanna was frequently assured by a variety of persons that her son would one day amount to something in the world. Almost all such stories should be regarded as later inventions, prophecies after the event. It may well be true that Francis was blessed by a tramp or beggar who came to his parents' door, took the baby into his arms, and promised that he would do great things; Bartholemew of Pisa alleges that it was so, and there is no reason to doubt him. Tramps and beggars have been ingratiating themselves with doting parents in this way ever since there have been house doors

---

* Unfortunately, however, the claims for the other 'traditional' site are nearly as convincing. It puts the original home of the family where the Chiesa nuova now stands: the 'new church' was built in the seventeenth century with funds provided by King Philip III of Spain on the site of an old property belonging to a family named Bini, who claimed that it had once been owned by Pietro Bernardone. The only claim publicly made for the site when King Philip's emissaries purchased it was however that it had once belonged to the Bernardone family, and no reference was made to Francis's birth and childhood there when the new church was dedicated to 'the Conversion of Saint Francis and all the saints of the Minorite Order'. The further claim that Francis had actually been born there was not advanced until after the church had been completed. A third possible site lies right over on the far side of the town, between the Benedictine church of St Paul and the church of San Nicolo di Piazza, in the San Giacomo quarter, close to the great basilica of Saint Francis. This site certainly once belonged to the Bernardone family, as the town's archives prove, but nothing else is certain.

to knock at in search of a dole. But that this particular tramp was an angel in disguise, or had been specially inspired with a divine message, as some chroniclers later than Bartholemew claim, is at best undemonstrable.

Pietro and Giovanna's son was baptized Giovanni at the episcopal church of Santa Maria Maggiore, in the upper town at Assisi, where all baptisms were then performed. The 'new' cathedral of San Rufino, where the font is preserved, had been begun in the 1140s, but in the eighties had still not yet been consecrated.*

The official *Life of Saint Francis*, written by Saint Bonaventure, the Minister General of the Franciscan Order, after the chapter of 1266 at which it was decided that such a life was needed, because of the proliferation of apochryphal and spurious lives, records that Francis was sent to school to the priests of Saint George's, also in Assisi. But he seems to have learned little from them except enough Latin to read with difficulty and write with great labour. In later life, the clerkly Brother Leo usually acted as his secretary; although an example of his signature survives, he preferred to make his mark with a Greek cross, the letter *tau*, the cross used by the crusaders. However, somewhere – probably in the first instance from his father and his father's business acquaintances – he learned enough French to be able to converse in that language, and earn himself the nickname *il Francesco*, 'the Frenchman', although whether it was given him by his father, as pious legend has always maintained, or by the wits of Assisi, is uncertain. Whoever gave it to him, it was the obvious name for a boy wearing French cloth, talking with French visitors, and singing French tunes, the songs of the troubadours and jongleurs. John Bernardone became 'Francis' early in life, and has remained Francis throughout the years since.

Which dialect of French he spoke is unknown. Because he was called 'the Frenchman' and called his language 'French', it is

---

* For another view, see Fortini, *Nova vita di San Francesco*, vol. 1, 1, 106. Over many years, Fortini, a lawyer by profession, has researched into the records of Assisi for traces of persons and places mentioned in the various *Lives* of Saint Francis, publishing his results in several volumes; his material is of the greatest interest, though the conclusions he has drawn from it have been challenged on many points, especially by Franciscan historians.

usually assumed that his dialect was that of the north and the Ile de France, not the langue d'oc of the county of Toulouse, which further west towards Navarre shaded into early Spanish. But although he once himself proposed to go to Paris, most of the traces of 'French' influence in his life seem to relate to southern France, and there are no proofs that Pietro Bernardone's travels in search of business took him further north than the great fairs at Toulouse, Lyons, and Montpellier. The question remains open.

Francis's everyday language must have been the current Umbrian dialect: not yet Italian, but a mingling of late Latin and dialect words from which Italian was rapidly emerging. He died just thirty-nine years before the birth of Dante, the first and greatest of the Italian vernacular poets.

According to Thomas of Celano and later chroniclers, the upbringing Francis received from his parents was not one to find approval from strict Christian moralists, and the best efforts of Saint George's priests did little to mitigate its evil effects. At that time, the *First Life* says (I Celano, 1) there had 'spread everywhere among those bearing the name Christian the most depraved custom of trying to bring up their children from the cradle without any training or discipline. ... As soon as infants started to talk ... they were taught by word and action the most shameful and odious things. By the time they were weaned, they had been forced not only to say but to do gross and indecent things ... [so that finally] a rotten tree from a rotten rootstock [they were] left with nothing of Christianity but the name'.

What truth there is behind this it is impossible to say. Almost all medieval writers make the worst of the moral climate prevailing outside the religious orders to which they so often belonged. They were especially inclined to exaggerate when their subject was the life of a holy man, converted from 'the world' to a different way of life. There is no evidence to suggest that Assisi was morally more corrupt than any other part of Italy in the late twelfth century, or that the twelfth century was more impure than any other. Men like Thomas of Celano joined religious orders because they believed that the most ordinary ways of the world led to damnation.

However, regarding Francis's upbringing, Celano goes on to

say that 'until his twenty-fifth year, Francis went further in his
enthusiasm for frivolities' than any of his contemporaries, and
hence was 'universally admired' not only because 'he struggled to
outdo others in his display of worldly magnificence, in pranks, in
fashion, in lewd and asinine talk, in songs, in his flowing style
of dress', but also because he was 'a very kind man, thoughtful
and amiable' (1, 2).

Taking these passages together, we are less shocked than Celano
obviously feels we ought to be. If the Bernardones taught their
son to be 'very kind . . . thoughtful and amiable' in an age when
arrogant haughtiness was the mark of a gentleman, they had not
done badly by him, at least by our standards. However, Celano
and Francis's later biographers thought differently. Not only did
they habitually present the palest of moral greys as black but
also they tended to see the world as so corrupt as not to be worth
thinking about. This view was strictly speaking unorthodox, and
probably none of them would have been willing to express it so
bluntly, but it did colour much of their thinking. In the opinion
of medieval proto-puritans generally, children should be baptized
and then not brought up in this world, to live it to the full, but
led through this world to heaven. Anything that did not serve
this end was imperfect if not actually evil.

Francis's parents obviously disagreed. To them, and hundreds
of thousands like them, it was important that their eldest son in
particular should learn to be a man living in the world of men, fit
one day to succeed his father as the head of the family business.
Francis showed no inclination to be a monk. His manifest
destiny was to work hard at wresting a living from a hard
world. He deserved what few pleasures the world offered, the
comfort of good clothes, music, and laughter.

As for Celano's allegation that Pietro and Giovanna deliberately
taught Francis 'gross and indecent things', till with others of his
generation he became 'a rotten tree' growing from a 'rotten rootstock', it is probably safe to ignore it. Celano was all too obviously
biased against Pietro Bernardone, and his strictures recall those
of some contemporary clergy against the freedom, which they
call licence, with which many children are brought up today.
Had Thomas of Celano lived to attend the Second Vatican Council, he would undoubtedly have been listed among the blackest
of the conservatives.

If there were ever any stories to support the assertion that Francis sank deeper into moral turpitude than any of his contemporaries, they have disappeared. Later Franciscans deliberately suppressed surviving details of Francis's early excesses, and in 1260 purged the office of matins on his feastday of a line declaring that he went 'further than his teachers in immorality', substituting for it the thought that 'by the graces of God, he was mercifully restrained'.* His secretary Brother Leo was strongly censured in a dream for allowing himself to wonder whether Francis had been celibate all his life.† For those ready to accept Bonaventure's authority, his *Life* settled the question by roundly declaring that Francis 'never yielded to the flesh' (1, 1). Despite this, Francis himself said in his *Testament* that he had lived 'in sin'. But what was 'sin' in a world where almost every human activity apart from work and prayer was roundly condemned at some time or another? Even laughter was suspect, although joy was a Christian virtue.

As early as the fifth century, St Augustine – whose influence was very powerful in Francis's day – had expressed satisfaction at the Christians' somewhat cold style of joy, saying that their serene and non-dissolute happiness (*serena et non dissoluta hilaris*) was one of the things which had converted him to Christianity from his orthodox pagan beginnings. The serene smile characterized the true Christian. The great Saint Bernard of Clairvaux condemned laughter. So too later in life did Francis himself, at least according to the *Mirror of Perfection*, in which Brother Leo, after relating how Francis rebuked a brother who looked miserable, telling him 'always be joyful in the presence of me and the others' adds the gloss 'not that we should understand or think that our father . . . would have had that joy expressed in laughter, or in the least light word; that would not show spiritual joy, but emptiheadedness and folly'.‡ The serene, not to say insipid, smile of the Angel of Rheims and so many other Gothic works of sculpture and painting was no accident, but really did express the

---

* Cf. O. Oliger, *De ultima mutatione officii S.F.*, in *Archivum Franciscorum Historicum I*, 1908, pp. 45ff.

† Cf. *The Considerations of the Holy Stigmata 4*, Eng. translation in R. Braun, *The Little Flowers of Saint Francis*, Garden City, New York, 1958.

‡ *The Mirror of Perfection*, c. 96.

accepted ideal. A century later, Dante, that great admirer of
Saint Francis, was to write of the most holy trinity itself as
'smiling'.

If laughter was suspect, uncontrolled singing and dancing were
even more deeply frowned upon. Dancing had always seemed to
the clergy a very dubious occupation, and no doubt for perfectly
valid reasons from their point of view, not least among them the
fact that the pagan opposition to the spread of the church still
surviving in the countryside centred on the festivals of the old
religion with their associated dances: sowing, midsummer,
harvest, and midwinter, under their various, often Christianized,
names. All medieval moralists would undoubtedly have agreed
with the author of the *Speculum morale*, in whose view dances
are 'an invention of Satan, frequent occasions of sin, insulting to
God, and times of foolish lightheartedness'.

Foolish lightheartedness had above all else to be avoided, so
singing (often a sign of it) was also considered dangerous. Of
course, the angels and the spheres sing. So too do monks. In fact,
the art of church music reached new peaks of eloquence and
excellence in the twelfth and thirteenth centuries. Unfortunately
for the moralists' peace of mind, however, secular music also
made great strides during the same period. This was the age of the
troubadours and jongleurs, the age of the Courts of Love. What
puritanical mind could fail to be concerned when boys learned
to sing such provocative songs as the notorious *Suscipe flos florem*,
written at about this time (and preserved in the Manuscript of
Benedictbeuren):

> Take, O Rose, this Rose
> It is the flower of love,
> And by this very Rose,
> I captive am of love,

or the love-songs in early French which, within a few years were
to inspire Guillaume de Loris' *Romance of the Rose*?

Thomas of Celano sadly records that before Francis's conversion
his songs were better than anyone else's, and writes elsewhere of
his singing 'in French'. An ability to sing the French songs of
the period was not one to endear the boy to the priests of
Saint George's. Typical of them is this verse from *The Definition*

of Youth and Age, Per velha teno domna puois qu'a pel latge, by
Bertram de Born, who fought for Henry II of England in the
French wars:

> I hold a woman for old once she has an ugly skin
>   Old when she has no cavalier.
> I hold her for old once she does not share herself between
>   two lovers
>   Old when she gives herself to a base fellow.
> I hold her for old if she loves in her own castle
>   Old when she has no use for love-charms.
> I hold her for old when jongleurs bore her
>   Old when she herself will talk too much.

It is doubtful if they would have approved even of this hymn to
the beauty of nature from the *Litany of Love* by Piere Vidal of
Toulouse, which became famous while Francis was in his teens,
and may have inspired some of his ideas about the natural world:

> *Be m'agrada la convinens sazos*
> So pleases me the gentle season
> And pleases me the gentle summer weather
> And please me the birds, singing so much,
> And pleases me the flowers in bud,
> So please me all that pleases the courtly
> And most of all please me deeds of chivalry,
> I undertake them joyfully
> Bending all my heart and mind to them right willingly.

Obviously, men who sang of bending all their hearts and minds
to deeds of chivalry were not giving much thought to reaching
heaven.

Moreover, not only were these songs themselves an incitement
to lasciviousness and worldly interests, in the eyes of the moralists their singers too were often suspect, especially the troubadours
and jongleurs of Provençal origin who taught the ethics of the
Courts of Love in Germany and Italy, and were accused also of
spreading heresy with the aid of excerpts from the scriptures translated into the vernacular languages. Although the Courts of Love
taught a very rigid morality – the morality of the knight errant

and his pining, but untouchable and often much-married noble mistress – that morality was not Christian, and the atmosphere in which it was discussed was one of highly-charged, barely suppressed sexuality, wholly antipathetic to the Christian puritan, and bound in his opinion to lead to unorthodox views, even when it did not actually spring from heresy itself.

The twelfth century found the source of this unorthodox thinking on sex and marriage in the Frankish Kingdoms of the Near East established after the first crusade, holding them responsible for the invention of both chivalry and romantic love. It was during this century that there arose both the custom of hallowing a squire before he became a knight (usually, though not inevitably, by laying his sword on the altar of the chapel where he kept vigil for at least part of the night before he received knighthood) and the intricate system of rules governing courtly love.

Fucher of Chartres, a proto-puritan if ever there was one, laid full blame for what the stricter clergy saw as the gross immorality of the times squarely on the plump, smooth shoulders of the courtesans, concubines, and semi-official wives of the crusaders:

> He who was once a Roman or a Frank has become a Galilean or a Palestinian ... married to a woman who is not of his own country: a Syrian, or an Armenean, or even a Saracen who has not received the grace of baptism.... They speak different languages, but have already learned to understand one another. ... It was well written indeed: the Lion and the Lamb shall lie down together.*

What the crusading lion learned from lying down with the eastern lamb was a delicacy in sexuality going far beyond the mere coupling to extinguish lust and beget children grudgingly permitted by the fathers of the church. From the commingling of the races, the moralists would have us believe, came all manner of evils with a sexual slant; among them they list taking baths, wearing soft clothes, singing romantic songs to strange eastern

---

* Fucher of Chartres, *Gesta Francorum Iherusalem Peregrinantium*, ed. H. Hagen Meyer, Heidelberg 1913.

melodies (or even worse to 'borrowed' hymn tunes!), and loving for love's sake, or for the sake of honour.

Scandals like Queen Eleanor's affair during the second crusade with her uncle Raymond of Poitiers, the Prince of Antioch, or Abelard's tragic infatuation with Heloise during the same generation, gave ammunition to the preachers, but added spice to the lives of students at the new universities of Paris and Bologna, and to the songs and stories that Pietro Bernardone brought home with him from France, along with the latest eccentric fashions in materials and cut of clothes.

It is a little surprising that Bernardone himself was apparently never accused of heresy. Anyone who wandered from place to place was suspect; cloth merchants were especially so, from their necessary contact with the weavers, who were often – and probably with justice – suspected of spreading the dualistic doctrines of the Cathars. And in country places like Assisi, a man who consorts with foreigners is usually even more suspect than the foreigners themselves. However, the worst charge that was ever brought against him was that he was a bad father. After his death, there were many like Thomas of Celano ready to attack him for teaching his son how to make money (as a youth, Francis was 'very well off') and how to spend it ('and did not hoard money avariciously, but squandered it openhandedly'), so that he seemed 'a very kind person', a gay and gallant young man, in the best style of the new convention.

The puritanical Thomas even found fault with the fact that Francis was openhanded and friendly, on the grounds that his generosity brought him unsuitable acquaintances: 'for this reason, many followed him who were upholders of evil and instigators of crime' – the implication being that he both laid himself open to corruption and encouraged his companions in their criminality by his freedom with his money.*

If such a sentence were written today, its natural meaning would be that Francis was a real troublemaker, leading a gang of delinquents in frequent orgies of lust and crime. In fact, however, it probably means no more than that he was a leader of fashion in the town: light-hearted, liberal with his father's money, always well dressed, always familiar with the latest songs and

---

* I Celano, 1, 12.

newest gossip, welcome at any party, not seen in church as often
as his mother; in fact, just the kind of young man that twentieth-
century, middle-class parents are secretly so proud of, until the
day when they drop out, and become flower people, or beautiful
people, following cults of their own in exhibitionist protests
against the world that has given them the best it knows. And
parents and teachers are left asking: why?

Early in the thirteenth century, Pietro Bernardone tasted that
same bitterness. His son dropped out of contemporary society to
become first seemingly a madman and afterwards manifestly a
saint. And Pietro Bernardone was left asking: why?

3

Becoming a man of God

After Duke Conrad of Urslingen had surrendered his Italian holdings into the ready hands of Pope Innocent's legates, Innocent entrusted the government of the duchy of Spoleto to Cardinal-Rector Gregorio Crescenzi. Papal policy was to encourage local elected authorities while discouraging separatism, thus in effect dividing and ruling the estates and fiefs passing into papal hands as German power waned in central Italy. At Assisi, the elected senate of the commune continued to govern the day-to-day business of the city, and was represented in 'foreign' affairs, dealings with the Rector and other cities, by its two elected consuls. There was no detectable change in the electorate, apart from the disappearance of so many of the *boni homines*. The senate was chosen by the merchant class, while the lowest class struggled along with what it had always had – next to nothing. Its day would come later.

So although the change from German to papal rule was politically important, it at first made very little difference to the life of the average citizen of Assisi. The Lombard towns generally were pleased to be rid of the Germans but did not welcome the pope's men. As at Assisi, many rebelled in the name of freedom. The covert policy of dividing to rule did prevent the formation of an effective Lombard League, but the emphasis put on local authorities tended to magnify local pride and exacerbate inter-city rivalries. Perugia and Assisi now shared the same ultimate overlord, but their differences did not vanish overnight on that account. Nor was their disappearance in the interests of those of Assisi's *majores* made homeless by the rebellion. Perugian policy remained aggressively expansionist; the master plan – understood by all loyal citizens, even if never put into writing – called for an attack on Assisi following successful reduction of Perugia's yet more accessible neighbours in the plain of the Tiber. These preliminary campaigns occupied 1200–01. The attack on Assisi was timed for 1202. Promised restoration of their property in the event of a Perugian victory, Assisi's exiled *majores* co-operated enthusiastically in the war against their home town.

The papal forces which should have defended these cities against one another's excesses were fully committed to guarding the pope's furthest-flung frontiers, and Innocent's attention was divided between his plan for a great crusade in the east and the measures he was taking to combat a new threat from the south, where Markward of Anweiler, the former Marquis of Ancona, had succeeded in uniting the Germans of Sicily against both the pope and the resurgent Norman nobility. It was of only minor importance to him whether or not Perugia attacked Assisi, as long as both cities remained loyal to his bigger causes.

The news of the coming war could not be kept secret from the Assisians. How could they defend themselves? The Germans had gone from the *rocca*. Their own revolt had deprived them of the knights the *majores* usually put into the field in fulfilment of feudal obligations. The Assisian senate did what it could to make good the deficiencies of the defence by calling the sons of the *minores* to arms and promoting them to the status of knights if their families were rich enough to equip them with a horseman's arms and armour.*

Among those so promoted in the militia was Francis Bernardone. His father equipped him richly, as befitted the family's pretensions. It was as well that he did: the first skirmish in the campaign, close to Saint John's Bridge over the Tiber, saw Francis unhorsed and taken prisoner. Because he was armed and mounted like a gentleman, he was not imprisoned with the rabble but with those it was worth making some effort to keep alive, the knights whose families could be expected to find ransoms for them as part of any peace settlement.

Little is known of the conditions under which Assisian prisoners

* Cf. Fortini, *Nova vita di S.F.*, I, pp. 157ff.

were kept at Perugia.* From the few surviving stories of Francis's imprisonment, it seems that they lived in a common compound, probably in the lower levels of the castle, but were not put to slave labour, as the poorer prisoners were. Their present was uncomfortable and their future uncertain, but Francis seems either to have had no understanding of the gravity of their situation, or to have been indifferent to it. His lighthearted acceptance of captivity grated on the others' nerves. They told him they believed he was mad, and asked him what he thought there was to be happy about. He countered: 'Why am I happy? Because one day all the world will reverence me.'

He was a prisoner until some time in 1204. In having to waste less than two years in prison, he was more fortunate than most of the Assisians captured with him; they regained their freedom only when a truce was signed between the cities in August 1205. Someone obviously ransomed Francis, or else he would have remained in Perugia until the truce; equally obviously, his redeemer can have been only his doting and prosperous father. The terms of the redemption were probably arranged through Perugia's 'Prisoners' Aid Society', the *Congregatio et Societas Captivorum Amulatorum* known to have existed there since at least 1164.

Although the terms of the truce reached in 1205 did not directly affect the course of Francis's life, they are interesting for the light they throw on conditions in Umbria in this year of his conversion. The vanquished *minores* were to permit the exiled *majores* to return to their homes and to restore their property, but were themselves to be given a voice in Assisi's affairs through representatives on the senate. The lot of the serfs and peasants living outside the town was not discussed. No one had been fighting for the peasants' welfare. The 'citizens' demanding freedom and citizens' rights in towns like Assisi in these years were the new capitalists, men like Pietro Bernardone, who were gaining confidence as their wealth grew and they discovered the full range of the opportunities money and leisure time afforded. The treaty of 1205, confirming Assisi's shopkeepers in the right to vote directly on their own future was a sign of change over an area

* On Francis's imprisonment generally, see O. Englebert, *St Francis of Assisi*, Franciscan Herald Press, Chicago, 1965, Appendix VI; Fortini, *La Guerra di Perugia*, in *Nova vita di S.F.*, 1, pp. 151ff.

far wider than Lombardy. All over Europe, the feudal aristocracy had barely reached the height of its glory, but already its power was under attack. Future centuries would belong as much to the Bernardones, the forerunners of the Medicis and the Fuggers and their like, as to the *boni homines*, a fact which the *majores* of Assisi were tacitly recognizing in 1205 when they did not insist on the dissolution of the rebel senate that had so effectively kept them exiles for six years.

When Francis returned to Assisi, a year before the treaty was agreed, he was either twenty-one or twenty-two years of age. Being a prisoner of war had apparently changed neither his attitude to life, nor his determination to be a famous and success-ful soldier. He continued to play the gentleman on his father's money for several months to come. As Celano puts it, 'until his twenty-fifth year, he wasted his time woefully'. Then he fell ill.

In retrospect this sickness could be seen to have played so decisive a part in his development that it seemed to Celano that it could only have been a heaven-sent intervention in his affairs: 'God suddenly decided to deal with him. . . . For some time, he was laid low by sickness, the just deserts of human perversity'. When he was fit enough to walk again, leaning on a stick, he took a very bilious view of the world: 'The beauty of the meadows, the delight of the vineyards, and all the lovely things there are to see gave him no pleasure' (I Celano, 1, 3). 'The sudden change in himself puzzled him', yet he found himself thinking that anyone who did find enjoyment in the beauties of nature must be very stupid.

Sabatier, in his great *Life of Saint Francis*,* speculated that it was the round of parties following his redemption and homecom-ing that proved too much for his health. Dissipation may have weakened him, and delayed shock at having been a prisoner may also have played its part in his depression. There was, however, much more to it than that. Celano was right to see it as no mere liverishness, a hangover followed by a long period of morbid remorse and daily half-hearted vows of reform. In Celano's Christian terms, God was dealing with Francis. The decisive period in his development had come. In the terms of Jungian psychology, his ego-consciousness was suffering an invasion from

---

* P. Sabatier, *Life of Saint Francis*, Scribners, New York, 1903.

the depths of the unconscious mind, the undifferentiated self that we all share, the ground substance of our human nature and mind. Such an invasion is bound to lead, for better or worse, to apparent personality changes, at least until it is accepted. In Francis's case, the invasion was so overwhelming, so shattering, that by the time its effects were fully apparent, his ego had all but ceased to exist. In Saint Paul's phrase, Francis 'put on' Christ; he became the Cosmic Man. At the end of this evolution, his 'christification', to use Jung's word, was complete, and was seen to be complete in the physical manifestation known as the stigmata, the reproduction in his limbs of Christ's wounds on the cross, as they were visualized in Francis's times.

Francis's illness and depression thus marked his first attempts to adjust to the 'threat' to his ego from within. He withdrew from the world, to fight the interior battle for control of his own destiny. A little later, in August 1205, he tried to force himself to return to 'normality' by volunteering to join a military expedition into Apulia. In the event, he did not fight in the south, because he had 'lost' the battle within himself. His depression in 1204 marked the first step in his definitive conversion from the world. Celano says that God deliberately made him ill 'putting a stop to his false thinking by making his soul unhappy and his body sick': the whole man, body and mind, was involved in his struggle for survival.

As the story is told by all his near-contemporary biographers, Francis's life from this time onwards was punctuated by a succession of divine interventions: crucifixes that spoke; revelatory dreams; and supernatural cures. Some writers went further, looking back through his sickness and its outcome to see his cheerfulness in prison and his apparently illogical conviction that one day the world would reverence him as harbingers of divine favours to come, or – as non-Christians might prefer to think – of the coming breakdown and reconstruction of his personality from within. But as Celano half realized, it was Francis's illness and subsequent withdrawal that was crucial to his conversion, and not any of the 'miraculous' things which are alleged to have happened around him. He was 'converted' from within, rather than by a voice from the famous crucifix at Saint Damian's. It shows Celano's insight that in his *First Life* he does not mention the speaking crucifix, though by the time Bonaventure's official biography came to be written, the miracle had become the kernel of the whole story.*

His world's reaction to his depression was natural enough. It wrote him off as insane. His father bore with him longer than most people, and encouraged his decision to re-enlist for the Apulian war by buying him new equipment. But ultimately even he was forced to the conclusion that his son was mentally disturbed when, a few months after his 'illness' began, he stole part of the family's stock-in-trade, sold it, and gave the money away. At this stage, Pietro Bernardone reacted as those closest to the insane often do, with anger, blame and guilt, beating his son and locking him up.†

The period immediately before this theft, the months from August 1205 to the summer of 1206 which Francis spent in the twilight world after his failure to escape into more soldiering, is especially significant. Until he tried to fight back to normality by winning 'glory and riches' in Apulia, he became, the *First Life* says, 'ever more contemptible in his own eyes'; then when he could not bring himself to go and fight, he withdrew completely from 'the business of the world', going to a cave and praying there alone day after day.

At this stage, he had one confidant, 'a man dearer to him than anyone else', but typically did not give even him his full confidence. Instead, he talked of having found 'a wonderful, precious treasure' in the cave, although he would not allow his friend to see it, but made him stand guard over the cave's mouth, while he went in alone to gloat over his new-found riches.

Here the story reaches back beyond traditional Christianity to the mysteries of paganism, and especially those at Pythagoras and Orpheus, and Isis/Osiris/Serapis, in which the novice 'hearer' became an adept by spending a period alone in a dark place, returning to the womb, as so many have pointed out, and discovering there the great treasure of enlightenment and rebirth to eternal life.

Though described by Francis himself and his biographers in Christian terms, his 'conversion' was not specifically and uniquely Christian in form. It was not directly connected with any church

---

* Bonaventure 2, 1; see also II Celano 10, where the story does appear.
† Cf. I Celano 1, 8–10.

organization, or the personality of any winning clergyman, but had a universality the importance of which cannot be over-emphasized.

Inside the cave, Francis 'devoutly prayed ... to God to guide his path: he suffered most extreme agonies of soul.... All kinds of ideas went through his head.... The fire of God burned in him. ...' When he re-emerged into daylight 'he was so exhausted that he seemed a different person'. After months of such be-haviour – it may, in fact, have lasted as long as a full year – his friends concluded that he was love-sick in the best courtly tradi-tion. They asked him if he planned to marry. He replied: 'Yes. A bride more beautiful and noble than any of you has ever seen.'

He could not, of course, maintain this way of life indefinitely. The pattern broke quite suddenly with his apparently irrational theft of his father's cloth. 'When the appointed day came', as Celano put it, 'he followed the pious impulse of his heart, to tread underfoot all worldly desires, and gain the perfect good.' Moved by the sight of the sufferings of the poorest during an epidemic, he took 'some scarlet cloth' and rode to Foligno, intend-ing to sell the stuff on the market, and buy medicine with the money. However, once at Foligno, he sold the horse as well as the cloth and, experiencing a sudden revulsion against all property, decided to rid himself of the burden of money as soon as he could. He seems to have forgotten the very existence of the poor whom he had set out to help. Walking back from Foligno, he reached the ruined church of Saint Damian, an out-chapel of the Benedictine monastery then standing on Mount Subasio high above Assisi. Entering the chapel, he tried to persuade the resi-dent priest to accept the money for its restoration. The priest would not touch Bernardone money, so Francis 'threw it on to a windowsill' and talked the priest into letting him stay at the church.

News of his whereabouts soon leaked out – Assisi was only about a mile away – and his father came with a party of friends to carry him home, by force if need be. But the party betrayed its approach by the noise it made, and Francis hid in a nearby cave, staying there for about a month. Darkness and isolation worked their usual effect on a susceptible mind. He entered the cave hunted, afraid and miserable. Suddenly, after so many days alone, he was 'filled with an ineffable joy' which 'so inspired him' that he left his lair and went boldly back to the city.

His month as a fugitive had done nothing for his appearance. 'When people who knew him saw him looking like that ... they called him raving mad, and threw mud and stones from the road at him'. His father rescued him from the street urchins, dragged him home, locked him up in a darkened room for several days; then pleaded with him, beat him, and finally put him in chains.* Nothing had any effect. His return to the womb of Mother Earth in the cave had been definitive. His old life was over.

* All in I Celano 1, 11–21.

4

The world well lost

Francis's interior drama was played out against a backcloth of world events which themselves bore all the marks of high tragedy. He was apparently cut off from those events by his imprisonment and illness, and the voluntary withdrawal following them, but it is obvious from his later actions and attitudes that they did affect him, even if only indirectly. When in 1206 he went to live at Saint Damian's, the chapel was close to ruins, because the duchy of Spoleto was close to ruin, Italy in chaos, and the whole of European civilization apparently on the point of collapse.

Innocent III's call in 1198 for a fourth crusade at first met with very little response. Shortly after 1200, his expansionist policy in Italy had led to endemic rebellion in the Lombard cities, and a union against him of the Germans remaining in Italy and Sicily under Markward of Anweiler. In the wake of Saladin's successes in the Holy Land, the Christian leaders of the surviving eastern Franks were hopelessly divided. At Constantinople itself, power was in the hands of a usurper calling himself Alexius III, whose blinded brother, the legitimate Emperor Isaac II lay in prison, while his son, also confusingly named Alexius, was in Italy urging Innocent to rescue his father and save the eastern empire.

Innocent was always a pragmatist, and fortunately at this stage in his career he still had the patience the situation called for. Gradually, his legates gathered a crusading army, finding recruits mainly in France. In Italy, too, he found allies, men as antagonistic to the Germans of the south as he himself was. Chief among them was Walter of Brienne, son-in-law to Norman Prince

Tancred of Sicily, once an enemy of the papacy, but always an enemy of the Germans, whose accession to power in Apulia, where his estates lay, had made him a landless man.

It was probably in support of papal aims in southern Italy, and not merely in search of 'glory and riches' that an otherwise unknown 'nobleman of Assisi' planned the expedition into Apulia in 1205 which Francis was tempted to join. *The Chronicle of the Three Companions** makes the point that it was not just a raid in search of plunder, but part of a larger and well-planned military expedition, in short, the war that Walter of Brienne began that year for vengeance's sake, but in the pope's name and with his blessing.

The levy from Assisi was to fight under a certain 'Count Gentile', who mustered men at Spoleto. If Francis had ridden to war under Count Gentile, he might have found the fame he dreamed of, for Markward of Anweiler had died in September 1202, and though the army he had inspired was prepared to fight on without him, by 1205 German resistance was on the point of collapse.

Meanwhile, amid countless intrigues the infamous fourth crusade to the East had at last got under way, sailing from Venice because its originally designated home port in Sicily was still in German hands. By now, however, so too was the crusading army itself, the meddling hands of Philip of Swabia, whose envoys were active during the debates at Corfu in the spring of 1203 which finally determined the barons to lead their men not to the Holy Land, but to Constantinople. The outcome of their enterprise is notorious. After camping for months at the gates of the city, while two revolutions rid the scene of all those with title to rule there, they lost whatever little patience they had ever had with Byzantine promises, stormed the city, and sacked it. On 16 May 1204, Baldwin of Flanders was solemnly enthroned as the first Latin Emperor of Constantinople at Hagia Sophia; he wrote to Innocent saying that if the pope would send Latin priests and monks to the new empire, the reunion of the churches could quickly be achieved, and promising that the crusaders would then march on triumphantly towards Jerusalem.†

---

* *The Three Companions* 5; cf. Bonaventure 1, 3; Anon. Peruginus 5.

† Cf. S. Runciman, *The Crusades*, vol. 3; *Cambridge Mediaeval History*, vol. 4, c. 14.

Innocent was not convinced. The Greek Church, he wrote to his legate, with the crusaders 'would hate the Latins like dogs – and they would be right ... [the crusaders] have spared neither religion, nor age, nor sex. They have repeatedly committed adultery and fornication ... emptied the treasuries ... and violated shrines'.

The news that God's own army had sacked the Christian city shocked all Europe. At first, the crusaders were universally denounced, but within months the pragmatic Innocent had reconciled himself to their atrocities, comforting himself with the thought that his authority was at least now nominally recognized from the Atlantic to the Black Sea. The knowledge gave him added confidence – if any were needed – in the struggle against the Germans in Italy. He declared that war a crusade also, offering crusader's blessings to all who would join in it and calling on every Christian in Italy to fight with Walter of Brienne for God and the victory of the church.

Walter of Brienne died of wounds received in a siege early in the campaign. His death was a bitter blow to Norman separatist hopes. It left the pope as the only focus of the anti-German movement, so that when the south Italian crusade prospered despite the loss of its general, Innocent gradually gained control of the whole region. He had declared Henry VI's heir, Prince Frederick, his ward, and now won physical control over him, making himself during Frederick's minority sole arbiter of affairs from the March of Ancona to Sicily.

Francis of Assisi dreamed of fighting for the right, and the pope had declared that the war in southern Italy was God's holy cause. Why, then, did he finally decide not to fight with Walter of Brienne? Celano claims that the decision was spontaneous. He describes Francis as 'fascinated' by 'visions of great renown' and dreaming that the house was 'full of weapons', but nonetheless withdrawing from the expedition at the last moment because he realized that, whatever his dreams, he was not a natural soldier and to force himself to be one would be 'to do violence to himself' (I Celano 1, 5).

This explanation is quite satisfactory as it stands, but later writers unnecessarily heighten the drama by supplying Francis with a vision to warn him that war was not his calling. In Bonaventure's *Life* the simple dream that the house was full of arms has become a fully-fledged prophetic vision rewarding an act of charity: during the period of Francis's convalescence, the story runs, he one day met a soldier 'of noble blood, but poor and badly clothed' and impulsively shared his clothes with him; the following night he dreamed of a palace full of arms and armour, all marked with the crusader's cross, and was told by a voice from heaven that they belonged to him and his men (Bonaventure 1, 2). He took this as a sign that he was to join the Apulian expedition, and set out for the muster at Spoleto. But when he had reached Foligno, he heard God ask him during the night 'in the voice of a friend' who could do more for him, the lord or his servant, a rich man or a poor one? When he replied that a lord or a rich man could obviously help him the more, the voice asked him why then he was leaving 'the lord for the servant, the rich God for the poor mortal?' and told him to return home, and fight the spiritual crusade from there.

Back at Assisi, his first battle was with himself. He had to teach himself contempt for the world, and self-dedication. He won this fight by forcing himself to embrace a leper he met while riding over the valley of Spoleto, kissing the man's diseased hand and pressing money into it. Moments later, the leper disappeared: Bonaventure does not actually claim that he was an angel, but leaves the reader in little doubt of it.

His next experience was the vision of Christ crucified, which he interpreted as a direct invitation to deny himself, 'take up the cross' and follow Jesus to perfection. From that time on, he deliberately sought the company of lepers, visiting their hovels, giving them money, and sharing his clothes with them.

Of all this, there is nothing in the *First Life*, but when Celano came to write his *Second Life* in response to popular demand after the General Chapter of the Franciscans in 1244, he knew that Francis had reached Spoleto on his way to the wars, and says that he fell sick there. This psychosomatic illness drove him back to Assisi; no vision was needed, and Celano does not mention one. He was surely right to omit the miracle stories. It was Francis's deepening investigation of his own true nature that led him to reject military crusading as a career. Unfortunately for Celano's complete credibility, however, he also omits stories which are more likely to be true, and so distorts the picture a little, especially in his earlier work, where the impression is given that

Francis did not leave Assisi between his release from Perugia and his momentous visit to Foligno to sell his father's cloth. In fact, not only did he probably try to join the army at Spoleto, he almost certainly also made a pilgrimage to Rome some time during those two years.

The Chronicle of the Three Companions and Bonaventure's Life mention this Roman journey only because it affords an opportunity once more to emphasize Francis's concern for beggars. The square before old Saint Peter's swarmed with them; Francis changed clothes with one of them and sat all day in rags, begging at the church door.*

The omission of this story from the First Life suggests that the visit to Rome meant little in retrospect to Francis himself. If it had made a deep impression, he would have talked of it often enough for Thomas to feel that he should include it in the story of his hero's conversion. The probable truth is that after Francis had given up all thought of a military career, and before his stay at Saint Damian's, he was too wrapped up in his own self-exploration to notice much of what was going on around him unless it related directly to his own interior conflict: he did not remember Rome, but only Rome's beggars. It was left to the Three Companions – allegedly men of Assisi themselves, and not entirely dependent on Francis's conversation for the facts of his early life – to recall that Francis learned at Rome what it was to beg and be rebuffed.

The later histories even find it impossible to leave unadorned the story of Francis's stay at Saint Damian's. As it stands in the First Life, it is perfectly credible and psychologically satisfying; his friends, the poor, were in danger; he, their champion, rode out with the only weapons he had, some rolls of cloth, to bring them aid from Foligno (Thomas makes the point that before starting out, he 'fortified', 'armed', himself with the crusader's cross); at the market, he forgot the poor, he forgot everything, except his new-found hatred for the encumbrance of possessions; on the road home, he came to Saint Damian's and stayed there 'for the love of God'.

By the time Bonaventure's Life was composed, a cheap holy picture, in the form of a miracle story, had been pasted over this

* The Three Companions 10; cf. Bonaventure 1, 6; II Celano 1, 8.

snapshot of a man at the crossroads of his life; according to this version, what drove Francis to Folingo was not pity, but the voice of God speaking to him directly from a crucifix in the semi-ruined Saint Damian's where it was his habit to meditate. The voice told him three times: 'Francis, rebuild my house; as you see, it is falling into total ruin.' He was actually being called to reform the church, but thought that he was being ordered to rebuild Saint Damian's, so he took part of the stock of the shop, sold it at Foligno, and offered the price he received for it to the resident priest at Saint Damian's, who refused it for fear of his father's anger. His father tracked him to the church; he hid in a cave until inspired to go home. Assisi received him with stones and insults, and his father locked him up.

The speaking crucifix is preserved at the church of Saint Clare in Assisi, where over the centuries it has inspired much genuine piety. It may be that Francis did 'hear' the crucifix speaking, but if he did, it was after the visit to Foligno market, while he was hiding in the ruined church from his father and the world his father represented. In Christian terms, Francis's first vocation was to save himself from his own nature and the world; his second, to make himself a brother to the poor and helpless; and his third to inspire the poor by his example to 'rebuild', reform and restore, the church.

He had no opportunity of doing anything towards fulfilling this third part of his vocation while he was locked up, loaded with chains, in a small, darkened room, undergoing the treatment for madness universal until the nineteenth century. It was his mother who gave him the chance he needed. When Pietro Bernardone was away on a business trip, she first tried to talk her son out of his fixation, then released him, although she knew that he was not 'cured'. He went straight back to Saint Damian's.

The outcome was inevitable. The pattern has been repeated a million times in the last twenty years alone. Pietro, coming home to find Francis gone, decided that he had endured as much as he could bear. Guessing where Francis would be, he went to have it out with him. Would the boy forget all this nonsense and come home? He would not. Then his father was finished with him. Francis realized that. Then he owed him the price of some rolls of cloth and a good horse. The money still lay on the window-sill, where Francis had thrown it weeks before. Angry and frustrated, Pietro took the money and — because, one senses, that victory had been too easy — took a final step, one that he had in all probability not contemplated when he had set out: if Francis really would not pull himself together, would he come to the authorities and formally renounce all his legal claims as the eldest son of the family? No, said Francis (according to *The Three Companions*), he would not. He did not recognize the power of the authorities. They were only man-made. Now thoroughly exasperated, Pietro asked: if the senate and the consuls would not suit him, would he accept the authority of the Bishop? Francis said that he would — as Thomas of Celano says, 'gladly'.

The bishop, Guy II of Assisi, granted an audience, and in his presence Francis not only made the formal renunciation required of him, but went on to strip himself naked, so that he had nothing left that his father had given him (his life, he would have said, was a gift from God). Bishop Guy covered him with his own cloak till a servant brought a peasant's tunic and Francis put it on, after having first, Bonaventure says, chalked a cross on it, so 'taking the cross' as the crusader of the poor.*

The tragedy of this scene is missed by the early biographers. They see only the religious significance of Francis's total stripping off of 'the things of this world' (Thomas of Celano actually quotes the relevant passage from Saint Paul). Bishop Guy, it is claimed, also saw it in this light, or at least went so far as to surmise that God had inspired what 'the Man of God' had done. Perhaps only a father whose son had so contemptuously dropped out of his world could describe Pietro Bernardone's feelings adequately: from his point of view, the scene is horrifying; Francis not only totally rejects him, but also publicly sneers at him, doubly insulting him by stripping naked, both flouting convention and scornfully refusing to be further contaminated by what he had worked to earn and enjoyed giving. The action is not that of a praiseworthy man, but a self-willed child. The surprising thing is that when Francis behaved so badly, he was not fifteen but twenty-five.

Fortunately, his adolescence was nearly over. He had not yet come to terms with the invasion he had suffered from the totality of the self: he would never do that. But it had forced its terms on

* I Celano 1, 13–15; Bonaventure 2, 4.

him, and he had surrendered to it. Henceforward, he was committed to the quest for perfection, a perfection medieval Christianity saw in terms of the poor Christ, living in poverty and dying in pain. What that quest entailed for him is the real subject of the rest of this book. But before following him on it, it would be valuable to look briefly at the life of an older contemporary of his, Joachim of Flora. Joachim's experiences and teaching may have influenced Francis himself and certainly affected the later development of the Franciscan Order. Moreover, his conclusions about the pattern of world history have striking consonances with some thoughts of Professor Jung's about what happened to Francis at his conversion and afterwards.

Joachim of Flora* died in Calabria when Francis was aged about twenty. Later Franciscans proclaimed him the second John the Baptist, paving the way for Francis, their own second Christ. Joachim's life was full of action and movement, but his revolutionary teaching inevitably looks dull to any but specialists today, because he couched his arguments in biblical language and images. This makes it difficult to give any real sense of how revolutionary his approach and teaching seemed to the men of his own times. But in the 1190s controversy raged around him, and a hundred years later there were wars over his ideas.

He was born in the mid-twelfth century in Calabria, an area which today is part of Italy's problem and strife torn *mezzogiorno,* but in Joachim's youth, although poor, was the crossroads between west and east, the place where Italian, Byzantine, Norman, Eastern Frankish, German and – though usually indirectly – Arab influences met more freely than anywhere else in the world.

As a young man, Joachim was quite rich, and enjoyed 'the world', but it soon began to bore him, and he became a monk in the strictest of the existing religious orders, the Cistercian, founded at Citeaux in 1112 by the austere Saint Bernard, whose sometimes over-warm eulogizing of the virginity of Mary seems to have been the only relaxation he allowed himself apart from making capital gains in money and land for his order and thinking up new ways of tightening the regulations binding his monks. Before Joachim put on the cowl, however, he had experienced both the best and the worst the world had to offer. He had visited

* Cf. M. W. Bloomfield, *Joachim of Flora, A Critical Survey,* in *Traditio* 13, 1957, pp. 249ff.

the glittering Eastern outpost of the western world, Constantinople, and while there had experienced all the horrors of a major
outbreak of plague. Then he had followed the crusaders to Syria,
and visited all the holy places, falling victim to the charm of the
Saracens so completely that he came to prefer their company to
that of the Palestinian Christians – a preference which earned
him not a little suspicion. However, he was Christian enough, or
natural mystic enough, to want to spend a holy Lent with the
hermits on Mount Tabor, the Mount of the Transfiguration. On
Easter night 'when Christ rose, the conqueror of hell', he had a
vision, as a result of which he first tried physically to retrace
Christ's path over all the Holy Land and then, returning to his
native Italy, began to preach, although unlicensed to do so, before
taking vows at Cortale near Catanzaro, becoming first prior and
then abbot of his monastery, so growing familiar with both the
financial and disciplinary problems of Cistercian monks.

According to medieval orthodox thinking, the monastic life
was the most perfect open to man. Joachim's restless spirit did not
let him agree. The modified Benedictine rule binding the
Cistercians stressed the importance of the vow of stability, forbidding monks to move from place to place. Neither it, nor the
demands made on his time by the work of ruling the monastery,
could hold him in one spot for long. He was by nature a tramp,
part wanderer, part hermit, now longing for solitude to think and
write, now longing for company and minds against which to
sharpen his own wit. In 1181, he appealed to Pope Lucius III for
a dispensation from his duties and from the vow of stability, so
that he could travel; somewhat surprisingly it was granted,
although he remained a member of the Cistercian Order. Fortunately for himself, he took the precaution of having his dispensation confirmed first by Lucius's successor, Urban III –
whose friend and confident he became, wandering with him as
far as Verona when Rome was occupied by anti-papal forces –
and then by Clement III. That step saved him when, after followers began to attach themselves to him, the Cistercian Order
grew restive and in 1192 summoned him to attend its general
chapter and answer charges of heresy and contumacy, in an
attempt to force him to return to his own monastery, where he
would be too busy to write and teach. His papal licences and his
own eloquence were too much for his accusers. The chapter

released him, and he went south, to Monte la Sila, the so-called Black Mountain, east of Cosenza. His disciples sought him out and he formed them into a new religious community to which, in about the year 1195, he gave the name Fiore, 'the flowers'. The mystical name of Rome, dear to astrologers and magicians, was Flora; was Joachim building a new Rome, a new centre of hope, in the mountains of Calabria?

His teaching at Fiore was not wholly unorthodox, but a suspect mixture of mystical prophecies based on obscure biblical texts with calls for the reform of the church and, especially, a return to the poverty of Christ. He claimed to be the loyal subject of the pope and in the year 1200 being, as he said, 'always ready to observe what is or shall be decreed by the pontifical throne', submitted his writings to Innocent III as the supreme judge in matters of faith. Innocent, not a man usually hesitant to pass judgement, let months go by without a word, until Joachim died in 1202, neither justified nor condemned.

The key to his prophetic teaching was the text from *Revelations*, 'I saw another angel flying through the midst of heaven, having the everlasting gospel to preach ... over every nation and tribe and tongue and people' (14, 6). Joachim saw himself as this angel's spokesman. His message to the world was the final version of divine revelation, the everlasting gospel. He never tried to produce 'The Everlasting Gospel' as such – as, for instance, Aldous Huxley tried to summarize *The Perennial Philosophy* in a single volume similarly introducing western thinkers to eastern ideas. He tried to let the message of the everlasting gospel show through his teaching in other, often very practical, matters.

He attacked the Benedictines, the most powerful and richest of the religious Orders, reminding people of the provisions of Saint Benedict's Rule on monastic poverty, and declaring: 'If they were true monks, they would live by the labours of their hands; they would abstain from flesh meat...: Let them possess nothing of their own.'

He attacked the rich: 'There are some rich people – though very few – who have great households of men and women servants yet reach the Kingdom of Heaven nonetheless, because they have pity.... But the rest do not behave so.... They meet a murmur of complaint [from the lower classes] with terrible sneers, calling them evil slaves, and ignorant people, and liars.'

Holding that God had established the papacy, he refused to attack the pope; but he made it inevitable that his followers should clash with Rome by teaching that 'where the Spirit of the Lord is, there is liberty'. A legalistic pope like Innocent, or an arrogant one, like several of his thirteenth-century successors, could grant no one liberty, except the freedom to obey or suffer the consequences.

Joachim's revolt was probably the mildest (at least superficially) against the systematization of European life under the law proceeding so quickly in his day. Dante set him in the second circle of paradise, at Bonaventure's side, together with Rabanus Maurus, a ninth-century scholar and one-time archbishop of Mainz: 'Raban is here, and at my side there shines Calabria's abbot, Joachim, endowed with soul prophetic.'

'Where the Spirit of the Lord is, there is liberty'; the fundamental idea underlying Joachim's prophecy was that the Christian faith ought to be free, as a dynamic, growing plant is free, and not a static, unchanging building, the edifice built by lawyers and exegetes bound by precedence. Speculating on the thought that the Old Testament was followed by the New Testament, the law by the gospel, and that Jesus promised a new world ruled by the Spirit, he added up the generations from Adam to Christ in the genealogy of Jesus, and decided that they represented a period of 1260 years. Logically, then, he argued, the age of the gospel, the age of faith and the Son, should also last about 1260 years. When their time was run – within a couple of generations of the time at which he was writing – men could expect to see the end of the gospel age and the beginning of a new world order, the age of the third person of the Christian trinity, the age of the divine, freedom-loving Spirit – the age of the everlasting gospel.

In the age of the Father, married men had led the world: Adam and Abraham, David and Solomon, and the Jewish priesthood. In the age of the Son, the secular clergy had guided mankind. When the third age began, true monks, with the hermits in the van, would lead the human race to God by contemplation and mystical prayer, and through the influence of sacred songs as he himself had collected in his *Psaltery of Ten Strings*. But their true leadership would be perfect freedom, for the third age will be the age of love and the Spirit 'that bloweth where it listeth', when all men will live in equity, brotherhood and peace.

The personality of Abbot Joachim and the appeal of his semi-mystical, semi-practical theorizing to half-educated minds still not far from paganism goes a long way towards explaining the welcome given to his everlasting gospel. But Joachim's emphasis on the word freedom was perhaps the chief reason for his success. He promised freedom from oppression by either kings or priests, freedom from want and freedom from fear. His everlasting gospel was a liberation movement, comparable to those so familiar today, though its vocabulary was so different. In his time, no less than our own, people were afraid not only of sickness and death, but also of the continual, crushing pressure of conformity. In only a few years' time, Innocent III was to set in train the developments which were to lead to the establishment of the Holy Inquisition, ordering, among other enormities, that the lay members of the church were to confess their own sins once a year at least and to denounce those of their neighbours. The twelfth and thirteenth centuries were the age of law: the Roman Law, edited by Gratian and commented on at the universities, and the Canon Law of the church, both exerting pressure towards conformity to accepted standards in every aspect of life. No wonder then that the underground had such appeal, and the promise of a coming great time of freedom by one preaching with an abbot's authority, but a most unabbotlike impudence in using it, was welcomed by those who felt themselves to be the victims of the age.

The passage of time proved that Joachim's prediction of the coming of the age of the everlasting gospel in the year 1260 was ill-founded. Yet his movement lived on. One of the reasons why it lived on was that though his prophecy of the occurrence of certain external events on a certain date was nonsensical, his theorizing nonetheless reflected a profound truth about human development. He made the mistake of exteriorizing into the physical world an evolution which is naturally interior. When this is realized, the closeness of his experiences to Francis's becomes apparent, as also does the surprising depth of his own insight into them.

The symbol of the trinity has universal and not merely Christian significance. Discussing its universality and the insight it provides into individual human development, Jung came very close to a statement of the everlasting gospel, and was led on to formulate a theory about the *stigmata*, the appearance of Christ's wounds in the hands and feet of such as Francis of Assisi. 'Generally speaking', he wrote,* 'the Father denotes the earlier stages of consciousness, when one is still a child, still dependent on a definite, ready-made pattern of existence, which is habitual and has the character of law'. Joachim claimed that the first age is the age of the Father and of the law when married men lead the world. The second age is the age of the Son, the age of detachment from the Fathers. Jung wrote: 'Legitimate detachment consists in conscious differentiation from the Father.... The Christianity symbolized by the "Son" therefore forces the individual to discriminate and reflect.'

The third age, Joachim said, is that of the Spirit. Jung maintained that the Spirit 'raises the subsequent stages of consciousness to the same level of independence as that of the "Father" and the "Son". The "Son" represents a transitional stage, an intermediate state, part-child, part-adult. He is a transitory phenomenon, and it is thanks to this fact that "son"-gods die an early death.'

Joachim's third age is that of freedom and insight, when the mystical hermits will rule. Jung wrote: 'The advance to the third stage means something like a recognition of the unconscious, if not actual subordination to it.... It is clear that these changes are not everyday occurrences, but are very fateful transformations indeed. Usually they have a numinous character, and take the form of conversions, illuminations, emotional shocks ... or their equivalents.' Francis agonized in his cave, found his treasure, was so 'exhausted' by his experiences that he seemed a different person.

In the course of this discussion on the nature of the adulthood achieved by submitting to 'the spirit of one's own independence' – by recognizing or even becoming subordinate to the subconscious – Jung said something of vital importance for understanding Francis's pursuit of the perfect good, and the effects of that quest both mental and physical:

This third stage ... means articulating one's ego-consciousness with a supraordinate totality, of which we cannot say that it

* C. C. Jung, *Psychology and Religion*, pp. 181ff.

is 'I'. . . . Hard as it is to define, this unknown quantity can be
experienced by the psyche and is known in Christian parlance
as the Holy Ghost, the breath that heals and makes whole.
Christianity claims that this breath also has personality. . . . For
close on two thousand years history has been familiar with the
figure of the Cosmic Man, the Anthropos, whose image has
merged with that of Yahweh and also of Christ. Similarly, the
saints who received the stigmata became Christ-figures in a
visible and concrete sense, and thus carriers of the anthropos-
image. They symbolize the workings of the Holy Ghost among
men. The Anthropos is a symbol that argues in favour of the
personal nature of the 'totality', i.e. the self.

Francis was in fact the first known 'carrier of the anthropos-
image' in the form of the stigmata. His stigmata appeared towards the end of a life devoted to making himself an acceptable
Christ-figure, and his self-dedication to the pursuit of this perfection began in withdrawal after his imprisonment at Perugia – a
spiritual retreat, at first into sickness and later into the isolation
of a cave, from whence he emerged, set on a new course of life.
'It is clear', Jung said, 'that these changes are not everyday occurrences, but are very fateful transformations indeed'. To Francis,
they were not only fateful, they were in a real sense fatal. He did
not merely become a bearer of the anthropos-image. He was
transformed, or he transformed himself, into that image, that
archetypal symbol. The archetype, the anthropos-image, made a
successful take-over bid for the man, the human personality
Francis of Assisi. Francis 'put on Christ' so completely that one
of his friars was later to say that in his dreams Christ was Francis
and Francis Christ. Both were so powerful an expression in
'Christian' terms of the universal anthropos archetype that the
good friar could no longer distinguish between them.

5

The pursuit of perfection

Freed, about the spring of the year 1206, from everything tying him to what theologians called 'the world', Francis was poised to begin his life's work at last. There was one difficulty, however. He still did not know what that work was.

Though freed from the world, he was still totally dependent on it for food, drink and clothing. He took a job as a dishwasher in a monastery – probably a subpriory of the Benedictines of Mount Subasio – but he felt that he was being badly treated there, and left, crossing the mountain to the village of Gubbio, where an old friend took pity on him, giving him food and clothing. One wonders if this bitter experience sharpened his animosity towards the established religious orders. He certainly had little time for them later in life, although he owed much to Subasio's Benedictines. Returning to Assisi, he started work on the rebuilding of Saint Damian's, lodging with his friends among the lepers.*

In prison, years earlier, he had claimed that one day he would be universally reverenced. At Spoleto, he had become convinced that he must do a crusader's work in Assisi. Now he was more than ever certain that some special task awaited him. He was filled with the joy of the new convert. Celano is surely right to place immediately after his renunciation of the world the story of how, when walking in the forest clothed only in a loincloth and 'singing to God in French', he was ambushed by outlaws who demanded to know his name and business, and told them

---

* I Celano 1, 16; Bonaventure 2, 6.

that he was 'the herald of the Great King', only to be thrown into a ditch for his impertinence. The tale may not be authentic: it reads like one of those pious stories invented by later Franciscans to underline the New Testament character of their hero, although it identifies him with John the Baptist rather than Christ. But it perfectly mirrors the sense of release felt by someone who has at last made a decision over which he has been agonizing because he knows it will change the direction of his life.

While working on the restoration of Saint Damian's, Francis also continued his attempts to help the lepers, who at this time were still outlawed and counted dead by most of the world. Since the first crusade, their numbers had vastly increased, though whether their disease was true leprosy or not is a matter of dispute. In the mid-twelfth century Pope Alexander III had founded an Order known as the Crossbearers, *Crucigeri*, to tend them, at first in the Near East, and later in Europe. By Francis's day, there were forty of the Order's lazar-houses in Italy alone; one of them, San Salvatore della Pareti, stood outside Assisi, at the place still called *Ospedaletto*, 'the little hospital'. Francis shared the general horror of leprosy. In embracing lepers, living with them, and even exchanging clothes with them, he was not only performing acts of charity but also driving himself to his own limits and beyond, compelling himself to do what in the world he found it hardest to do. As he himself wrote in his *Testament*: 'While in sin, it seemed to me a thing repulsive beyond measure to see lepers, so the Lord himself led me to them, and I stayed with them a little while' (or, in another version of the will, 'and I showed mercy to them').

To rebuild Saint Damian's, he begged stones – and, of course, food – from his father's friends in Assisi. Their pity must have been as hard for Pietro Bernardone to bear as anything he had yet endured on Francis's account. The Three Companions say that father and son were now so totally estranged that Pietro swore at Francis whenever they met. Francis knew the damage he had done and – whether from superstition or bravado – to quieten his conscience persuaded a beggar to walk around with him, sharing the alms he received, and bless him whenever his father cursed him. Whatever Francis thought he gained from such behaviour, Bernardone can only have concluded that he was being mocked, especially as Francis called the beggar 'father'.*

When Saint Damian's was safe from collapse, Francis turned his attention to another country church, dedicated to Saint Peter (not the Romanesque church still standing at the west corner of Assisi's city walls, but a chapel in the fields). And when he had done all that he could there, probably some time in 1208, he undertook the restoration of Saint Mary of Jehosophat, the famous 'Little Portion', Portiuncula.†

Saint Mary of Jehosophat was the smallest and poorest of the out-chapels of the abbey on Mount Subasio. Lying in the middle of a little wood, far below the town on the edge of the plain of the Tiber, it had reputedly, though not in fact, been built in the fourth century – long before Benedict wrote the first Rule for western monks – by four pilgrims returning from the holy places recently explored by the Empress Helena. Why it was named 'Blessed Mary of Jehosophat' is not known; nor how it came into Benedictine hands. According to the Old Testament and Jewish apocalypses, the valley of Jehosophat, outside Jerusalem, will be the scene of the last war at the end of the world and the place of the last judgement. Lying in the plain, on the frontier between Spoleto and Perugia, and so in the path of countless armies down the centuries, Blessed Mary of Jehosophat had witnessed numberless rehearsals for the war of Armageddon. One of the reasons for its neglect was that constant skirmishes and pillage had driven the population away from the area. Another was that an aura reputedly hung over the place itself: its popular name was Saint Mary of the Angels, because it was said that angels could sometimes be heard singing there.

The chapel of Blessed Mary of Jehosophat is now totally enclosed in the gaudy basilica of Saint Mary of the Angels, on which work began in 1569, and its exterior is so covered in decoration that it is difficult to imagine it as it was when Francis began to restore it. By this time, the genuineness of his attempt to achieve personal holiness had been recognized, and the Abbot

---

* *The Three Companions* 23; cf. II Celano 12.

† On the fabrication of the legends of Portiuncula, see E. d'Alençon *Des origines de l'église de la Portioncule, etc.*, in *Etudes franciscans 11*, 1904, pp. 585ff.

of Mount Subasio appointed a chaplain to say mass at Saint Mary's for him, as was the custom for hermits.

It was during the reading of the gospel at one of these masses that Francis realized what his vocation was. The gospel for the day came from Matthew 10, the account of Christ's injunctions to his apostles when he sent them out to preach, including the command: 'Preach, saying the Kingdom of Heaven is at hand' and 'Have no gold, nor silver, nor money in your purses, nor scrip for your journey, nor two coats, nor shoes, nor a staff'. Francis had probably heard these words dozens of times, but now they seemed to be addressed to him personally. Unless he followed them to the letter, he would, he convinced himself, fall short of perfect discipleship.

Comparison of the various missals then in use in Benedictine houses in Italy has led Bollandist scholars to the conclusion that the date was probably 24 February 1209. Celano says that Francis immediately put into practice what he had heard, taking off his sandals, throwing away his staff, putting on the oldest tunic that he could find, tying it round with a piece of rope as cheaper than the leather belt he had worn until then. So dressed, 'he began to preach penance to everybody', actually starting at Saint George's, where he had been to school, a fact that Celano found significant, as it was also the place where he was first buried. As he preached, he did not look at his audience, but gazed up into the sky, as though expecting the supreme judge to appear there at any second. His first words, on that occasion, and whenever he preached later, were, 'The Lord give you peace' (I Celano 1, 23).

It was the literalness of Francis's attempt to make himself the perfect disciple that struck his contemporaries, and has given him his appeal through succeeding centuries. The attempt was perhaps a naive one. The later history of the Franciscan Order shows how impossible Francis's ideal was as a practical way of life for a large number of men. Interpreting all developments in terms of morality (and in black and white at that) the Order's earliest historians over-emphasized the good will or evil intentions of those who tried to perpetuate Francis's ideals, or interpret them more practically, after his death. Once the Order grew, social and economic pressures made change inevitable. Christ could ask his twelve followers to accept the possibility of starvation or death by exposure; the church found it impossible to make the same demands of twelve thousand or twelve million. Similarly, Francis could interpret the gospel literally for himself and his first few brothers; but how literally dared a whole Order of brothers interpret it? This was the question which divided the Franciscans in the thirteenth century, and still divides them today. A hundred years after Francis's death, the argument over whether all Christians ought to practise the poverty of Christ and the Apostles almost split the church. But to Francis himself, in Lent 1209, the question was not whether he should pursue total poverty and preach penance, but how best could he fulfil what he believed to be his absolute duty? He was a fanatic, totally devoted to the achievement of Christian perfection as he envisaged it.

The quest for perfection is never easy. In the early thirteenth century, it could be dangerous as well as difficult. Others in the recent past – Joachim of Flora among them – had tried to make themselves hermits, or perfect disciples, or holy ascetics. The failure of those who had attempted to do so within the church, and the apparent success of at least some of those who had tried outside the framework of orthodoxy, had cast suspicion on the very idea of seeking perfection long before that February morning when Francis took off his shoes and wished the people of Assisi the peace of God.* In fact, it would scarcely be going too far to say that by 1209, Philip of Swabia being dead and Guelph Otto IV the undisputed emperor of Germany, the only real opposition nearer than England to the fulfilment of Innocent III's vision of a Europe united under the pope came from the underground 'perfectionist' movements. Innocent could contain and control local rebellious leaders and rulers, like John of England, but fanatics are uncontrollable; they can only be destroyed.

The underground perfectionist movement in the twelfth and thirteenth centuries did not present a united face to the growth in power of the capitalist state and church. It was made up of many disparate elements, ranging from the near-orthodox to the neo-pagan. How far Francis was consciously influenced by any of them is uncertain. But their undeniable popularity proves that he was not an innovator in the sense that he was fired by an idea

---

* Cf. S. Clasen, *Armutsbewegungen* art. in *Lexikon für Theologie und Kirche*, I, pp. 88ff.

A. C. Shannon, *The Popes and Heresy in the Thirteenth Century*, Villanova, Pennsylvania, 1949.

which had never occurred to anyone before. His originality lay elsewhere, chiefly in his success in keeping his own expression of the quest for perfection within the pale of orthodoxy.

Even Joachim of Flora only just escaped condemnation during his lifetime. Other contemporary reformers and preachers of freedom were not so mild as Joachim, though some of them started off with wholly orthodox intentions. One of the most influential of them was Peter, called Waldo, leader of the Poor in Spirit, a movement with remarkable similarities in its origin to Francis's own.* Until his conversion, nine years before Francis's birth, in 1173, Peter was a prosperous merchant at Lyons. What moved him to examine his life and find it wanting was the story of Saint Alexius as told on a street corner one Sunday morning by a professional storyteller, a *joculator*. His self-examination led him to consult a priest. The priest quoted to him the text: 'If thou wilt be perfect, go and sell all that thou hast, and give to the poor'. Peter took the injunction literally, and forthwith made himself the first 'Poor Man of Lyons', providing for his wife before setting off to beg his living, but leaving himself with absolutely nothing.

His movement's most dedicated enemy, the Dominican Etienne de Bourbon, later said that his followers 'called themselves the Poor in Spirit, because the Lord said, "Blessed are the poor in spirit".' He also records that Waldo had the scriptures translated into French, first for his own use, then for the members of his sect: first the gospels, then 'many books of the bible' and afterwards 'proof-texts from the saints, arranged under heads, which they call sentences'. The Poor in Spirit learned by heart their favourite passages from the scriptures and quotations from the saints supporting their interpretation of the gospels, using them to preach to the poor in their own language. Peter's initiative in having the scriptures translated was one of the root causes of later Roman suspicion of the vernacular bible. He used his French gospels to attack ecclesiastical capitalism, preaching apostolic poverty, and arguing that as Christ and his apostles had been poor men, so popes, cardinals, bishops, monks and priests ought also to be poor.

He was suspect because he preached to the poorest, suspect

---

* Cf. G. Gonnet, *Enchiridion fontium Valdensium*, Torre Pelice, 1958.

because he preached in French, and most suspect because he urged others – people of all the lowest occupations, Etienne of Bourbon complains – to preach without licences from their bishops, or any formal training.

The worst fears of the authorities regarding the Poor in Spirit were quickly realized. These medieval demonstrators soon found other banners to carry as well as the message of apostolic poverty. They were accused of every kind of heresy, as well as of preaching revolution, but in 1179, at the Second Lateran Council, Peter temporarily silenced the opposition by obtaining from Pope Alexander III a dispensation for himself and his followers to preach wherever the local priest allowed. Three years later, however, Archbishop Bellesmains of Lyons banned the sect from his archdiocese, and in 1184, frightened by the movement's continued advance, Pope Lucius III condemned it altogether.

Lucius's decree, promulgated at Verona Cathedral on 4 November 1184, simultaneously with an Imperial Constitution against heresy issued in the name of Frederick Barbarossa, should be regarded as one of the most notorious documents in Christian history. It marked the beginning of the transformation of the theoretical rule of Christ into an actual reign of terror.

Centuries had passed since a heretic had been burned in the West for his opinions alone, and although the popes, as secular rulers of the states of the church, did not hesitate to use armies to enforce their authority, they had traditionally used force only to compel political obedience. When in 1169 Arnold of Brescia,* who had declared that the pope and the bishops should own nothing because everything belonged to the people, was executed at Rome for heresy and rebellion, churchmen everywhere were shocked and dismayed. 'Evil though his doctrines were', Gerhon the Provost of Reichersberg had written, 'I could have wished that Arnold had been punished with prison or exile, and not by death; and now that he has been killed, I could wish that it had been in circumstances in which neither the Roman *curia* nor the church could have been held responsible'.

Alexander III's Lateran Council had laid down a procedure for identifying heretics, with a view to converting them, but Lucius

---

* Cf. A. Frugoni, *Arnaldo da Brescia nelle fonti del seculo XII*, Rome, 1954.

III's decretal of 1184 sowed the seeds of later persecution. It condemned not only the Poor in Spirit, but also a whole host of other sects, together with anyone who advocated unlicensed preaching or taught differently from the church on baptism, the eucharist, the forgiveness of sins, or marriage.

It was one thing to ban the Poor in Spirit, ordering bishops to seek them out, and local imperial courts to punish them: it was another to make the new co-operation between church and state effective. Peter's Poor Men already had many loyal friends among the poor, and early attempts at persecution drove them into alliance with other sects on the banned list. The Poor in Spirit survived, continuing to preach apostolic poverty, until long after Francis Bernardone had made it at least temporarily respectable to do so. But by then they were also teaching a variety of other revolutionary doctrines, which he certainly would not have approved, especially the voluntary separation of husbands and wives (without either submitting to the 'higher' discipline of the monastic life), and the right of every good man to preach and celebrate the eucharist. Driven into the hills of eastern France by continual pressure from the authorities, they had to organize themselves to survive, and so naturally in orthodox eyes became schismatics as well as heretics, a menace to the whole unitary fabric of medieval life.

Joachim of Flora and Peter Waldo were not the only preachers of apostolic poverty and Christian freedom in the half-century before Francis began to preach. Arnold of Brescia's followers proclaimed him a martyr to poverty, justice and freedom, and continued to work against the growing power of the church in Italy; they too were denounced at Verona, together with another group, later called 'the Humble Men', *humiliati*, whose movement was strongest in Lombardy, where at times its teaching also assumed anti-papal political overtones.*

As Innocent III later recognized, many of the Humble Men were strictly orthodox. They merely wanted freedom to live simple lives, imitating the life of Christ as they imagined it. They therefore rejected any form of profit as usury, and worked as farmers or labourers to earn enough to eat, wearing the plainest

---

* Cf. A de Stefano, *Delle Origini e della natura del primitivo movimento degli Umiliati* in *Archivum romanicum 11*, 1927, pp. 31ff.

undyed clothing, and joining together for prayer and mutual encouragement. A few among them progressed from denunciation of the church's wealth to condemnation of the clergy as such. Their revolt was spearheaded by a man named Hugo Speroni, who had once studied with the noted theologian and canon lawyer Master Vacarius, and was afterwards three times consul of his native city. From Vacarius's refutation of Speroni's teaching, it is clear that by about 1180 he wished to overthrow the whole hierarchical and sacramental system of the church. A herald of the later Society of Friends, he preached interior baptism and spiritual communion; without sacraments or priesthood. Few were willing to go so far with him. Lucius III's condemnation of their movement temporarily drove the Humble Men out of the church, but between 1199 and 1201 Innocent III succeeded in reconciling many of them to his rule, sensibly permitting them to keep their distinctive dress and meetings for prayer. Some, however, remained outside the church, even after further negotiations had led to another group of them, the Poor Catholics, submitting to orthodox clerical direction in 1206.* By that time, those who had strayed furthest from orthodoxy were already being identified in popular thinking both with the Poor in Spirit and what to Innocent and his advisers seemed the biggest and most dangerous threat to European unity under the papacy, the 'church' of the Albigenses, the Cathari, the Pure.†

So much has been written about Cathars, most of it – until this present century at least – by their enemies, that it is difficult to pick out fact from fiction with regard to them. To Innocent III, at least, they were the arch-enemy, a menace to both his political and religious authority. Their faith was much older than Christianity itself. Its essence was that matter, the physical world, is evil: only the clean, the *catharoi*, who have freed themselves from all worldly concerns and from all ties between the soul and the physical universe, can ultimately be united to God. Their ideas were thus related to those of the pre-Christian and Christian gnostics, the Manichees of the third century, and the neo-Platonists of the fourth and also, it is often claimed, to those

---

* Cf. Clasen, *op cit.*, and E. Werner, *Pauperes Christi*, Leipzig, 1956.
† Cf. A. Borst, *Die Katherer*, Stuttgart, 1953.

of the old religion of Europe which the church called witchcraft and satanism.

Whether Catharism was originally a loosely-knit creed is uncertain. The first organized Cathar churches to trouble the orthodox authorities emerged in Bulgaria in the eleventh century, before the definitive split between the eastern and western branches of Christianity. In Bulgaria, they were known as the *bogomils*, god-bearers. But when they appeared in Asia Minor, they were 'the carriers of the scrip' – that is, beggars. It was as 'a beggar' that Basil of Bulgaria was burned for heresy in the hippodrome at Constantinople in 1118. Despite persecution, however, by the time Innocent III became pope in the West, the Cathar movement was so strongly entrenched in the East as sometimes to seem dominant there, and worse still, from the pope's point of view, had established itself firmly along the main trade routes of Europe, in Bosnia, Lombardy, and southern France.

How far the western Cathars were organized into a church is still debated. It has been said by their enemies that they duplicated the whole Roman system, with a pope of their own and territorial provinces and dioceses, each with its own 'bishop'. Their organization may well not have been as formal as this suggests, but their strength lay not so much in their organization as in the facts that, first, they were opposed to papal sovereignty in religio-political affairs and so had national appeal, and second that their Perfect Men, the adepts of their faith, set themselves so high a standard of asceticism that they could not fail to attract anyone disgusted with the hypocrisy – as it so often appeared – of Christian leaders, preaching acceptance of poverty to the poor, but themselves often living in great style, arguing that their social or political position demanded it.

The Perfect Men genuinely did live without meat, marriage, or property. They were pacifist to the point of avoiding not simply war, but even argument. Yet they allowed total freedom to their congregations, on the grounds that as any contact with the physical world was totally corrupting, a simple believer could not harm himself further whatever he did. He was already totally corrupt. His only hope was that communion with the Perfect in this life would help him in the next, whether reborn into this world or into another. Hence the accusations of concubinage, sodomy, gross blasphemy, and treachery brought against the sect, despite the admitted asceticism of its leaders.

The only 'sacrament' offered to Cathar believers was the *consolamentum* received by most only at the hour of death. By it, the believer, receiving bread, water, and probably a fish from a Perfect Man, shared in the general holiness of the Cathar body. Only those wishing to attempt to live among the Perfect received the consolation earlier in life, and those who found themselves incapable of pursuing perfection after receiving it were urged to free their souls from the prison of the body at the earliest possible moment, not actually by killing themselves – all killing was forbidden – but by allowing themselves to starve to death, undergoing complete 'mortification' of the body, in the Christian word, through the ceremony significantly called *endura*.

The Cathar church offered freedom from the pope and his bishops and abbots; freedom to choose one's own path to God; freedom to use one's own language in worship. Its appeal, though not immediately obvious today, was very real during Francis's lifetime. In France, and especially in Languedoc, it was strong enough by the mid-twelfth century to hold 'church' councils of its own. There was one at Saint-Felix de Caraman near Toulouse in 1167, only four years after Pope Alexander III had held a council at Tours where the sect was banned. The council of Saint-Felix is said to have appointed new 'bishops' and set up a commission to fix boundaries for their 'dioceses'. Its appointee to the Diocese of Albi, Barthélemy of Carcasonne, was so famous for his asceticism that Cathar believers ultimately came to be known as Albigenses in that part of France, although elsewhere they were commonly called *textores*, weavers, because it was so often among textile workers that the sect found its most ardent adherents.

By the time of Pope Innocent III's accession, another factor had entered the situation in France, with the succession of Raymond V to the county of Toulouse. In constitutional theory, Toulouse was the most Catholic of all the multitude of petty principalities, duchies and counties making up what is now France, and in consequence its bishops were left free to conduct church affairs as they thought best. Intellectually, its court was one of the most brilliant in Europe. Its music was famed throughout the western world. The chivalry of its knights captured imaginations all the way to Acre. As the popes saw it, however, the counts of Toulouse had for several generations held the moral attitudes of the eastern Franks of Ultramar. Too many of them had spent too long in the Holy Land. The Court of Toulouse was *the* Court of Love. Although Raymond V was a feudal lord like any other, and a very successful capitalist, there was a freedom about Toulouse not to be found elsewhere, and the combination of Oriental freedom at court with Manichean freedom among Cathar believers in the county was too much for the strict legal moralist Innocent III to stomach. When early in the thirteenth century he decided that the time had come to stamp out heresy once and for all time, it was with the Albigenses of Languedoc and the county of Toulouse that he began the war, ordering Philip Augustus of France proper to lead a crusade against them.

On 21 July 1209, four months after Francis began to preach perfection at Assisi, 7,000 old men, women and children, seeking refuge in the Madeleine church at Béziers, were murdered there in circumstances of the utmost horror. The Cathedral church of Saint-Nazarenius was razed. The war that destroyed a civilization and a pope's integrity had begun.*

In France, the Poor in Spirit and orthodox Catholics died with the Cathars. In Lombardy, both Cathars and Humble Men came under the gravest suspicion. It was not a good year, on the face of it, in which to start preaching perfection through poverty and denial of the world. It can only have been because Francis was so obviously guileless and unmenacing that he was permitted to teach at all. There is no evidence that he ever directly attacked the monastic ideal (although he fought to prevent the

---

* Some have attempted to justify Innocent's share in the horror of the Albigensian crusade. Thus E. K. Mann, in his *Lives of the Popes in the Middle Ages*, vol. XII: *Innocent III* (1925): 'It assuredly is a pity that the salvation of Christendom should have cost so much blood. But many more lives have been sacrificed for ends much less valuable than those for which Innocent invoked the swords of the Christians of the North. Innocent was striving to maintain the principles on which must rest all human society to the end of the world. . . . No voice was raised against the action of Innocent in his own age: but on the contrary, his moderation in the Albigensian struggle was praised by men whose sympathies were with the Court of Toulouse.' (pp. 260ff.).

Franciscans from adopting a monastic rule) and he was generally respectful towards the clergy, especially the pope. But his preaching of the quest for perfection in a state of total poverty was itself an indictment of the prevailing system.

Francis soon attracted attention, and acquired his first follower, Brother Bernard (I Celano 1, 24). This forced him to amplify his over-simple rule of life. He did so by adding two more texts to the charge to the Apostles which had been his original inspiration. Significantly, the two he chose were: 'If thou wouldst be perfect, sell all' (the very passage which had moved Peter Waldo to make himself the first Poor Man) and, 'If any man will come after me, let him deny himself, and take up his cross, and follow me'.

Little is known of the early life of Brother Bernard, later called 'di Quintavalle', except that, having often relieved Francis's poverty with alms, and come to admire him, he finally joined him at Blessed Mary of Jehosophat, and asked to be allowed to stay. Francis told him to sell everything he had and give the proceeds to the poor. He obeyed. Later, he was one of the Order's first missionaries.

Thomas of Celano says that the Rule followed by Francis and Bernard was a divine gift to them. Francis opened the book of the gospels three times at random, and put his finger on the three verses of the primitive Rule. While it is perfectly possible that the two men went through this solemn ceremony to discover the divine will for them, the coincidence is very difficult to accept, especially in the light of the prevailing revulsion against medieval capitalism. It seems even more unlikely if one has read the story of Saint Augustine's conversion from paganism in his *Confessions*. Augustine says that one day a child playing outside his house sang over and over again the phrase 'Take it and read it!' and moved by he knew not what he took up the first book that came to hand, and found himself reading a part of the Epistle to the Romans in which Saint Paul calls for conversion to a more ascetic way of life. In the thirteenth century, Augustine was one of the most influential of early Christian writers, and Celano's *Lives* contain several reflections of his thought and phraseology. That Augustine should by coincidence, or the finger of God, have lighted on the one text that could touch him is perfectly credible. That Francis and Bernard should have lighted upon precisely the three passages that epitomized Francis's ideals and summed up the aims of the general reforming movement is all but unbelievable.

The more likely truth is that in the first instance Francis had no plans to found an Order. His aim was personal holiness and perfection. When first Bernard and then others joined him, and needed precepts – 'sentences' in the jargon of both the lawyers and the Poor in Spirit – to guide them, he made them learn by heart these three texts as the touchstone of their actions in all circumstances.

The aim was perfection. The interesting thing about medieval Christian perfectionism with its emphasis on perfection through poverty is that there is no evidence that Christ and his followers the apostles practised total poverty as though it were an art to be perfected by constant attention to its skills. Maybe they impoverished themselves by giving alms and going out to preach instead of following their trades, but there is little or no evidence in the New Testament that they deliberately reduced themselves to beggary as a praiseworthy end in itself. Only Saint Luke, the gentile among the evangelists, makes Christ bless the poor. Christ used monied friends. Judas kept the common apostolic purse. The rich young man was told to 'sell all ... and give to the poor' not apparently because possessions as such were intrinsically evil, but because he worshipped his wealth.

It was the eremitical prophets, from Elijah to John the Baptist, who wooed and pursued poverty. Though the urge to make oneself 'like Christ' by imitating not him but the prophets living in desert places on next to nothing seems to have appeared early in Christian history, it would seem to be of non-Christian origin. It was the *illuminati* among the gnostics and neo-Platonists, and the perfect among the Cathars, who were bound by their creeds to free themselves as far as possible from material goods as in themselves evil. Whether the adoption of this ideal of perfection into Christianity was valuable remains questionable. Its popularity in Francis's time is explicable in terms of protest; over-simplifying – but not much – the argument could be summarized: our bishops and abbots are obviously rich, and obviously bad; therefore they are not Christ-like, because Christ was good; therefore Christ, who said 'It is easier for a camel to go through the eye of a needle than for a rich man to enter the Kingdom of God' must also have been deliberately poor; therefore 'poor' equals 'good' and absolute penury equals Christ-like perfection.

Christian perfectionism through poverty was a kind of fanaticism, and all fanaticism is dangerous. History records the stories of 'successful' hermits; how many broke down trying to be hermits, how many slunk back to the cities, how many went mad, how many starved to death, history does not record. Francis committed himself and Brother Bernard to a life of discomfort deliberately chosen, and of cheerful acceptance of whatever evil befell them. By his acceptance of the injunction to preach, he saved his movement from the fate of many earlier eremitical groups. If his brothers preached, they could not so isolate themselves from human beings that they lost their own humanity. That the brothers became super-tramps, in the style of Joachim of Flora, was thus of crucial importance, if only because it saved Francis himself from going on attempting to be a hermit and perhaps ultimately withdrawing altogether into himself, as he seems several times to have been in danger of doing. In Christian terms, he was 'called' to a 'mixed life' of prayer and action. In its origins, his movement was a reaction against the oversophistication of monastic capitalism, the quasi-aristocratic life of the higher clergy and, at the same time, the Christ-less-ness of ordinary Christians of the middle classes now becoming powerful. Having tasted poverty, it is doubtful whether he had any romantic illusions about the godliness of the poor, but his deliberate courting of poverty was a romantic rather than a pragmatic gesture. He was an extremist and, in his own way, a rebel. He carried his personal protest against the corruption of riches to extreme limits. There is a story in the *Mirror of Perfection* which, whether it is authentic or not, perfectly illustrates the romantic fanaticism of his devotion to his principles.

It relates that a certain novice who could read wanted permission to own a psalter. But Francis's ideal – which he later had to abandon in practice – was that his brothers should desire neither knowledge nor books, and knowing this, although the novice had permission from his immediate superior to own a psalter, he asked the founder what he advised. Francis replied, very romantically, that Charlemagne, Roland, Oliver and 'all the paladins' fought to the death for the faith and died martyrs to

it, but nowadays men were content to receive 'the praise of men'
for telling the stories of what the heroes had done: similarly there
were too many Christians ready merely to read what the Saints
had done. A few days later, the same novice again asked permission to own a psalter; this time Francis told him that if he
were allowed a psalter, the next thing he would want would be a
breviary, and when he had a breviary, he would sit on a chair
like a great prelate, and say to his brothers: 'Bring me the
breviary!' Then he poured ashes on his head, and said repeatedly: 'I – a breviary! I – a breviary!' Months later, meeting
Francis in the street, the same novice again tried to persuade him
to allow him a psalter; Francis told him to do whatever his
superior permitted. The brother went happily on his way, but
after a moment or two, Francis had second thoughts and running after him, took him back to the precise spot where they
had talked together, and there withdrew what he had said,
reiterating the rule of the Order as it then stood, that a brother
should have nothing beyond a tunic, a cord, breeches, and, in the
worst weather on the worst roads, a pair of sandals.

Both the words and the actions in this story ring true. The
Mirror has been variously dated between 1227 and 1318; it claims
to be the work of Brother Leo, who also collaborated in the work
of *The Three Companions*. Whether the *Mirror* is early or late
as a whole, in this story it does reflect Francis's mind admirably.
The stories of Charlemagne and the paladins, recently composed
in French in the *Chansons du geste*, had set Europe on fire with
the ideal of chivalry. Francis's own dream had been of becoming
a knight of Christ, going out and doing things; his own 'thing'
was preaching by word and example, and seeking perfection in
poverty; pouring ashes on his own head and taking the im-
portunate novice back to the very spot where he had misled him
to set him on the right path again were romantic, courtly
gestures in the grand tradition though on a minute scale; they
were *gestes*, the deeds of a paladin translated into another field,
the quest for holy perfection, and performed in the name of Lady
poverty. The contempt reflected in the story for the great abbots
and prelates of the church, sitting on their chairs and ordering
their brothers 'Bring the breviary!' is too obvious to need com-
ment.

Fittingly enough, the first paladins of Francis's new crusade remain shadowy figures, despite intensive research into their backgrounds. Of those who gathered around Francis in the first months, Thomas of Celano names only the very first, Bernard of Quintavalle, the third, Brother Egidio 'Giles', who out-lived Francis and was renowned for his obedience, hard work and prayer life, and the seventh, Brother Philip, who was a famous preacher. Later sources fill in the other names: Peter of Catania, then after Giles, Sabbatino or Sylvester, a priest, Morico, John of Capella, Philip, John of San Costanzo, Barbaro, Bernard of Viridante, and Angelo Tancredi. Already when Philip joined the brothers, the story runs, Francis foresaw that the movement would grow until the original eight became 'a great multitude'. Thomas of Celano says that as their numbers grew, Francis came to doubt his own abilities as a leader, a doubt that was to recur constantly. Typically, he withdrew from the rest, and sank into the depths of depression; then gradually, his spirits lifted, till he felt filled with certainty of success and was faint with joy. From the depths, he bemoaned his wasted years: 'O God, be merciful to me, a sinner!' At the other end of the scale, he was beside himself, ecstatic with joy, and in that mood went to the others telling them that failure was impossible: 'Frenchmen are coming! Spaniards hurrying! Germans and Englishmen running!' (I Celano 1, 27). He did pause long enough to warn them that things would not always be easy, before sending them out 'two by two' to preach, in conscious imitation of Christ, but obviously did not waste much time instructing them on coping with difficulties (I Celano 1, 29).

That first year, Brothers Bernard and Giles took the great pilgrim route north through Italy, then west across war-torn Languedoc to the shrine of Saint James at Compostella (I Celano 1, 30). Where the other three pairs went is not recorded. Within a few months, they were all back at Assisi, and Francis decided that the time had come to write them a formal Rule.

So Celano tells the basic story, and no doubt it is accurate, so far as it goes, but it is so oversimplified that the picture it gives is one of a little world too well-ordered to be wholly credible. In Bonaventure's account of this first summer's preaching, just one of the many difficulties is hinted at, that of communication between the brothers. According to the official *Life* Francis solved it miraculously with a prayer that God answered by sending each of the brothers a message of recall; not only the original eight reconvened at Portiuncula; four new converts also arrived from the world, so that the group numbered twelve, like Christ's original band of apostles.

The Chronicle of the Three Companions is more honest about the difficulties. It shows Francis himself at odds that year with both a priest named Silvester, who had sold him stones for the repair of Saint Damian's and claimed that he had not been paid enough, and also with Bishop Guy, who told him that living wholly without property was too difficult for any man. No doubt the bishop was afraid that his diocese was about to breed a new heretical sect of Poor Men. Francis was very curt with him, telling him that anyone who owned property was bound to defend it with weapons and lawsuits, a telling thrust as Bishop Guy was a litigious and quarrelsome man. Meanwhile the brothers, wandering about and sleeping rough, telling anyone who asked, 'We are Penitents, Men of Assisi' were treated, like the tramps they resembled, with universal suspicion and as potential thieves, who were possibly mad and certainly ought not to be let into any house in case they made off with the silver. *The Three Companions* tell the sad story of two of them – one of them Bernard of Quintavalle – who went to Florence. One night, they were offered a bench in a porch for a bed 'because there was nothing to steal there but the bench'. Taken for the down-and-outs that they had made of themselves, they had mud thrown at them, were pushed about and had their clothes torn, and were even mockingly challenged to try to change their luck by gambling. Their story reads like a tale from the early days of the Salvation Army, when the *War Cry* was hawked from bar to bar on Saturday nights.*

Story after story reflects their memory of how simple it had all seemed in those early days – the tale of the coming of Brother Giles, for instance, from the *Mirror of Perfection*: 'In the early days of the Order', when Francis, Peter and Bernard were staying at Rivo-Torto, a ruined and deserted leper-house an hour's walk from Assisi beside the road from Perugia to Rome, Giles

* *The Three Companions* 27–31; cf. Bonaventure III.

simply arrived 'from the world' and stayed with them. After he had been with them for several days, a man even poorer than the brothers came begging. Francis turned to Giles and said 'Give him your tunic'. Giles took it off, and the beggar put it on. His ready obedience showed Francis that Giles was a true brother at heart 'so he was received', and afterwards 'advanced to the greatest perfection'.

The conversion from the world of the fifth brother, Morico, was even simpler.* Morico was a member of the Order of Crossbearers, devoting his life to the care of lepers. When he himself fell ill, Francis sent him a medicine of bread and lamp-oil (together with a great deal of the faith that moves mountains), and the message that it was time that he joined the brothers. As soon as Morico was fit enough, he left the lazar-house wearing only his tunic, marked with the cross of his Order, and joined Francis. There is no echo in Bonaventure, who tells the story, of the legal battle there must have been with his former superiors over his defection, but we can imagine that Francis would have ridden very roughshod over anyone who tried to take his Brother Morico away from him. His conviction that he was called to lead a revolution in Christian thinking and action often made him an impossible man to deal with; whether one treated him as inspired or as mad, the only thing to do was give him his own way. He was convinced that God wanted him to have Brother Morico; the only way to have stopped him enrolling Morico among the penitents of Assisi would have been to execute one or the other of them.

The idea has grown up, probably on the basis of the legends related in *The Little Flowers of Saint Francis*, that Francis was a pleasant and gentle man. So he could be – when it suited him. But he could also be ruthless in defending his own vision and pitiless in making either his own brothers or outsiders feel and look fools, if he thought that would serve his ends. There is often humour in the tales related in the *Fioretti* – but it is frequently a very rough, coarse and rustic humour. If Francis had been soft, he could not have created the Order of Friars Minor, writing

* The order of the names of Francis's earliest followers is very uncertain, though much effort has been put into trying to unravel the evidence; cf. Engelbert, *Life*, appendix 5, 1.

its rule himself and personally persuading Innocent III to approve it at a time when the pope was fighting all innovations except his own. Yet that is precisely what he did next.

6

The first rule

Before Francis could go to the pope and obtain official sanction for the existence of his Order, he had to give it a name and a definite Rule of Life, so that it could become a *religio*, a legally constituted religion, comparable, for instance, to the Order of Saint Benedict, or the Religion of the Knights of Saint John of Jerusalem.

Normal procedure would have been for him, the founder, to have appealed to his bishop for temporary and local approval of a provisional rule and the appointment of a chaplain, who would also act as a watchdog for the authorities over the activities of the brothers. The bishop would then forward the rule, together with his own report on both it and the brothers themselves, to Rome where, after suitable investigations had been made, and usually, suitable amendments imposed, a papal bull would be sealed giving the new religion the right to exist.

There were several reasons why Francis could not follow this pattern. Not least important was the fact that he had already clashed with Bishop Guy of Assisi on the main provision of his *religio*, that the brothers should own no property. The occasion when Guy condemned Francis's way of life (*religio*) as too hard may indeed have been when Francis attempted to persuade the bishop formally to recognize the rule, though it is recorded as merely a personal disagreement between the two men.

Moreover, the Order already had a chaplain, in practice if not in law, the priest from the abbey on Mount Subasio who said mass for Francis at Blessed Mary of Jehosophat. As was not uncommon, the bishop and the abbot were not on friendly terms.

They were later to quarrel so violently over who should receive
rent for a certain patch of vineyard that a papal court had to
decide the question.* It is unlikely that Bishop Guy would
have been willing to appoint a chaplain to a group already under
the wing of the Benedictines, or that the Abbot of Mount Subasio
would have been happy to allow him to use the Benedictine
chapel standing on the Benedictine Little Portion.

But probably most important was Francis's personal conviction
that what he was doing was not a thing of merely local importance. He was a man in a hurry, with no time for legal conven-
tions. Certain, once he had overcome his initial self-doubt, that he
was starting something destined to spread all around the world,
he naturally decided to go right to the top in person to obtain
approval for it. Given Francis's bulldozing approach to life, it
is interesting to speculate what would have happened if Innocent
had refused to sanction the new religion: the church might well
have found itself with a new order of heretics and schismatics on
its hands, despite Francis's frequent verbal assertions of total
loyalty to ecclesiastical authority.

In the centuries since Francis died, the Franciscans have often
wondered what precisely was the form of the Rule that Francis
and his brothers drew up for the pope in 1210. Many suggestions
have been proposed, but the truth is that no one knows. Thomas
of Celano merely says that he wrote 'a Rule and Order of Life in
a few, simple words . . . mainly from gospel texts, as his heart's
single desire was gospel perfection', adding only 'a few things
. . . absolutely necessary' (I Celano 1, 33).

Bonaventure's *Life* quotes this passage almost literally, with
no additional information. Almost certainly, the first Rule, which
soon had to be modified, was very brief indeed. Its main provisions can hardly have been anything else but the three texts
from the gospels which Francis adopted for himself, Peter and
Bernard during the first weeks of their communal life, and
among the few additions to them were, probably, notes on the
dress of the brothers, a simple injunction to them to eat whatever
was offered to them, inventing no complicated rules of fasting, a
statement of loyalty to the pope and bishops, and the formal
name of the Order.

* Correspondence in Horoy, *Honorii III Opera*, 1, 163 and 200.

To have legal existence, the Order had to be a corporation under the law, with a name to identify it, even though the principal provision of its character was to be that it should have no property over which there could be any lawsuit. The brothers' name at this stage was probably that by which they called themselves when preaching, 'the Penitents' or 'the Penitents of Assisi'. The primitive Rule in all probability also bound the brothers to allegiance and obedience to their own chosen leader.*

Armed with this policy-statement, Francis walked to Rome to present it and himself to the pope. How many of the brothers actually accompanied him is not known. Thomas of Celano says that they all did, adding that by this time there were eleven of them besides Francis. This may well be true: they were all equally interested in the outcome of this adventure.

According to the early Lives and Legends, Francis had little difficulty in winning a hearing from the pope, though gaining his approval for the Rule was not so easily accomplished. The brothers' first official contact was with the Cardinal-Bishop of Saint Sabina, Giovanni di San Paolo.† The brothers had an unlooked-for encounter in Rome with their own bishop, Guy of Assisi, and possibly also met 'the Lord Hugo, Bishop of Ostia', then Cardinal Hugolin, later Pope Gregory IX, Francis's great champion in later conflicts with authority.

The Lives suggest that Bishop Guy was delighted to meet the brothers in Rome and that he did all he could to help them (cf. I Celano 1, 32). It seems more likely that he did his best to persuade the authorities to have nothing to do with them, especially as the Cardinal-Bishop of Saint Sabina was chosen to investigate their Rule. He had a great knowledge of contemporary heresy in general and Catharist perfectionism in particular. The suspicion overhanging Francis is obvious. The Cardinal-Bishop's first objections to the Rule were almost identical to Bishop Guy's:

* Cf. I Celano 1, 32; L. Casutt, *Die älteste franziscanische Lebensform*, Graz, 1955.

† I Celano 1, 32; John of Saint Paul was a Benedictine who had studied medicine at Salerno and written a treatise *On the Virtues of medical simples*. He was made Cardinal of Saint Prisca in 1193. Firmly anti-German, he served Innocent III as legate to Markward of Anweiler, and in 1201 was made legate to France, with instructions to oppose the Cathars there. He became Cardinal-Bishop of Saint Sabina in 1204 and died in 1215.

the Rule was too hard, too demanding; no one could live wholly without property. According to Bonaventure, 'some cardinals' argued against the Rule as 'an untried thing' and 'too hard for human strength', whereupon the Cardinal-Bishop John tried to persuade Francis to drop it in favour of one already approved for an eremitical or monastic order. The suggestion was to be made again and again in the controversies of the next ten years. Francis's reply was always essentially the same: that his was not an eremitical or monastic order, it *was* a new thing, and needed a fundamentally new rule. At length, after questioning Francis closely, the Cardinal-Bishop was won over and took it upon himself to act as the brothers' patron with the pope.

It was a signal victory for Francis. It is a pity that the Lives make so little of it, representing merely as a victory for personality what must have involved a good deal more. Cardinal-Bishop John was not a man to be won over by charm alone, or even charm combined with obvious sincerity.

Innocent III had grave doubts about the Rule, as the bare phrase 'after due consideration' in Celano's skeletal account of his grant of provisional and qualified approval for it is enough in itself to prove. His misgivings were unconcealed when he told the brothers to 'go with the Lord and preach' and come back later, to petition him for greater privileges than the bare right to exist 'when they had increased in numbers and in grace'.

Gossip, as reported by Alberic della Tre Fontane, had it that Innocent was a man who lived on 'a great quantity of lemons'. The story may have been inspired by the pursed-up, thin-lipped face he shows to the world in surviving portraits. There certainly was an acid quality about him, and the last few years had been bitter. Though his German policy appeared to be bearing fruit – Philip of Swabia was dead, and he himself had spent the previous summer of 1209, at Verona with his ally Otto of Brunswick, whom he had crowned there as the Emperor Otto IV – very little else was going right for him. In the early years of his reign, he had laid great emphasis on the value of 'word and example' (*verbum et exemplum*) in the conversion of heretics to orthodoxy; his first mission to the Cathars and the Poor in Spirit had been conducted on this basis, with no element of coercion, by Cistercian monks living under a rule specially modified by Innocent himself to fit them for it. But in the ten years since, experience had soured him; though there had been successes, notably with the Poor Men and Humble Men of Lombardy, conversion by word and example alone had not fulfilled the high hopes he had once entertained for it. In 1208 he had been driven to call for a crusade in Languedoc. 1209 had seen the obliteration of Béziers. Now, in 1210, here was Francis asking papal approval for a rule which would make his brothers Poor Men in all but name, fanatical ascetics and untrained preachers. True, the Cardinal of Saint Sabina could not find traces of heresy in their opinions, but. . . . No wonder Innocent hesitated. It is surprising that he did not reject Francis and his Rule out of hand.

That he did not was probably due in part to the fact that Francis's 'untried thing' was not in reality totally untried. Earlier in his reign, Innocent had given permission for another group to attempt the attainment of perfection through poverty and preaching. On 7 November 1206 he had sealed a bull addressed to his legate in the Midi, authorizing him to appoint 'tried men' who 'imitating the poverty of the poor Christ', 'humbly dressed' and 'inspired by an ardent spirit', 'will not be afraid of approaching the lower classes' to preach 'by word and example' in Navarre and wean the masses away from the Cathars and the Poor in Spirit. The suggestion in this bull that the clergy were then afraid to approach the lower classes is a terrible indictment. A year earlier still, Innocent had called his clergy 'dumb dogs who will not bark'. Papal policy was failing at the grass roots. The 'tried men' in Navarre were to attempt to make good the deficiencies, and close the gap between the middle-class and aristocratic church on the one hand and the poor on the other. The leaders of Navarre's 'tried men' were already selected before the bull of 1206 was written. They were Bishop Didacio of Osma and his chaplain, Dominic, the founder of the Order of Friars Preacher.*

Now, in 1210, if Francis and his brothers remained loyal to the pope and orthodox in their teaching, they could provide the material for another experiment in conversion by word and example, this time chiefly among the Poor Men of Lombardy. *If* they remained loyal and orthodox. The odds were against it.

---

* Inevitably, the origins of the Dominican Order have given rise to controversy. The basic document is Jordan of Saxony's *Life*, ed. J. J. Berthier, Freiburg, 1891.

The main difference between Dominic in 1206 and Francis in 1210 was that in 1206 Dominic was already a 'tried' man, whereas Francis in 1210 was an unknown quantity, whose only recommendation apart from his obvious sincerity was the fact that he had asked for recognition before his movement had grown very large, and so demonstrated at least a desire to be thought loyal.

Dominic's loyalty, like his ability, was beyond question. A canon regular of the diocese of Osma in Aragon, bound by the Rule of Saint Augustine to an ordered life, he had already more than a decade of experience in the work of reconciling heretics before ever he met the pope. His bishop, Didacio, had devoted much of his life to debates with 'reformers' in Aragon and Navarre, debates which had led ultimately to the rehabilitation of many of them within the church as fraternities of 'Poor Catholics', following their own ascetic way of life, but loyal to papal authority and the dogmas of the church. Dominic may actually have helped the Poor Catholics' leader Durand of Huesca to draw up the rule of life followed by these communities and certainly took a lasting interest in the charitable foundations to which they devoted their lives. In 1205, he accompanied Bishop Didacio on a visit to Rome, the aim of which appears to have been to persuade the pope to set the bishop free from his diocesan duties to go on a mission to the Cumans of western Russia; papal permission would also have been needed for Dominic to accompany him, because as a canon regular he was bound to remain throughout his life a member of the cathedral chapter to which he had been first appointed. The pope diverted their attention from the pagan Cumans, directing it towards the Cathars and Poor Men of Languedoc. Thus the origin of the Friars Preacher lay with the pope himself, but it was Dominic who shaped it into an order of wandering and begging 'friars': the 'Black Friars'.

Didacio and Dominic began work with a force of forty brothers 'going out humbly, acting and preaching after the example of the Master, walking on foot, without gold or silver, imitating in every way the example of Christ' as the *Historia Albigensis* puts it. Their authority was the bull of 1206 and, faithful to it, they showed no fear of 'approaching the lower classes'.

Obviously the aim of their mission from the outset was to demonstrate that the Perfect Men among the Cathars and the best of the Poor Men had no monopoly of holiness as the lower classes understood it; that there were, in fact, orthodox Christians, licensed to preach, who were not the hangers-on of rich abbots living on their rent-rolls, or of bishops who if the Apostles had come begging at their palace doors would have ordered their chaplains' servants to drive them away. As Innocent put it, these missioners preached *verbo et exemplo*, by word and example, not by exhortation alone.

Bishop Didacio died in 1207, but Dominic continued the work in the Midi with limited success. He had already found that without centres to operate from it was impractical to co-ordinate either his mission's preaching or the rehabilitation of reconciled heretics. Many of the Albigenses were women and girls, who appear to have found the unwashed, half-starved, sexually dormant, and semi-crazed Perfect wholly fascinating. When one of the Perfect was reconciled to the church, his girl followers would also return. The only way to re-absorb them was to accept them as a community, and allow them to continue their lives of self-inflicted austerity. Dominic established the first community of ex-Cathar nuns at Prouille in 1207, though it was held in such suspicion that it was not granted a charter until 1211. Meanwhile, Innocent had lost faith in conversion *verbo et exemplo*, and the Albigensian crusade had begun. Not until the Council of the Lateran in 1215 was Dominic able to present his Rule of the religion of Friars Preacher to the pope in the form in which experience had proved it viable. After six years of war, Innocent's reaction was not favourable, although he had inspired Dominic's mission in the first instance. According to Dominic's ardent advocate Jordan of Saxony, he told Dominic to 'go back to his brothers and when he had discussed the question fully with them, choose by unanimous consent some Rule already approved, after which he might return to the pope to receive confirmation of all that they had done.'

At this point, the problem of the authenticity of the sources becomes acute. Jordan of Saxony's memory of Innocent's words to Dominic in 1215 so closely resembles Thomas of Celano's record of the Cardinal-Bishop of Saint Sabina's suggestion to Francis in 1210 – that he should accept an already sanctioned monastic or eremitical rule – as to throw doubt on the accuracy of both stories. This doubt gathers strength when these accounts are compared with the thirteenth canon of the Lateran Council of 1215 which reads:

> For fear that too great a diversity of religious orders would lead to grave confusion within the church of God, we formally forbid the foundation of new religious orders. Anyone who wishes to become a monk should enter an order already approved. Likewise, anyone wishing to found a new religious house must accept the rule and organization of an order already sanctioned.

Inevitably, one must wonder if Thomas of Celano (and perhaps also Jordan of Saxony) has not allowed this canon to colour his remembrance of what the pope actually said to his hero sixteen years before he wrote it down. But the truth is that already in 1210 the situation looked so dangerous and the church was so much on the defensive that it is perfectly possible that a formula, a stock answer, had already been evolved for those wishing to establish new religions. Innocent III and his legally trained contemporaries were happier with what they knew than with innovations. Though Innocent's early acceptance of Dominic's plan for the conversion of heretics by winning them over *verbo et exemplo* by wandering preachers shows that he was not always hidebound by precedent, a view of him confirmed by his acquiescence in the plan to allow the Humble Men to follow their own way of life within the church, his primary aim was always to defend and strengthen the church as he had inherited it, not to reform it radically; and as a lawyer, devoted to precedent, nothing is more likely than that he would have repeated the same thoughts in the same words year after year. The 'untried thing' might prove valuable: it was more likely to prove dangerous. There were many still living who could recall that Alexander III had once given approval to Peter Waldo's 'untried thing'. And everyone could see for himself where that had led.

Grave as Innocent's doubts about Francis were, however, and strongly though the cardinals may have argued to reinforce them, he put the penitents of Assisi on probation, as it were, rather than ordering them to disband. Let them go and prove themselves: let them see if they could both fulfil their own harsh rules, so as to 'grow in grace', and attract new members to their community; then he would think about them again (I Celano 1, 33).

Later Franciscan writers found it so incredible that Innocent gave even such hesitant approval to the first rule at such a time that they had to invent reasons for his doing so. Characteristically, they could only imagine that he had received a warning from heaven convincing him that Francis must be given his chance. The story, as it appears in Bonaventure's *Life*** is a typical medieval dream sequence: the pope imagined that he saw the Basilica of Saint John Lateran, Rome's cathedral and thus the unmistakable symbol of papal christendom, crumbling and about to fall down; suddenly 'a short, common-looking man' appeared, and took the weight of it on his shoulders: so all was saved. Remembering his dream when he woke, and warned by the Cardinal-Bishop of Saint Sabina that to condemn Francis's attempt to live as Christ was believed to have lived would be to blaspheme against Christ, the great example, he granted Francis's petition 'there and then'.

Actually, Innocent's approbation of the rule illustrates his generally pragmatic approach to the problems of ruling the church. If Francis and his penitents attracted any followers at all, they were likely to be people of the kind which, if these orthodox perfectionists did not exist, would be seduced away from the church altogether by their admiration for the extreme asceticism of the Cathar Perfect and the devoted Waldenses. With the opposition to Catholic orthodoxy so strong, Innocent needed all the voluntary help he could find, whether its style appealed to him personally or not. At this stage, Francis did not strike him as the kind of man to save the church; but there were only eleven of the brothers, their names were known, they had no rich friends (such as the French Cathars had); if they looked like proving troublesome, it would be easy to round them up.

There was a peculiar and distinctive quality about the encounter between the tramp Francis Bernardone and the Prince Lothario di Segni. Its flavour is well conveyed by two stories about it which, although probably apocryphal, both illustrate how high-handed Francis could be when he thought the situation called for it. One of these stories found its way into the canon

---

* Bonaventure III, 10; cf. II Celano 17; *The Three Companions* 51-2.

of Franciscan legend, through *The Chronicle of the Three Companions*; the other, the Franciscans could not accept.

The authorized story related that when praying for guidance at Rome, Francis was inspired with a parable about poverty which he related to the pope: There once lived in the desert a woman who was very poor but very beautiful. The Great King saw her and longed to make her his wife, because he was convinced that his children by her would also be beautiful. The marriage contract was signed and the marriage consummated, and the king had many sons. When they grew up, their mother told them: You have nothing to be ashamed of, my sons: you are the children of the king. So now go to court, and he will give you everything you need. When they reached the court, the king admired their good looks and thinking that they resembled himself asked them, Whose sons are you? On their replying that they were the sons of the poor woman living in the desert, he joyfully embraced them and said, Fear nothing; you are my sons; if strangers eat at my table, so much the more should you, my legitimate children. Then he sent to the woman to tell her to send all her sons to court, so that they could be cared for there.

'Most Holy Father,' Francis concluded, driving home his point with a sledgehammer, 'I am the poor woman whom God, by his love has condescended to make beautiful, and by whom he has been pleased to beget legitimate children. The King of Kings has told me that he will maintain any children he has by me – for if he maintains bastards, how much the more is he bound to support his legitimate sons?' *

What the bastard clergy and monks, those strangers at the Great King's table, thought about this (it must have been they who were under attack: the fact that Bonaventure preserves only a watered-down version of the parable probably indicates that he realized this) is left to the reader's imagination. Ubertini of Casali, writing about the year 1300, says that at one stage the cardinals sneeringly asked Francis: 'Are you so much better than our fathers, who gave us our incomes (*temporalia*)?' If Francis called them bastards, and his followers God's only legitimate sons, it is not surprising that they opposed approval of his Rule.

The other story of Francis's battle with the pope is not found

* *The Three Companions* 50f.; cf. Bonaventure III, 10.

in any early Franciscan source, but was told by Matthew of Paris, St Alban's historian, only a generation or so after Francis's death. It relates that after Francis had made his petition for recognition of the Rule 'so very hard and impossible to fulfil', the pope 'bearing in mind his shapeless clothing, his comtemptible face, long whiskers, unkempt hair, and black, shaggy eyebrows', thought the matter over carefully, then looked down at him and said, 'Go away, brother, and find a pig – for that is what you ought to be compared to, rather than a human being. Stay with him where he wallows, and offer him the Rule you have devised, and so fulfil your task of preaching.'

'When Francis heard this', Matthew Paris continues, 'he bowed his head and went out, and having at length found a pig, stayed with him in the mire long enough to get filthy from the soles of the feet upwards, till his whole body was covered. And returning to the consistory in that state, he presented himself before the pope and said: I have done as you told me. Now, please, grant me what I ask'.*

It is an unlikely story, yet there is a feeling of psychological truth about it. Innocent was the pope who called his clergy 'dogs' and who reputedly lived on lemons: it is said that when he died, the whole world rejoiced. Francis was a man so direct in his approach to life that if he felt he could have his own way (which he was convinced was God's way) only by shaming the pope into giving it to him, by taking him at his word and rolling in muck with a pig, he would do it, so at a stroke unmasking Innocent's arrogance and proving his own absolute loyalty to the concept of papal sovereignty over himself and his Order.

Grudging and restricted as Innocent's sanction for the Rule was, when the brothers left him they had secured what was most

---

* *Chronica maiora*, quoted in Limmens, *Testimonia minora saeculi XIII*, Quarrachi, 1926, p. 29; if this rather doubtful story is in fact not authentic, it should perhaps be traced back to a story told by Pope Innocent IV in 1239–40: Innocent IV was Innocent III's nephew, and was himself minister general of the Franciscans in 1274–9, before being elected pope. Innocent said that Francis's first meeting with his uncle at Rome was accidental: they encountered one another in a corridor. Francis tried to raise the question of the Rule there and then, but the pope, worried by the Albigensian trouble, brusquely sent him away. The story may be found in an appendix to Bonaventure *Legenda maj.* c. 3, n. 9; 98, n. 1, in the Quarrachi edn., Rome, 1898.

essential to them, immunity from arbitrary interference with their experiment in 'apostolic' living. The actual record of Innocent's grant to them has been lost, but it must have been recorded in a bull addressed, probably, to the papal rector of Spoleto, and couched in similar terms to that granted to Bishop Didacio and Dominic Guzman in 1206, or the bulls authorizing the Poor Catholics to maintain their congregations and preach wherever the local clergy gave them permission. The Cathar expert, Cardinal John of Saint Sabina, was confirmed in his position as the Order's protector, both representing it at Rome and overseeing its activities on Rome's behalf.

In exchange for the right to exist, the penitents of Assisi had put themselves and their future entirely in Innocent's hands. In fact, although they did not realize it, Francis had sworn away the 'freedom' of God's 'legitimate sons', binding them to the service of his 'bastards' the clergy. But when they left the pope with his qualified blessing on their enterprise, the brothers did not feel enslaved. According to Thomas of Celano, they were 'elated at the gracious grant' made by their 'Father and Master'. From the Lateran Palace, they went straight to the tomb of Saint Peter at the Vatican on the other side of the Tiber, and after praying there, set off for Spoleto, full of plans for a glorious future (I Celano 1, 34).

One of their first communal acts as a legally constituted religion was to break their own rule, or rather, casuistically, and no doubt with some delight at their own cleverness, make it impossible for themselves to keep it. Instead of returning immediately to Assisi, they spent a fortnight at Orte and, as they literally owned nothing, and were close to starvation, begged their food in the town. But so that they should not have to share what little they were given with other beggars even worse off than themselves (as their Rule would obviously have required them to do), they lived in a cemetery outside the town, and kept their store of food in an old tomb, 'because the place was lonely and deserted, and few or none ever came there' (I Celano 1, 34). It was very human of them – but very ominous for the future.

7

The first hard years

For the penitents of Assisi, their return to the duchy of Spoleto with Pope Innocent's approval for their first Rule was both a triumph and a challenge. Not even Bishop Guy himself could now command them to disband and return to their secular way of life. Francis may actually have received the monk's tonsure at Rome, the universally recognized token that a man was under the church's protection, and owed it allegiance.* But the Order had still to prove its worth, growing in virtue and numbers as Pope Innocent put it, and the preliminary signs were that this would be no easy task.

Perhaps naturally, the early biographers make light of the difficulties. So, for instance, at this point in his story, Thomas of Celano suddenly loses all sense of chronology, and follows his account of the return to Spoleto with a rhapsodic description of the restoration of paradise consequent on Francis's preaching, with drought giving way to bumper harvests on the farms as the harvest of souls was reaped in town and country alike. However, even in this glowing account of the Order's development there are hints of the nature of the troubles the brothers endured, especially the constant problem of trying to live without possessions in a materialistic world which could not believe them when they said they laid claim to nothing, yet ate constantly at other men's expense.

They spent only a fortnight at the disused cemetery outside

* Bonaventure III, 10; cf. II Celano 193; *The Three Companions* 52; for the controversy whether the brothers were *clerici* or *laici*, cf. Egelbert *Life*, appendix 7.

Orte partly because Assisi was their home and they longed to see it again, but partly also, Celano says 'for fear lest extending their stay there might make it appear that they in some way laid claim to the place'. If they had stayed very long, they would have seemed to be establishing squatters' rights over the cemetery. This might have led to a lawsuit and their ejection; if it had not, they would eventually have found themselves legally endowed with title to it, which Francis did not want, but manifestly could make other people believe he did not want only by moving away. It was a minor incident, but significant as the first manifestation of a problem that was constantly to arise, until ultimately the Order had to give way to the economic and legal pressures of the age, and accept legal ownership of real estate property.

Another problem, one apparently more pressing at the time, presented itself within a matter of weeks. This was the question of how best to fulfil the pope's injunction to 'grow in virtue'. For Francis himself, there was presumably no problem: his aim was to be the perfect, penniless, propertyless disciple, preaching penance and the Kingdom, and whether he starved to death, or was stoned, did not matter. But the most perfect men the brothers knew were the Catholic monks and Cathar perfect, living in enclosed communities, and the hermits, living in wild places, totally withdrawn from the world. Some of them argued that only by imitating this retreat from the world would they advance to perfection. Francis, however, was adamant: gospel perfection as he understood it involved living an ascetic life in the world, combining preaching with penance, as he believed the apostles had done. In other words, the penitents of Assisi were to continue the experiment of converting the world 'by word and example', although the pope himself showed every sign of having lost faith in the system.

Returning to Assisi, they walked straight into a civil crisis. The peace between Innocent III and the Germans had not long survived Innocent's crowning of Otto IV in October 1209, and by the middle of 1210, the pope had excommunicated the emperor and put those remaining German lords in Italy owing allegiance to them both in impossible positions. Otto made matters worse by claiming the right to grant lands and titles in areas which had for years been under papal control. Innocent's appointee to the much-disputed March of Ancona had been Azzo IV, Marquis of Este, and actually a distant cousin of Otto's. The emperor had annulled the grant made to him by the pope, then reinstated him in his own name, so making Azzo in theory a traitor to the pope, and binding him in feudal service to himself. In the duchy of Spoleto, he had acted even more provocatively. While angling for the support of the German electors, he had himself confirmed the church's possession of Spoleto in a document known as the Diploma of Neuss, dated June 1201. Now, in 1210, he revoked the Diploma, expelled the papal rector, and made duke in his place the man who was perhaps Innocent's most implacable enemy in Italy, Diepold of Vohburg.

It was Diepold who in 1205 had killed the pope's champion in the south, Walter of Brienne, at the moment of Walter's victory. For years, he had terrorized southern Italy, acting like a land-based pirate, hardly worthy of the name of guerilla, although he had made his living by sacking papal-held cities in the name of an absent king. When, in 1208, Innocent had declared Frederick of Sicily adult, and therefore eligible to rule in Sicily, Diepold and his followers had ignored the declaration because at that stage the young prince had seemed so obviously the pope's man.

Diepold was to all intents and purposes a brigand, and his acquisition of the duchy of Spoleto could only mean terror, or civil war. He intended to rule as a feudal lord in the harshest sense. To the once-powerful and still-rich *majores*, whose expulsion from Assisi at the time of Duke Conrad's submission to Pope Innocent had led to the war with Perugia in which Francis was taken prisoner in 1202, it seemed that their chance had now come to annul the concessions they had been forced to make to the *minores* at the end of the war. To the *minores*, with whom Francis had fought, the moment was one of depression and fear. Before Diepold could tighten his hold on the duchy, there were riots at Assisi and elsewhere. In the autumn of 1210, when Francis and his penitents settled back at the old lazar-house at Rivo Torto outside Assisi, they found themselves confronted with the arduous task of preaching peace in their own city before they could preach penance to the world.

It has always been claimed that in fact Francis did play a leading part in the establishment of the peace between the *majores* and *minores* of Assisi formalized in a document dated

9 November 1210, in the name of God, the Emperor Otto and Duke Diepold. Under it, both *majores* and *minores* swore not to make any agreement or treaty with any king or pope or emperor, or their delegates, unless all classes had been consulted. In addition, feudal duties were commuted to money payments, tax-rates were fixed, villagers were declared the equals of townsmen (and thus were in theory no longer tied to the soil) and protection was promised to foreign travellers and merchants.

This peace treaty was in fact comparable to an English borough charter of the same period, such as that granted by the King to Bristol in the year 1200. What it meant in practice depended on the quality of the local overlord at any given time. At the end of 1210, it united the people against their new German lord, and made it possible for them to combine with like-minded inhabitants of neighbouring cities to help papal forces expel Diepold the following year.

No doubt Francis and his brothers did preach peace in Assisi that autumn, but whether in fact he played the leading role ascribed to him in reconciling the factions is undemonstrable. If the claim also sometimes made is true, that it was from this time that the penitents of Assisi began to call themselves the *fratres minores*, it is unlikely that Francis arbitrated effectually in the quarrel. At Assisi in 1210, *fratres minores* would not have been taken to mean 'the lesser', that is, more humble, 'brothers', but 'brothers of the *minores*'; it would have been a political label, as suggestive of commitment as 'the Workers' party' or 'the workers' brotherhood' might be today. Francis had fought with the *minores* in 1202 and he was committed to poverty; but he had not damned the rich for their wealth, as Joachim of Flora had done, and it is unlikely that he would have begun his mission to the world by deliberately alienating a significant faction in his native city.

When and how the penitents did in fact come to change their name to Friars Minor remains a mystery. The tradition as Thomas of Celano knew it was that one day when what later came to be known as the First Rule was being recited in Francis's presence, and the reader came to the words, 'Let the brothers, whenever they find themselves called to work or serve, never accept an office setting them above others, but let them always be the lower ones, *sint minores*', he interrupted with the exclamation, 'I want this religion to be called the Order of *Fratres Minores*, Friars Minor' (I Celano 1, 38). The name may well have been a sudden inspiration, but when it occurred is problematical. Almost certainly, if the circumstances were as described by Celano, it was not in 1210, when the Rule being followed was that very simple collection of gospel precepts recently approved by Pope Innocent. Yet it is here that Celano places it, to link the name of the Friars Minor firmly with the paradise-on-earth brought into being when the brothers returned from Rome and the charter was given to Assisi.

Actually, both these accounts of the origins of the name Friars Minor are to be regarded as rationalizations after the event. There probably never was '*a* moment when' the penitents of Assisi became Friars Minor once and for all time. They always thought of themselves as a band of brothers, *fratres*. *Minores* may well have been a half-mocking, half-admiring nickname applied to them by those among whom they worked. The Humble Men and the Poor Catholics were already well known in Lombardy: now, here were Francis and his brothers trying to be even humbler, even poorer, even lower – even more minor than the rest. The *fratres minores*, in fact. Once the name had come into use, whoever initiated it, Francis would have welcomed it as the briefest possible definition of what his religion was all about.

Whether or not it was the unsettled political situation in 1210–1211 that kept the brothers outside the town at Rivo Torto, they did not remain there long. Thomas of Celano's story of their leaving the place is that a poor man with a mule moved in, and they promptly moved out, so that there could be no dispute over property rights. It is the story of Orte cemetery over again (I Celano 1, 43). Despite later modifications of the Rule, there can be no doubt that Francis's own view on property was that which he expressed to Bishop Guy at the very beginning of his preaching: if a man has property, he has to waste time and energy defending it. The first friars had nothing, and were expected by their founder to want nothing but spiritual perfection.

Driven from Rivo Torto, whether by a counter-claimant or for some other cause, they moved back to the protection afforded by the Benedictine Order – protection they seem never to have acknowledged in so many words – returning to the little chapel in the wood at Portiuncula (I Celano 1, 44). It suited Francis very well in that it did not belong to him, but no one would want to take it from him. He used it as his semi-official headquarters for some years – until, in fact, he withdrew from 'the world' for the last time. Numbering too many now to live in the chapel's tiny sacristy, the brothers built themselves huts among the trees, so that while they were at Portiuncula they lived as a community of individuals, neither monks nor hermits, but more like Saint Anthony of the desert and his Egyptian friends in the fourth century than like any other Order previously seen in the West.

How fast the Order actually grew after the return from Rome is another mystery. The early *Lives* record the names of some recruits who became famous in later days, but are not precise about the moment when individuals joined Francis in the quest for perfection.

The year 1212 was one of crisis everywhere. In the outside world, Otto IV, excommunicated by Innocent and declared deposed, withdrew his army north of the Alps, a papal rector returned to rule the duchy of Spoleto, and in what at the time looked like a master-stroke of diplomacy, Innocent proposed Frederick of Sicily as the new German emperor, but made the prince swear to abjure the throne of Sicily the day that he came to power in Germany, so that never again would the papal states be squeezed between German armies to the north and south. It was not, however these highly-charged political events which presented Francis with his greatest challenge, though later they were to be highly significant to the Order, but the arrival at the Portiuncula of the first women to seek perfection among the lesser brothers, Brother Rufino of Assisi's cousin Chiara of Offreduccio, and a cousin of hers named Pacifica di Guelfuccio.*

Chiara's father, Favarone di Offreduccio, was one of Assisi's *majores*, brother to the clan-chief Monaldo Lord of Cariano, a leading citizen since the revolution, one of Assisi's richest men. Her mother Ortolona was a pious woman who is said to have made the same three pilgrimages as Giovanna Bernardone, to the Holy Sepulchre, the tombs of the Apostles, and Saint Michael on Monte Gargano. Again like Francis's mother, she had also

---

* I Celano 1, 18; cf. Thomas of Celano, *Life of St Clare*, ed. Battelli, Milan, 1952; and N. de Robeck, *St Clare of Assisi*, Milwaukee, 1951.

been assured by mystical (or at least, mysterious) experiences long before that her child would amount to something in the world, would be in fact 'the light' to souls her name proclaims her.

Chiara found Francis as irresistible as the women and girls of Languedoc had found the Cathar perfect, obviously for the same obscure psychological reasons. Having impressionable girls fall in love with them is one of the earliest perils that would-be mystics and ascetics have to learn to deal with. The indications are that Francis nearly failed this test. There are hints and stories enough in the *Lives* and the *Mirrors of Perfection* to show that he always found celibacy difficult.

The fact that Chiara's devotion to Francis did provoke a serious situation has generally been obscured because the ultimate outcome was a happy one from the Order's point of view. The tragedy of Heloise and Abelard was not re-enacted in Umbria, probably because Francis was too simple a man to allow himself to be ensnared into too much cerebration about Chiara and himself. His one goal, perfection, could fill his thoughts to the exclusion of everything else most of the time.

Naturally enough, the first meetings between Francis and Chiara were clandestine. And even more naturally, his biographers skate lightly over even the fact that they must have taken place before it could be arranged that on the night of Palm Sunday 18/19 March, Chiara should slip away from her home with her cousin Pacifica and join the brothers at Portiuncula.

Francis received them, cut their hair to signify their marriage to Christ, dressed them in coarse tunics like his own, and was wise enough to let them stay with the brothers only that one night. After mass in the morning, he took them to the Benedictine convent of Saint Paul, near Bastia. Not unnaturally, even their one night's stay with the brothers was too much for the girls' parents to accept a fitting. Chiara was Favarone's eldest daughter, and so far too valuable a property to be lightly abandoned to a set of tramps, even if they were allegedly holy. By next day, he had tracked her down. She refused to return home with him, unless he took her by force.

There is little in either of the best-known portraits of Saint Clare to suggest such a measure of wilfulness. Both that by the

Siennese Simone Martini in the lower church of Saint Francis at Assisi, and that by Tiberio of Assisi in the chapel of the Roseto at Saint Mary of the Angels show her as a nun and a saint, rather than as the head-strong teenager she was in 1212.

Within a fortnight, the nuns of Saint Paul's had found it expedient to rid themselves of her; she transferred herself to the convent of Sant-Angelo-in-Panzo, on the slopes of Mount Subasio, and there her sister Caterina, later called Agnes, joined her. Caterina was then aged fourteen and obviously, in her father's just estimation, in need of care and protection. He mounted a full-scale attack on the convent, and dragged her away. Somehow (the legends naturally say that it was with the help of a miracle) Chiara enticed her back. Francis claimed that he had given both Chiara and Agnes the veil, so making them nuns, but by what authority he did so is nowhere revealed. Nor, however, was his right to do so questioned. The nuns of Sant-Angelo-in-Panzo were in a very difficult position: they could not afford to quarrel with the di Offreduccio's and their powerful friends, nor could they tolerate having their cloister invaded by angry men. They did not actually expel the sisters and their cousin, but they made life as uncomfortable for them as they could. Chiara herself recalled in her *Testament* that they did not stay there any longer than they had to. Urged to it no less by Chiara than by Sant-Angelo's mother superior, Francis set himself the task of breaking his Rule by finding a permanent home for the sisters and several of their friends who, excited by their example, wanted to join them. Once again, the Benedictines helped. As several years earlier they had let Francis settle at Blessed Mary of Jehosophat, so now they offered the use of the first chapel he had repaired, Saint Damian's on the road to Foligno, as a home for the girls.

Once the sisters were housed away from the nuns it became immediately urgent to provide the material necessities without which they could not live. They had bound themselves by the brothers' vow of absolute poverty, but in 1212 it was unthinkable that they should wander about, as the brothers did, picking up a living as best they could. Neither law nor custom would permit them to go from place to place preaching, and scandal would soon have destroyed the whole Order if they had lived as the Little Sisters of the Poor do today, begging their food from door to

1. A fresco by Simone Martini of Saint Francis, in the Basilica of St Francis at Assisi. Compare the earlier pen-portrait on p. 131

2. Thirteenth-century (?) fresco of Saint Francis in the chapel of St Gregory
at Subiaco

3. Saint Clare, by Simone Martini

4. The meeting of Saints Francis and Dominic. Detail from Benozzo
Gozzoli's painting in the Church of St Francis at Montefalco

5. Berlingheri's painting of Saint Francis in St Francis's Church, Pescia. At the left, the vision of the seraph (p. 156) is shown above the preaching to the birds

6. In the square before the Lower Basilica of St Francis at Assisi, a procession commorates the dead of the Franciscan Order – with that pomp which Francis so deplored

7. 'Franks' storming Constantinople in 1204. Constant civilian fear of siege and sack by disciplined troops is vividly reflected in this primitive work

8. The fall of Constantinople to the Crusaders the same year. Both from a mosaic at Ravenna

9. Assisi

10. God the father in glory, with the Blessed Virgin and Saint Regimus. The decorative panel above the main door of the Cathedral Church of Assisi; a 'new' work when Francis was a child

11. The interior of the Lower Church

13. Saint Francis before Honorius III, by Giotto

14. Saint Francis scattering the demons of Arezzo, painted by Gozzoli. In the Museum

15. Giotto's death of Saint Francis. The ceiling is cut away to permit illustration of the vision described on p. 14

16. Saint Francis renouncing his father's clothes, by Giotto

door. Once Francis had accepted these girls as members of his religion, his brothers had to take it on themselves to provide for them, and in fact the problem of doing so was to prove one of the factors slowly eroding the cardinal rule of the Order that no member of it should ever own anything either personally or in common with anyone else. In the end, social and economic pressure towards providing homes for the female branch of the Order from which it could not be expelled proved too great to be resisted and the convents of the Second Order came to be regularly organized and endowed. But Chiara herself never admitted that there was a Second Order: in her own mind, she was always simply a member of Francis's brotherhood, although barred by her sex from some of the aspects of its life. After 1232, when Elias became Minister General of the Order, she wrote to him as 'the Reverend Father, our Brother Elias, Minister General of the whole Order', emphasizing his authority over herself.

There must from the first have been some modification of the original Rule approved by Innocent in 1210 to cover the special requirements of the girls at Saint Damian's. But if Francis ever wrote an amended Rule for them, no copy of it now exists. The way of life at Saint Damian's cannot really have been very different from that of other convents of the time, apart from the fact that at Saint Damian's the law against property was strictly kept. At least in the early months 'our brothers' called often and the sisters visited them, though Francis himself soon introduced rules limiting these visits.

Probably because of Offreduccio's opposition and that of the secular clergy led by Bishop Guy, still no admirer of either Francis or the Benedictines protecting him, it took four years to win from Innocent official sanction for the 'Poor Ladies of Saint Damian's' to live without possessions, in the unprecedented grant known as the *privilegium pauperitatis*. The privilege proved to be a burden impossible to sustain, and the rule was in fact modified only three years later, in 1219, when a new Rule drawn up for the Poor Ladies by Cardinal Hugolin forced them to become 'enclosed' nuns, no longer able to mix freely with their brothers a couple of miles away at Portiuncula.*

---

* Cf. I. Brady, *The Legend and Writings of S. Clare*, p. 12f. and p. 103f., New York, 1959.

However, in 1212 the fight led by Chiara to preserve the Poor Ladies' freedom to be poor lay hidden in the future. For the time being, she was safe at Saint Damian's, free to come and go as she wished and Francis allowed, visited often by Francis and the brothers, and soon protected by two brothers especially appointed to the task, with the title 'Zealots of the Poor Ladies'. Unable to marry Francis, she had married Christ, and in romantic terms had become the embodiment of the Lady Poverty for whom he fought all his battles.

Not unnaturally, perhaps, none of the difficulties resulting from the acceptance of women into the religion of the brothers are spelled out in the early Lives of its founder. To their authors, Chiara and her nuns were always what the later painters portrayed them as, saintly women, untroubled by the world or the flesh, dedicated to perfection, and on the point of achieving it. Bonaventure called Chiara 'the virgin most dear to God', 'a snow-white spring flower' and 'an exceedingly bright star'. But it was a long struggle that finally led to such recognition.

8

The crusader

The year that Chiara joined the Order, Francis was once again gripped by the urge to become a crusader. Typically, he went about it in his own way, taking only one companion and no weapons, but that he went about it at all reflects the strength of the crusading urge then endemic in Europe. Fear that the Muslim tide would not be turned in the Balkans and in Spain, a genuine desire to do the pope's will and see the holy places freed, a lively spirit of adventure (the Holy Land was the Wild West of the High Middle Ages), dreams of fame and fortune in this world coupled with a well-indulgenced entry into the next; all these factors influenced men to crusade, though not all of them weighed equally heavily with every crusader. What did influence every one of them was what might be called the psychological atmosphere in which they lived. It was as though there were a crusading virus, as infectious some years as plague or influenza, and often as deadly in the long run.

The crusading-bug struck different sections of the population of Europe at different times. In 1212 it was tragically the turn of the children.* Excited by Innocent III's constant demands for a crusade to free the East, demands disseminated with a good deal of pulpit bathos by every parish priest, and numbers of itinerant special preachers, and encouraged perhaps by highly-coloured tales of the great victory won by the Christian arms of the Kings of Castile, Aragon and Navarre at the Battle of Las Navas de Tolosa, a young shepherd from the Vendome con-

* Cf. T. C. van Cleeve, *The Fifth Crusade* in *A History of the Crusades*, vol. 2, Philadelphia, 1962.

vinced himself that God was calling him to liberate the Holy Sepulchre, and raised an 'army', put in some accounts at as many as thirty thousand strong, composed wholly of adolescents and children, and set off towards Jerusalem. The hysteria spread to the Rhineland, where twenty thousand more children left home to march to the East.

The afflicted children, unarmed, unskilled in war, disorganized, without money, and without a ration train, were doomed from the moment they set out. Few ever returned to their own homes and none actually reached the Holy Land, unless it was as a slave. Unlike today's flower children and anti-war demonstrators, they were not protected by public sentimentality, or paternalistic government agencies, or even by voluntary welfare services. Some died of starvation, others died of disease. The rest were taken by slave-dealers and sold for what they would fetch in the Balkan markets.

Francis's personal crusade that same year was almost as badly mismanaged, though its outcome was not so terrible. His last attack of the crusading virus had struck him in 1205, when he had planned to join Walter of Brienne's expedition into Apulia. His conversion to the quasi-knightly quest for perfection had since made him a monk of sorts and freed him from the desire actually to bear arms, but it had not made him immune from the universal crusading disease.

Like the children of Tourraine, he naturally went to war unarmed – or at least armed only with his obsession. He set out not to kill, but in the hope of being killed, 'burning with longing for martyrdom' as Bonaventure put it (*Life* 9, 5), though he hoped for time before he was killed to preach the gospel in the simplest terms to the Muslims, so that his teaching and his death together would effect the conversion of many thousands of them. He must have hoped also that his French would be generally understood, for there is no evidence that he tried to learn any Semitic language.

It was probably in the late summer of 1212, when the first furore created by Chiara's impetuous joining of his religion had died down, that he took the road to the coast, with a single brother as company, and begged a passage to Syria. But his ship never left the Adriatic. A storm blew up, and the master was forced to seek shelter in one of the ports of Dalmatia, where he discharged himself of any further responsibility towards his passengers. Uncharacteristically, Francis's strength of purpose could not withstand this set-back. After wandering about for some time, looking for a ship to take him East, he suddenly threw in his hand and tried to beg a passage back to Ancona. When this attempt also failed, he stole a passage by stowing away, helped by a friend and one of the sailors.

Even this rather sordid little incident was gilded with a miracle story by Francis's biographers. Celano says – and Bonaventure repeats the story – that between Dalmatia and Italy this ship also ran into a storm; before it blew itself out, the sailors had run out of food, and were only too pleased to find that they had stowaways aboard with a seemingly inexhaustible supply of provisions. Emptied every night, by next morning Francis's scrip was always full again. So all came safe to land 'giving thanks to Almighty God' (I Celano 1, 55).

However, not even two Adriatic storms were enough to dampen Francis's ardour for a crusade *verbo et exemplo*. Either in 1213 or 1214, while the memory of two papal letters on the urgent need for a new crusade was still stirring men from one end of Europe to the other,* he decided to make a personal attack on the Islamic leader Mahommet en-Nasir, defeated three or four years earlier at the battle of Las Nevas and allegedly still licking his wounds in Morocco. The companion he chose for this journey is named by the biographers as Bernard of Quintavalle.

Brother Bernard, Francis's second disciple, belonged to a family well known at Assisi, and played an important role in the early history of the Franciscan movement. He may also have been Francis's companion on the abortive mission in Dalmatia, and was very closely involved in the drama surrounding Chiara's admission to the Order. Later in life, he was the founder of the first Franciscan house in Bologna, and stood out firmly against the 'luxury' of Father Elias, who had the temerity as minister general to ride not merely a horse, but a good horse, instead of walking like a true Franciscan.

In 1213–14, walking in the mode of Francis almost proved to much for Bernard. Francis constantly ran on ahead of him 'like

---

* Innocent III, *Epist. XVI*, 28 and 29.

one drunk with the Spirit' (Bonaventure, IX, 6), so that he had
to appeal to him to slow down. But once again, Francis's im-
petuosity proved greater than his strength. In Spain, he became
so ill that he could not go on, and was forced to return to Italy.
The early historians agree that it was 'by the will of God' that he
fell ill. The illness was clearly psychosomatic. By going to
Morocco, he was again doing an injury to himself, giving way to
the romanticism of crusading; giving up his life as a martyr in
the fight against Islam was not his *métier*. He recovered his
health when he returned to the task to which the self or his
God had called him, the care of his 'family' in Italy. But
apparently being forced by weakness to give up the planned
mission made him speechless with anger and frustration: 'Because he could not go to Morocco as he wished, he was gravely
ill', Celano wrote in his *Treatise on the Miracles of Saint Francis*
(c. 34) 'and he lost his voice completely for three days'.*

That the missions of 1212 and 1214 were aberrations seems
clear from the fact that whereas they were grotesque failures, the
work in Italy in these same years made excellent progress. This
period in Francis's life was that of the popular 'miracle' stories
of the *Little Flowers* and other legends, relating such incidents
as the preaching to the birds,† the 'conversion' of the hare that
followed Francis everywhere like a puppy, and the taming of
the wolf of Gubbio, which he forbade to be wicked in Christ's
name, persuading it to stop feeding on the dogs and people of the
town as long as the town gave it rations, which promise it kept
for two years, until its death from natural causes.‡

More important, perhaps, though not to the Francis legend
over the centuries, were the adherence to the Order of Brother
Albert, Brother Agnello of Pisa, and Brother John Parenti of
Florence, the Minister General of the Order from 1227 to 1232,
the crucial years immediately after Francis's death. Brother John
had studied law at Bologna, and at the time of his conversion
from the world was judge at Civita Castellana.

---

* There seem to have been two illnesses in Spain: one preventing the
journey to Morocco, the other regretting the impossibility of that journey.
Francis was to lose his voice again later in life, when things went very
wrong for him.
† *Fioretti* 16; cf. Bonaventure XII, 3.
‡ *Fioretti* 21.

More significant still in Francis's own evolution was his acceptance of generous gifts from Messer Guido of Cortona, who entertained Brothers Francis and Bernard 'as though they had been angels from heaven', committed himself to providing cloaks and tunics for all the friars during his lifetime, and finally himself became a hermit at La Celle, emerging from his cave only rarely, when he felt the need to preach penance, in accordance with the primitive rule. Messer Guido taught Francis that there was grace in accepting a gift as well as in giving one. The *Little Flowers* says that Francis was full of praise for Guido's 'courtesy' in giving, and that he matched that courtesy with equal courtesy in receiving, with the result that when another gift was offered to the Order, he was already predisposed to accept it gratefully and gracefully, rather than angrily rejecting it.

This new gift was the peak of Mount Alverna. It was assigned to the friars in perpetuity by its owner, Count Roland of Chiusi-in-Casertino on 8 May 1213. Francis's acceptance of it marked the completion of the revolution in his thinking begun when he had to provide a home for Chiara and her companions. In 1210, he had moved out of Rivo Torto because a man with a mule had moved in, and he wanted no dispute with him over property-rights. Now he was ready to accept a gift of land, the very kind of property over which most medieval wars were fought and lawsuits launched. No matter that the stony and infertile peak of Mount Alverna was of no use to anyone but a hermit: the point is that it was real estate property, and Francis permitted the friars to own it. Later in life, he moved back from this position to his former attitude, attacking those friars who accepted gifts of property and advocated that the Order should not accept gifts and bequests; but in 1213, he himself accepted the gift of Mount Alverna.

Alverna is a spur of the Apennines not far from the source of the Tiber, some fifty miles north-north-east of Assisi and thirty miles west of San Marino. As the *Little Flowers* tells the story of its gift to Francis, it came about quite by chance as the result of an impromptu sermon he preached at Montefeltro during the festivities marking the lord of Montefeltro's ennoblement of a local boy. Francis took as his text two lines from one of the songs of the troubadours, *Tanto é il bene ch'aspetto/Ch'ogni pena m'é diletto*: (So great is the treasure to which I aspire/That all pain is to me a delight). He talked, naturally, about the difficulties of the quest for perfection, and the rewards it offered, especially the joys of contemplation.

Count Roland of Chiusi-in-Casertino, who was one of the guests at the celebrations, was so moved by Francis's account of his 'treasure' — perfection-in-and-through-poverty and the imitation of Christ — that he offered the summit of Mount Alverna to the Franciscans as an ideal place for contemplation. The date is fixed by a deed authenticating the gift, signed by Count Roland's sons in 1274.*

It must also have been during this period that Francis passed a Lent alone on an island in Lake Trasimene (I Celano 1, 60). It is said that his first plan was to spend all the forty days of the fast without any food at all, but that he finally decided to take half a loaf of bread with him, so that he should not detract from Christ's glory by matching too perfectly the austerity of His fast in the wilderness. The story would seem merely one of those exaggerations which so blur the image of the true Francis, if it did not fit in so well with Francis's attempt, both conscious and unconscious, to parallel Christ's life in his own. To Francis, Christ was the perfect man, as well as God, and therefore the perfect example, but to have matched His example too perfectly might have suggested spiritual pride, the worst of sins. Granted the whole incident may be apocryphal, but if it is not, it suggests a certain calculation in Francis's quest for perfection. It would ill behove the courtier to appear more regal than the king.

This period of Francis's life is not well documented. Though one of solid growth in the Order, there was nothing spectacular about it. The significance of such happenings as Thomas of Celano's becoming a friar could only be seen years afterwards.†

---

* *Fioretti: The First Consideration of the Holy Stigmatization.*

† I Celano 1, 56–7 for the date. Thomas of Celano joined the Order in 1214–15 as a very young man. His significance to the future of the Franciscans, as the first biographer of Francis, is beyond calculation, because the particular form he gave to his *Lives* has shaped the legend of Saint Francis ever since. His *First Life* is rather a gospel of Saint Francis the new Christ, than a biography in the modern sense. (It was very important that Francis saw himself as the *Imitator Christi* in his generation; it was equally significant that Thomas of Celano also saw him in that light, and presented him to later generations as what Jung called 'the Cosmic Man, the Anthropos.)

The big events of the day were happening outside the Order's ranks. The most significant of them for the Franciscans (and indeed for the whole church) was Pope Innocent III's summoning of the Lateran Council of 1215.

The primary purpose of this Fourth Council of the Lateran was to stiffen the discipline of western Christendom in preparation for a great crusade. Innocent had, he believed, solved the Albigensian problem by liquidating the Albigenses. He had brought King John of England to heel with the help of an interdict on the whole country. The Spanish war of reconquest was going well, and seemed set to rid the peninsula of the Moors. If the German problem was not yet finally resolved, Innocent had gone a long way towards its solution by declaring Frederick of Sicily of age, and setting in motion the machinery that would be bound to result in his election as a rival to Otto IV. It remained only to free the East and North Africa, and bring them under papal authority in the moral sphere.

For this to be achieved, Innocent thought, it was first necessary to strengthen western Christianity by disciplining both the clergy and the laity through regularization of the administration of penance and similar reforms. His chosen instrument of reform was a council. Its bull of convocation, signed on 19 April 1213, and addressed to all the patriarchs, archbishops, bishops, abbots, priors and kings of the Christian world, calls on them to assist the pope in extirpating vice, implanting virtue, correcting excesses, reforming morals, eliminating heresies, strengthening the faith, assuaging discord, confirming penance, revitalizing freedom and so leading all Christian princes and peoples to decide to volunteer personally to serve in the coming crusade.* The council was called for November 1215, so that there should be plenty of time for it to complete its work before the crusaders sailed from Sicily for the East on 1 June 1217.

It was an impressive programme, and naturally only the less idealistic parts of it could possibly be fulfilled. Nevertheless, from Innocent's point of view the council was undeniably successful, if only because the attendance showed the world what influence the pope wielded. Presiding and visibly reigning over an assembly

* For the documents relative to the Fourth Lateran Council, see Mansi, *Sacrorum conciliorum, in loc*, Graz, 1960.

of archbishops and bishops from every country in Europe, together with the legates of their kings, Innocent was at the height of his glory.

Preliminary meetings of the council before its formal opening underlined the fact of papal sovereignty. The fathers accepted the homage of John of England and rejoiced to accept his kingdom as a fief of the papacy.* They approved the pope's confirmation of his ward Frederick's election as Emperor of Germany, refusing even to receive a deputation from Otto IV. They regulated the affairs of the Spanish dioceses freed from the Moors. It was a good beginning. In formal sessions, they were to achieve much more.

The council's final aim was always the success of the crusade, but its chief work was the reaffirmation of the faith in the face of heresy, and the establishment of rules for the punishment of those who broke the laws of Christian living. Innocent already carried the burden of thousands of lives in Languedoc; now he guided the council towards the adoption of a general policy which was to lead inexorably (though not in his lifetime) to the establishment of the Holy Office of Inquisition, with its malignant powers of arrest on denunciation and suspicion, and examination under torture. By the canons of Innocent's Lateran council, heretics were not only to have their possessions confiscated, their right to employment in public positions suppressed, and their contracts with their neighbours severely curtailed, as earlier laws provided, but were also to be handed over on conviction to 'the secular arm' for punishment. The clergy among them were to be unfrocked. The laity were to be expelled from their holdings by their lords, so that their property might pass to worthier men. Bishops were to oblige the faithful to denounce suspects (canon 3), and all Christians were to confess once a year at least to their own parish priests (canon 21), it being understood that any who refused to do so would automatically become suspect.

Suspicion was the keynote of the proceedings, and the approach throughout was legalistic, negative and oppressive. The winter of 1215 was obviously not the happiest moment at which to have to approach the pope with petitions for the confirmation of the

---

* In exchange, Innocent III had annulled the Great Charter, in a bull dated 24 August.

right to continued existence of those 'new' and 'untried' things, the friars. Yet Dominic of Osma and (presumably) Francis of Assisi were summoned to appear before the council and argue their cases before the pope and his advisers.*

Apart from the pope's legalistic preference for precedented action, the main obstacle to his welcoming the initiatives taken in founding the two Orders of Friars was that free speech, such as their preaching demanded, had so often proved dangerous to the unity under himself which he had worked so continuously to achieve. The council's general attitude on this point is shown by the fact that it accepted Innocent's instructions and condemned one of Joachim of Flora's free-thinking books, *De unitate seu essentia trinitatis*, and attempted to regularize all preaching under the authority of diocesan bishops.

Its ideal (canon 10) was that the bishop himself should do all the preaching in the diocese, but as this was obviously impossible (except perhaps in parts of Italy, where almost every town had its own bishop) provision was made for the appointment of assistants to the bishop 'not only to safeguard preaching, but also to hear confessions, distribute penances, and everything else touching the salvation of souls'. This somewhat loosely-worded canon could be seen merely as an attempt to put into words (and so legalize) the position of parish priests and their deputies, while reinforcing earlier rulings against unlicensed preaching. However, it can also, and probably should be, read as an invitation to every bishop to organize within his own diocese a group of priests, like Dominic's preachers at Toulouse, not under the control of any organization apart from that provided by the bishop himself. Dominic's Friars Preacher were subject to their own prior general, but local orders of preachers would have no prior general apart from their own bishop and could liaise with the preachers in the next diocese only through their own bishop; there would be no general rule governing their lives wherever they were in the world. Thus the policy towards preachers was to be to keep them divided, and so rule them.

If this was indeed the council's aim under this canon, it should have resulted in the collapse of both Dominic's and Francis's

---

* Cf. Gerard de Frachet, *Vitae fratrum ordinis Praedicatorum*, pp. 9ff., Louvain, 1896.

Orders of preaching friars. Dominic did, as we have seen, present a petition to Innocent praying him 'to grant Brother Dominic and his companions confirmation of an Order to be called the Order of Preachers, and to be that in fact'.* His initiative met with a double rebuff. Not only did Innocent tell him to 'go back to his brothers and after full deliberations with them choose, by unanimous consent, some Rule already approved, after which he might return to the pope to have his confirmation of all these things', but also canon 13 of the council in plenary session 'formally' forbade the foundation of new Orders. But this setback did not check Dominic's progress for long. Returning to Rome not many months after the council ended, and when Innocent was dead, he again laid his own Rule before the authorities, to have it approved 'fully and in every respect'. So by that date, at the latest, the plan to organize all preaching from the palaces of local diocesan bishops was already a dead letter. Dominic, however, was basically a conformist; the Rule for the Friars Preacher so fully approved in 1216 was not fundamentally new and untried, but a form of the Rule under which Dominic had himself lived so long, that of the canons regular of Saint Augustine, adapted to fit the life of the wandering preacher. Dominic was not the eccentric and original Francis.

It is not known whether Francis personally attended the deliberations of the Lateran council. Legend has it that he was at Rome in the winter of 1215–16, and that he met Dominic there. It is said that although the two men were so different in character and education, they agreed perfectly from the outset.

According to a Dominican chronicler, before Dominic met Francis, he saw him in a vision so clearly that when he did accidentally encounter him in the street, he recognized him immediately. In his vision, Dominic saw the Blessed Virgin present Francis and himself to Christ as the two men who would convert the world.

Thomas of Celano's *Second Life of Saint Francis* (c. 148) says that it was Cardinal Hugolin, the Franciscan's later protector, who brought the two founding fathers together, and put forward a proposal jointly with Dominic that the two Orders of Friars should combine, so that Francis's visionary magnetism and

---

* *Libellus de principiis ordinis predicatorum*, in Jordan of Saxony, vita.

Dominic's organizing ability should work together for the good of the whole church; when precisely this proposal was made, Celano does not say, though it was presumably after the council, when controversy over the future of the Franciscans became acute. Both the *Second Life* and the *Mirror of Perfection* (c. 43) relate how Dominic and Francis each rejected a suggestion by Hugolin that his friars should be eligible for promotion when prelacies fell vacant; Dominic on the grounds that 'if his brothers only realized it, they already had good positions'; Francis, similarly, because his brothers' vocation was to humility: they were *minores*, and called so in order that they should never be tempted to make themselves *majores*; they were called 'to walk in the footsteps of the humble Christ'.

The earliest sources do not describe these Roman encounters, no doubt because they never occurred, either at the council or later. They are designed to show how well the two founders agreed together, and are the products of a later time, when their successors were in bitter conflict. For that matter, none of the early sources mention Francis as present at the Lateran council, though the heads of all the religious orders were summoned to it, and he had every reason for being there, when the future of his religion was at stake. All that can be said with certainty is that the *fratres minores* did survive the suspicion of the fathers in council against untried things. Their protector at that time, Cardinal John of Saint Sabina, must have spoken for them, even if Francis was not there personally to do so.

There is, as one might expect, a later story telling how the Order was saved when the whole council was bent on destroying it. It exists in at least two versions, and related that, after the council had decreed in its canons that no new rules for religious orders would even be considered for approval, Pope Innocent personally declared, either before a formal session of the council, or in consistorial meetings afterwards, that the rules did not apply to the Franciscans, as he had personally approved their religion some years earlier. Naturally, his word was accepted as law. There may be a germ of truth in this tale, but there is no contemporary evidence for its veracity, beyond the facts that the Franciscans did survive the adoption of the council's canon 10, and that within little more than a year, when Cardinal John of Saint Sabina's died, they found themselves under the protection of one of the most powerful men in Rome, Innocent III's cousin, Cardinal Hugolin.*

Hugolin was not a man to waste his time with a movement doomed to destruction. Born Hugolin (or Ugolino) Conti, Count of Segni, trained as a lawyer, made papal chaplain and then arch-priest of St Peter's during the reign of his kinsman Clement III, he had been appointed Cardinal-Deacon by Innocent almost im-mediately after his election as pope, and Cardinal-Bishop of Ostia in 1206. Naturally ambitious, he intended one day to be pope – a position he later achieved, as Gregory IX – making use of the Franciscans (and every other legitimate group whose support he could win) in his underground election campaign.

That the Franciscan Order did survive the Lateran council and that Hugolin became its champion soon afterwards, suggests that in 1215–16 it was already too strong either to be suppressed without a crusade in Italy itself, or to be stretched on the procrustean bed of conformity. The time to force modifications of the Rule on Francis was not yet. By 1215 he had collected around himself a heterogenous mob of potential rebels against papal and military unity-in-uniformity; people like Chiara, who had deserted her home and defied every law and convention to be with Francis, or Morico, who had defied medieval legality to quit the Order in which he had made his religious profession to join the *minores*. By the strength of his personal appeal alone (in the first instance) Francis had wielded these individualists into an apparently loosely-knit but in fact strongly-united pressure group still, at this stage, totally loyal to himself. If by a false step authority had alienated that group from society (as the Poor Men of Lyons and so many others had been alienated) it would have become necessary to liquidate them. As matters stood, under the influence of Francis's imitation of the poor and humble Christ, the Franciscans were not so much protestors against monastic and mercantile capitalism and papal power, as protestants of poverty, humility, and the ready acceptance of suffering in imitation of the Suffering Servant of God. All their energies were contained and channelled in the relatively harmless direction of seeking

---

* The date when Hugolin became the Franciscans' protector is disputed, but it cannot have been much later than 1217; cf. S. Salvatore, *Gregorio IX*, Milan, 1961.

and preaching perfection. But one false move on Innocent's part could have turned them into fanatics ready to die defying the church they now championed.

Innocent III was pragmatic enough to realize that whatever the Lateran council might decree, he could force on Francis and his followers no more conformity than they were willing to accept, unless he himself was prepared to wreck the unity he had spent so long building in preparation for the great crusade to the East. By contrast, Dominic's was not a popular movement; it could be controlled more directly, and was so controlled by the imposition upon it of the Rule of Saint Augustine. With Francis, there was no middle way. His movement could only be accepted or rejected, unless he could be persuaded to modify his Rule himself. And he was not yet willing to make changes. He believed that his religion was based directly on the gospel, and that the gospel is not to be modified by mere men. So the pope had either to declare war on the Franciscans, or leave them severely alone. He chose to leave them alone.

Innocent's whole being was fixed on the needs of the imminent crusade. But he was not destined to bring that great enterprise to fruition. He died at Perugia on 16 July 1216, at the age of fifty-five, struck down by a fever while on a journey north through Italy to make peace between Pisa and Genoa, so that the men of those cities would feel free to take the cross.*

According to Thomas of Eccleston, writing some forty years later, among those who prayed beside his body before its burial was Francis. He had once more taken the familiar road from Assisi to Perugia to pay his last respects to the pope who, though unable to share his vision, had at least not compelled him to compromise it.

That same day, the newly named bishop of Saint John of Acre, Jacques de Vitry, arrived in Perugia for his consecration. What he found there horrified him. Hardly had Innocent died, he wrote in a letter to friends, before his courtiers deserted him to take part in the intrigues preceding the election of his successor; when the time came to bury the body next day, it was discovered that during the night thieves had stripped it of every-

---

* Cf. *Gesta Innocenti III Papae*, Migne, *Patrologia latina CCXIV*; and H. Tillmann, *Papst Innocenz III*, Bonn, 1954.

thing except a loin-cloth. 'It was that day', he wrote, 'that I truly comprehended the emptiness of glory in this world'.*

The gossips later said that in some monasteries the monks sang the *Te Deum laudamus* because Innocent the Oppressor was dead. But Francis cannot have rejoiced. Convinced though he was that God planned a glorious future for the Friars Minor, he must also have been aware of how much would depend on the character of Christ's next vicar on earth, and the attitude he adopted towards the brothers.

* Jacques de Vitry's letters are reprinted in Rohricht's edition, in *Zeitschrift für Kirchengeschichte*, vol. XIV–XVI.

9

Abdication

In the event, the new ruler of Christendom proved more positively friendly towards the friars than his predecessor had been, and so, paradoxically, came closer to ruining them, granting them too much and winning more concessions from them with smiles than they should have been willing to give.

Innocent's successor was the former tutor of the Emperor Frederick II, Cardinal Censius Savelli, who ruled as Pope Honorius III.* His election was an inglorious affair. The main impetus behind it seems to have been not the piety, learning and gentleness for which he was famed as the Cardinal of Saints John and Paul, nor his ancient and noble Roman blood, but the fact that he was old, and could be expected to live no longer than would be needed for the supporters of the two more credible candidates, Cardinal Bishop Guido of Palestrina and Cardinal Archbishop Hugolin of Ostia, to intrigue their way to the election of one or the other of them.

With fever stalking the city, none of the cardinals or their chaplains wanted to stay there a moment longer than was necessary. Given freedom of choice, they might well have gone back to Rome for the election. But they were not left free. Knowing the profits to be made from a papal election and enthronement, the Perugians rounded the princes of the church up and imprisoned them all together, setting a guard over them, and refusing to release them until they had elected a pope, threatening

* Cf. *Resgesta Honorii Papae III*, ed. Pressuti, Rome, n.d.; J. Clausen, *Papst Honorius III*, Bonn, 1895.

to reduce their rations day by day if they procrastinated in the hope of rescue. Under such pressure, it took the cardinal-electors only two days to shuffle the compromise candidate Cardinal Savelli on to the papal throne.*

Apparently, no one knew what Honorius's attitude would be towards any of the multitudinous problems confronting him. Early Franciscan tradition has it that Francis decided to go at the earliest possible moment to find out what future, if any, his *fratres minores* had under the new administration. It was a hopeful sign that Honorius was known to be very much aware of the dangers of wealth and had, as Jacques de Vitry wrote in a letter describing the election, 'given almost all his estate to the poor'.

That Francis did in fact meet Honorius several times is indisputable, but unfortunately there are two irreconcilable accounts of the circumstances in which their first meeting occurred. One of these stories, the tradition that has found favour among Francis's most ardent devotees, puts it firmly in the context of the death of Innocent III. The only near-contemporary evidence for it worthy of the name is Eccleston's remark that Francis went to Perugia to be present at Innocent's deathbed.† Yet there are still Franciscan scholars who argue for its truth. Briefly, the story is as follows: Cardinal John of Saint Sabina, the protector of the Franciscans, died a month before Innocent III, in May 1216, and Cardinal Hugolin immediately proposed himself as 'pastor and protector' of the Order, in which capacity he attended the annual spring chapter of the friars at Portiuncula on Whitsunday 29 May. It was probably in response to an urgent summons from him that Francis went to Perugia in July, to wait for Innocent's death and the expected election of his 'pastor' as the new pope. When the unexpected happened, and Savelli was elected, Francis promptly asked for an audience with him, certainly with Hugolin's connivance and probably at his urging. During their conversations, Francis effectively silenced the Order's critics by winning from the new pope a blessing on its work for the poor.

Naturally, in its 'received' form, the story is not as straight-

---

* Details in Giaconius, *Vitae Pontificium romanum*, I, 659.

† Cf. Little and Moorman, *Fratris Thomae ... de Adventu Fratrum Minorum in Angliam*, 1951, p. 95.

forward and credible as this. According to the legend as told by
Brother Francis Bartholi of Assisi* writing at the end of the
thirteenth century, the inspiration behind Francis's first visit to
the new pope was a vision of Christ and his Mother, and the
favour he requested from the pope was not merely a blessing on
the Order's existence and work, but the privilege which has
become known as 'the Indulgence of Portiuncula', under which
a pilgrimage to Saint Mary of Jehosophat was to be rewarded
with spiritual gifts equal to, or exceeding, those offered to
pilgrims at Jerusalem, Rome, Compostella or Saint Michael's on
Monte Gargano.

Bartholi's story is so unlikely that it is worth summarizing
as an example of the legends that later Franciscans wove around
Francis's life. He relates that some time in 1216, before the *curia*
left Perugia for Rome, Francis had a vision of Christ promising
an indulgence to whoever visited the Portiuncula chapel.
Emboldened by this promise, Francis hurried to Perugia to
demand from Honorius that 'anyone confessed and absolved'
entering the chapel on a given day of the year should 'without an
offering' receive 'remission of all his sins, both the guilt and the
penalty', so that, in theory at least, he was restored to the state
of primeval innocence enjoyed by Adam before the Fall in Eden.
This request not unnaturally shocked the pope, not only because
total remission of guilt and punishment was unheard of, but
also because he thought it 'only fitting' that anyone wanting an
indulgence should 'make an offering' in return for the privileges
granted. Canon 62 of the Lateran council which had finished only
a year earlier laid it down that no indulgence longer than a year
should ever in any circumstances be granted, on the grounds
that Peter's keys, with which he binds and looses sinners, would
'lose their value' if indulgences were too generous.

The cardinals reinforced Honorius's arguments with talk of
lost revenues at Rome if Portiuncula's indulgences were free.
Only when it became clear to Francis that Honorius would not
grant his petition for free indulgences on the strength of his
arguments alone did he mention the fact that Christ himself had
originally inspired the suggestion. Naturally, this changed the

* *Fratris Francisci Bartholi de Assisio: Tractatus de Indulgentiam
St Mariae de Portiuncula*, ed. Sabatier, Paris, 1900.

whole situation. When Honorius heard of the vision, he sanctioned the indulgence immediately.

Later versions of this story embellish it with miracles and additional visions. The whole thing could be dismissed out of hand as fiction from beginning to end were it not for the fact that in later times the indulgence of Portiuncula was unquestionably granted free of charge to all those who fulfilled the required conditions. However, precisely when it was first granted remains a matter for controversy among Franciscan scholars weighing considerations too remote from history to be discussed here. Whether this indulgence was already known in Francis's lifetime cannot now be ascertained, although several of the earlier brothers who outlived him were later prepared to swear that it was. Nor is its existence or non-existence at that time germane here, except in so far that Bartholi's story of its genesis bears witness to the strength of the tradition that Francis met Pope Honorius at Perugia, and so in 1216, for, once having left that city (some five months after the election), the *curia* did not return to it until after Francis's death.

All this would be much more convincing if Thomas of Celano, the Three Companions, and Saint Bonaventure had known the story and thought it worth using. Its emphasis on the needs of the poor and those unable to go on long pilgrimages puts both Francis and Honorius in a good light. Unfortunately, however, it is quite incompatible with Celano's account of the first meeting between Francis and the new pontiff, according to which the encounter took place at Rome, and so certainly months, and possibly more than a year after Honorius had been elected (I Celano 1, 73).

The story as told in the *First Life* is that during a visit to Rome on the Order's business, Francis was suddenly moved to ask Hugolin to arrange for him to preach to the pope and cardinals. Hugolin was doubtful as to the wisdom of his doing so, fearing that Francis's rustic naivety would provoke the princes of the church to laughter rather than devotion, but Francis insisted, and in the event everything went very well, although Francis was so full of the tension generated by zeal that he could not stand still, but hopped about while he preached, first on one foot, then on the other, as though he were dancing.

Celano does not expressly say that this was the first confronta-

tion between Francis and the pope, but clearly himself regarded
it as such. The passage is without indication of date, but the
context is a notable one. The scene is set with introductory paragraphs describing as all but total Francis's withdrawal from the
world into himself at this stage in his life. From 1216 onwards,
he did in fact gradually withdraw from the direction of the
Order, surrendering control over its development to Hugolin,
and its day-to-day operations into the hands of 'ministers'
appointed to various cities and districts, till only major crises
could recall him to his responsibilities as founder of the Order.
Spending days and nights in prayer and contemplation, and con-
centrating his attention especially, Celano says, on the wounds
Christ suffered at the hands of his executioners, he cut himself
off physically from the outside world, retreating to secret places
such as are beloved by hermits, and willingly emerging only to
preach, when he was sometimes so lost in his own thoughts that
he could not remember what he had planned to say (I Celano
1, 71).

Why such a withdrawal should have imposed itself upon him
at this particular time is not clear. There is no record that he
suffered any particular setback just before it began, as he had
at the time of his first attempt to become a hermit, after his
return from imprisonment at Perugia. There was, however, a
major development in the Order's growth at about this time, one
in which Francis was prevented from participating as fully as he
would have liked. This was the expansion of its work beyond
Italy, through missions to France, Germany, Hungary, Syria and
Tunisia, decided upon by the chapter general of the year 1217.*
Remembering how chagrined he was at his failure to reach
Morocco, it may be that his inability to lead any of these missions
himself forced him to a total reconsideration of his position, a
'withdrawal' from the world, and ultimately a decision to
abdicate from leadership of the Order, a step which he was soon
to take.

Francis certainly saw himself as leader of one of the missions
agreed in 1217, setting his heart on going to France. It would,

* Jordan of Giano, *Chronicle*, 3ff.; cf. E. J. Auweiler, *Chronica Fratris
Jordani a Giano*, Catholic University Dissertations, 1917; a convenient
English translation of the *Chronicle* is included in *Early Franciscan
Classics*, St Anthony Guild Press, 1962.

however, have been a most inopportune moment for him to remove himself several days', or even weeks', journey from central Italy, for the enemies of the Order were once again poised to destroy it. No doubt some of the wiser brothers tried to deter him, but according to Thomas of Celano, he insisted on appointing himself leader of the group travelling to France, and it was Hugolin who turned him back to his real duties, after he had already reached Florence on the journey to Paris:

> For once when [Hugolin] was acting as legate in Tuscany, Blessed Francis, still then without many brothers and wishing to go into France, came to Florence, where the said bishop then was.... As yet they were not yet bound together by extraordinary familiarity, but only mutually joined in charity and affection by the fame of [Francis's] blessed life.*

Francis followed his usual custom of making obeisance to the chief bishop of whatever town he was in, and so was brought to Hugolin, who asked him where he was going and why. On being told, he 'admonished Francis not to finish his journey, but give himself ... to the care of ... those the Lord had entrusted to him'. It was at this time that Hugolin 'offered to him his protection in all things' and Francis 'handed himself and his brothers over to him and committed them to him devotedly'.

Cardinal Hugolin was papal legate in Tuscany from 23 January 1217 to 14 September 1219, and again from 14 March 1221 onwards. If – in spite of the stories to the contrary – he had not met Francis before 1217, he may well have done so for the first time in March of that year, when he had just begun on his term of office as legate. He is known to have visited Perugia at that time, during his journey north towards Florence and Pisa, where he had special duties delegated to him by the pope. Celano seems to suggest, however, that Francis and he were already acquainted before this, though they did not know one another well: it was in the course of their accidental encounter at Florence that they began to be intimate friends. Hugolin used the weight of his

---

* I Celano 1, 74; cf. A. Callebaut, *Autour de la rencontre a Florence de SF et du Cardinal Hugolin*, in *Archivum Franciscanum historicam* 19, 1926, pp. 530ff.

authority to dissuade Francis from a foolishly ill-timed under-
taking. Francis not only accepted the advice as a command, but
also 'handed himself and his brothers over' to Hugolin, 'com-
mitting them' to him, almost as though accepting him as their
feudal lord.

From the surviving documents, it is difficult to decide whether
Hugolin had been officially appointed protector of the Order
before this, on the death of Cardinal John of Saint Sabina, or
whether the Order had existed since his death without an
official representative with the papal *curia*. My own feeling is
that Hugolin was already the Order's protector before the death
of Innocent III, and that at Florence in 1217 he was exercising
his official powers over Francis. If this is so, Celano's brief report
of the encounter at Florence conceals what was in all probability
an acrimonious confrontation, which ultimately resulted in a
better understanding between the two men, so that their hitherto
'correct' attitude towards one another warmed into friendship.
The actual date when Hugolin became formal protector of the
Order is not, perhaps, as important as the fact that when Francis
accepted the fact of his guardianship, he was prepared to give
everything into his hands. He had already tried once more to
make himself a hermit, now he was trying to 'escape' to France,
and that attempt failing, he 'committed' himself and his brothers
to Hugolin.

Henceforward, except when things went disastrously wrong,
it was Hugolin who was in Francis's eyes responsible for the
Order's affairs. 'The Cardinal in fact played the pastor's part,
doing the work', Celano says, 'but he left the name of pastor to
the blessed one'. It was Hugolin who argued the case for the
Order's continuance against its enemies, and Hugolin who persuaded Francis to give at least a minimum of his time to its
administration, instead of pursuing his own perfection exclusively
in contemplation and preaching. But here the cardinal was fighting a losing battle. Francis had no patience with administrative
detail, and would appear to have wished that there need be no
administration. There is a suggestion that on the first journey to
Rome in 1210 to win Innocent III's approval for the primitive
Rule he surrendered the leadership of the friars to Bernard of
Quintavalle, leaving him to pick the route and the stopping-
places. It is usually argued that it was Francis's humility that

made him subject himself to the rule of another: it may also have been in part his unwillingness to accept responsibility or face the demands of leadership. As time passed, he grew continually more irresponsible in this respect until, as is notorious, control of the Order's future passed out of his hands into those of Hugolin and such practical brothers as Elias.

It would seem to me that, forced to choose between Celano's picture of Francis's relations with Honorius and Hugolin, and that painted by Bartholi, we should prefer Celano's as truer to what is known of Francis's character. Throughout his life, he was a prophet rather than an administrator, an Elijah or John the Baptist rather than a Saint Paul, closer in character and spirit to Joachim of Flora than to Dominic of Osma.

To say this is not to deny that he might have visited Honorius at Perugia in 1216, but if he did, it was much more probably at the Cardinal of Ostia's instigation than on his own initiative. If he visited Honorious then, or during the following winter, it was more probably, as Celano suggests, to preach to him than to beg favours (such as the great indulgence) from him. The prophet comes down from the mountain when he has a message to proclaim. Francis was seeking perfection: he was not concerned with winning recognition and forbade the Order ever to accept privileges. His preoccupation with personal holiness led him in later years actually to betray the trust that the early members of the Order put in him. As early as 1219, he allowed Chiara and her Poor Ladies to be confined to their convents under a new rule drawn up for them by the cardinal protector, despite the violence that this did to the original spirit of their conversion. At that time, they still had the unique right to be poor conveyed by the *privilegium pauperitatis* marking them off from other nuns, but Hugolin was never happy with it. He could not annul it while Francis lived, but did try to withdraw it in 1228, when as Gregory IX he attended the ceremonies of Francis's canonization.*

Despite the fact the Hugolin was committed to bending the

---

* Though in fact then he confirmed it, under pressure, in the bull *Sicut manifestum est*; it was finally suppressed by his successor Innocent IV in 1247, after most of the existing houses of Poor Ladies had already voluntarily surrendered it.

Order in the direction of monastic convention – a commitment
he showed ever more openly as time passed – Francis always
saw him as the great protector he had at first promised to be. He
was Thomas of Celano's hero, and Celano describes him as
Francis's: his 'father' and 'mother' and 'master', his 'sword'
against his enemies, and his protective 'wall'. Francis leaned on
him, and leaned too heavily. There is absolutely no evidence of
actual malice on the cardinal's part towards Francis's vision and
the Order it created. Nevertheless, he damaged both Francis and
the Order, because his view of what a Franciscan ought to be
was not Francis's, but one more coloured by expediency and the
actualities of ecclesiastical politics. Superimposed upon Francis's
vision, it never succeeded in obliterating it, but did distort it
severely.

Practically speaking, of course, some form of organization and
control was necessary if the Franciscan movement was not to
degenerate into an anarchistic mob of beggars, saints and mounte-
banks, bound sooner or later to be wiped out either by an irritated
monarch or by starvation and disease. But any form of organization was bound to distort the simple quest for perfection of the
early days. In this sense, all expansion led inevitably to degenera-
tion, though this fact was not generally recognized at the time.
So the Whitsun chapter of 1217 at Portiuncula, the biggest and
most successful yet held, when it was decided that the areas in
which the friars worked should be divided into territories under
'ministers', was an unrecognized disaster.*

At later chapters, this first tentative step towards the hierarchical
structuring of the Order underwent a natural development. By
the time that Francis could be manoeuvred into writing a new
Rule, a second class of minister, the *custos*, had appeared. Later
still, heads of individual residences and hermitages were known
as 'guardians' (a title already found in Francis's *Testament*),
while friars controlling groups of friaries were *custodes*, and
groups of custodies were ruled by ministers provincial. At the
head of the whole Order was the minister general. When this
development was complete, the Franciscans had finally conformed

* On the development of the Order as an organization, see Gratien de
Paris, *Histoire de la fondation et de l'evolution de l'Ordre des Frères
mineurs*, Paris, 1928.

to medieval normality, adopting the pyramidal power structure envisaged by both Roman and Canon law as ordained by God.

In 1217, however, it seemed much more important to the friars that they unanimously agreed that the time was ripe for them to spread their activities abroad, both to the north, and to Muslim lands.

It is surprising that Francis's own choice as a field for mission work was France, and not Syria, where he could have fulfilled his old, crusading dream, as in fact, he tried to do later. The leader of the Syrian mission was Elia di Assisi, 'Father' or 'Brother' Elias, later notorious as the oppressor of the Order and general whipping-boy for all that went wrong after Francis's death.*

Yet despite his black record, Elias's early devotion to the founder and his vision was not obviously less than any other brother's. His origins and early history are controversial. Traditionally said to have been born at Beviglie near Assisi in the 1270s, he was over thirty when he joined the Order between 1212 and 1215. Previously, he had worked as a copyist in a lawyer's office at Bologna and may himself have tried to study law there; he had also spent some time at Assisi and worked as an assistant to his father, a mattress-maker. He has been tentatively identified with the Elias who was one of the first consuls of Assisi elected under the constitution of 1198, and may have received minor orders in the church. So Elias, the all-round-man, naturally felt himself in many ways a cut above Francis, just far enough above in age, education, experience of the world and achievement to come secretly to resent Francis's success, even though his loyalty to Francis's person remained unshaken.†

At the time of his mission to Syria, however, there was as yet no hint of troubles to come. The crusade so long worked for by Innocent III had at last set sail, not as a vast, coherent army, but as a dribble of ships and men. Its chances of achieving final victory for Christian arms were non-existent, but gallant men among the crusaders fought no less bravely for that. Elias followed in their wake, going first to Saint John of Acre, to found a very successful friary there, then, in 1218, to join the army of

---

* Jordan of Giano, *Chronicle* 9.
† For the story of Brother Elias, see A. Pompei, *Frate Elia d'Assisi*, in *Miscellanea Francescana* 54, 1954, pp. 539ff.; the reading of his character in this book is my own.

the King of Jerusalem, John of Brienne, at the siege of Damietta in the Nile Delta.

Meanwhile, Brother Pacifico, once a troubadour crowned King of Verses at an unknown Court of Love, had taken over leadership of the French mission from Francis, and succeeded in establishing a residence at Paris, after first being mistaken for a Lombard Cathar, and other misadventures. But a party of about sixty which John of Penna led into Germany met with disaster; Jordan of Giano says that their only word of German was '*Ja*' so they decided 'to answer any questions whatsoever "Yes" '; all went well until they were asked if they were Lombard Cathars, condemned heretics. Then 'some were jailed, some were stripped of their clothes, taken to a fair and made a butt for the people', so they beat an ignominious retreat into Italy (*Chronicle* 5). A mission to Hungary that same year fared no better. The brothers were robbed so often by that country's bandit-shepherds that they reached the point of despair. One of them told Jordan that he had 'lost his underclothes fifteen times... and overwhelmed by modesty and shame, and feeling the loss of his drawers worse than that of his other clothes, had dirtied his drawers with cow-dung' so that the next time the party was ambushed he would be allowed to keep at least this minimum covering. The ruse worked, but obviously a mission under these circumstances was impossible, unless the missioners were total fanatics, like the brother remembered in Celano's *Second Life*, who decided to play the role of a madman all his life, so that everyone would insult him for the glory of God. The Hungarian mission was made of more human stuff. The party left Hungary, sadder and perhaps wiser men (*Chronicle* 6).

Another mission to the Moors of Spain, which Jordan says set out that year (though later historians dated it in 1219), gave the Order its first five martyrs: on reaching Seville, then still in Muslim hands, the brothers were arrested for preaching against Islam in the crudest terms, actually in a mosque. They were naturally taken for madmen, and were offered repatriation to Italy, which they refused. Shipped to Morocco, they tried to convert the local commander, Amir al-Muminin Yusuf, by reciting the creed to him and commenting on it in terms he found grossly blasphemous. Al-Muminin had them executed (*Chronicle* 7–8).

In human terms, these missions were failures for the same
basic reason as Francis's own first missions outside Italy were
failures, because they were undertaken without due preparation, perhaps in the expectation that miracles would supply all
deficiencies. The missionaries were not prepared for their tasks
and the areas of their activities were not studied beforehand. In
both France and Germany, the brothers were taken for Lombard
Cathars; in both Germany and Hungary, they encountered in-
superable difficulties because none of them spoke the language.
By any standards except those of fanaticism, they behaved quite
irresponsibly, as also did those brothers martyred in Morocco. It
may have been realization of their irresponsibility, as well as a
desire to see the Order more firmly cemented into the church,
which impelled Hugolin to renew the struggle to persuade them
to change their Rule. As we have seen, he did manage to con-
vince Francis that he should not desert Italy to lead a mission
into France. On this occasion, Francis responded well, mainly it
would appear because Hugolin himself, rather than his reasoning,
appealed to him. But the fact is that he did not want to lead the
Order, though he did want it to succeed. As soon as he could –
actually, after the chapter of Pentecost 1219, at which there were
complaints from the ministers about the founder's neglect of their
difficulties – he sailed for the East, to join Brother Elias's crusading mission.* It has traditionally been said that he did not
formally step down in favour of Peter of Catania until 1220 (or
even 1221), but in practice he had abdicated in 1217, as Rosalind
Brooke has argued.† This explains why he felt free to go to
France, at a time when many were plotting to 'strangle the select
vine planted so generously by the Lord's hand'. He may
genuinely have believed that God and Cardinal Hugolin would
manage the affairs of the Order better than he could. Over-
reacting to criticism by resignation would not have been un-
typical of him, but even if his formal abdication should be
referred to 1220, from 1217 onwards he acted as though he were
already free of the burdens of leadership. It is from this time
that Celano dates Hugolin's domination of the Order's affairs.

While Hugolin could keep Francis at the centre of things,

* I Celano 1, 57; Jordan of Giano, *Chronicle* 10; cf. II Celano 30.
† R. B. Brooke, *Early Franciscan Government, etc.*, Cambridge, 1959.

there was little danger that the ministers' criticisms would become open rebellion or provide a lever for those outside the
Order who wanted to overturn it entirely. But almost immediately
after he had sailed from Ancona on 24 June 1219, those whose
fears for the future were greatest seized the opportunity to bring
their complaints into the open.

The grounds for their disquiet were indisputably valid. Francis
himself frequently seemed unbalanced, and his behaviour was
certainly idiosyncratic to an extreme degree. Not surprisingly,
his movement attracted many less stable though no less eccentric
than himself. Their eccentricities could only worry the more
rational and learned, who realized how little would be needed
to bring the whole Order under ecclesiastical censure. When
Francis left for the East, those remaining in control in Italy
were, not unnaturally, some of the brothers least like Francis
himself in spirit: practical men of affairs, whose devotion to
the Order was unquestioned, but whose practical outlook led
them to make realistic assessments of the needs of the situation,
rather than take daring leaps into the darkness of untried solu-
tions. Though Francis himself chose their leaders, Gregory of
Naples and Matthew of Narni, they were men so different from
him that their regency was bound to lead to conflict. Significantly,
Gregory of Naples was related to Hugolin, a fact which may have
played its part in his choice for the role he filled, and suggests
that Hugolin may have helped decide the way in which he filled
it.

Matthew of Narni acted as guardian of the Portiuncula. Little
is known of him, except that he supported Gregory, who acted as
the travelling arbiter of Franciscan affairs during Francis's
absence abroad. But it is tempting to speculate that it was
Matthew who permitted, or even encouraged, the people of
Assisi to build the church at Portiuncula which so annoyed
Francis when he saw it that he climbed on to its roof and tore
off the tiles.

The twin medieval passions, for order and property, passions
which Francis had always vigorously combated because he knew
the malignancy of their power, were given free rein in the months
that he was away. Hugolin started the process of rationalizing
Francis's religion by inspiring a bull named *Sacrosancta*, enclos-
ing the Poor Ladies, binding them under the Rule of Benedictine

nuns. The bull was not actually sealed until 9 December, but as early as 27 July, he himself signed a privilege, as papal legate in Tuscany, for the Poor Ladies at Monticelli, naming neither Francis nor Chiara, and allowing the sisters only Benedictine rights, with no specifically Franciscan freedoms. This was only a month after Francis had left the country.

It cannot have been much later when the minister in Bologna, Peter Staccia, founded the first Franciscan house of studies there, so deliberately flouting two of Francis's most cherished precepts: that against property and that against books.*

At about the same time, with or without Hugolin's approval, Gregory of Naples called a special chapter at Saint Mary of Jehosophat summoning to it, it seems, only those friars he knew to favour reform and the imposition of firm discipline. Someone – the finger of suspicion has always pointed at Gregory – put it about that Francis had died (Jordan's *Chronicle* 15). One feels that the crisis was deliberately inflated to prepare men's minds for the drastic measures to come. Jordan of Giano, who alone records the steps taken by the special chapter in any detail, concentrates on its modification of Francis's rule of fasting. The founder's rule was that the brothers should fast 'on Wednesday and Friday, and with (his) permission on Monday and Saturday also; and on every meat-day they should eat meat'. Gregory's chapter ruled that even on meat-days the brothers 'ought not to eat meat obtained by begging' but only that offered to them by 'the faithful ... voluntarily, of their own free will'. It also made Monday an obligatory fast-day, like all Wednesdays and Fridays, and ruled that on Mondays and Saturdays no friar should eat butter, milk or cheese unless they were pressed on him as a gift (*Chronicle* 11).

In themselves, these changes do not look very significant, and it has usually been supposed that they were accompanied by others which Jordan omits, though there is no satisfactory reason why he should have done so. In fact, even if they stood alone, they signalled a change which could only frighten and dismay Franciscans who did not share Gregory's view of the Order's future, for they brought Franciscan practice into line with that of the older religious orders, whose rules Francis had consistently

* Cf. II Celano 58; *Mirror of Perfection*, 6.

rejected. Coupled with Hugolin's moves against the freedom of the Poor Ladies, they augured ill for the future, especially in the pessimistic and tense atmosphere generated by the rumour of Francis's death.

Francis believed, and had taught his friars, that God himself had inspired him with the Rule and practices the Order followed. According to the *Mirror of Perfection* he had told the Chapter of the Mats in Hugolin's presence that God wished him to be 'a new covenant', which if he meant it literally implied that both the Old Testament and the New Testament had been superseded by Franciscanism, and the new world order foretold by such as Joachim of Flora had already come into being, with the advent of Francis of Assisi. The rules of Augustine, Benedict, and Bernard were anathema to him: the brothers were not so much as to name them to him (*Mirror* 68). This paragraph in the *Mirror* may not, of course, be a literal account of an actual conversation, but if it is not it is a record of what conservative Franciscans thought that Francis had taught, a summary, as it were, of his ideas about himself. Passages conveying the same ideas are frequent, especially in the legends. There is no reason to believe that they were not common currency during Francis's lifetime, especially among the simpler, and more fanatically devoted, of the friars. To such simple souls, seeing things always in black and white, any attempts on whatever grounds to tamper with the precepts laid down by the founder of the new covenant was manifestly inspired by the devil, and any attempt to bring Franciscanism closer to regular monasticism was an attack on God's 'new thing'.

In his own way, Gregory of Naples was as fanatical as Francis himself. When the conservatives in the Order reacted against the new rule by openly defying it, he tried to force obedience on the recalcitrant, inflicting punishments ranging, it is said, up to imprisonment and expulsion from the Order. Some of the brothers continued their rebellion; a few actually went into hiding. But most submitted, and seeing that Gregory's firmness brought its rewards, like-minded ministers started their own experiments with the rule, until as Jordan says 'the Order throughout Italy was troubled, both by the vicars (Gregory and Matthew) and by other friars who were experimenting with new ideas'.

If, as the admittedly rather meagre sources seem to imply, Gregory's actions during his vicariate were a planned attempt to subvert the Order Francis had created, the revolution was too hurriedly planned and clumsily executed for success. Despite what was rumoured, Francis was not dead, but still very much alive. It could only be a matter of time before he learned what was happening. But the question in many a brother's mind must have been: what will he do about it? He had an exaggerated respect for any authority whose rights he had admitted. Though he himself had appointed Gregory and Matthew to their positions, there was a very real risk that he would decide that he could not interfere with their government now that they were in office. However, that was a risk that had to be taken. A brave brother took it, acting on his own initiative, 'without the permission of the vicars' as Jordan says, setting out for Syria, taking with him a copy of the new constitutions, to lay the situation before Francis and appeal to him for help (*Chronicle* 12).

10

Francis in Egypt

Bartholemew of Pisa, writing a century and a half after Francis's death, says that it was from the port of Ancona that he sailed on 24 June 1219, the feast of his patron John the Baptist, in a vessel that made landfall first in Cyprus, then at Acre, to become a crusader at last.* Many brothers wished to travel with him: he left the selection of the twelve he agreed to take to a small boy he found playing on the quayside. Among the twelve the boy chose were Peter of Catania, Leonardo of Assisi (formerly Lord of Sassorosso, and one of the *majores* expelled from Assisi before the Perugian War), and Illuminato of Rieti, so constant a companion of Francis's that he was called as one of the formal witnesses at the process before Francis's canonization.

Random selection of the twelve was a typically Franciscan gesture. Although reason might reject Bartholemew's story as too unlikely for credence, Francis is in fact only too likely to have left the choice of his companions to the finger of God acting through a child, stipulating only that their number must be twelve, so that his imitation of Christ might be as perfect as possible.

The war into which the brothers so precipitately thrust themselves was a pitiful affair, made the more vicious by the bitterness of many who were unwillingly dragged into it. It had begun in a desultory way nearly two years earlier when John of Brienne, titular King of Jerusalem, had welcomed at Saint John of Acre in September 1217 the first wave of the flood of knights promised

---

* Cf. F. van Otroy, *S. François et son voyage en Orient* in *Analecta Bollandiana xxxi*, Brussels, 1912.

to him by Pope Honorius immediately after his election, a single shipload of men commanded by Duke Leopold of Austria. It was followed fairly soon by two shiploads under King Andrew of Hungary, a mighty relic-hunter but not a disciplined soldier. Meanwhile, thousands of more or less willing crusaders were stranded in Italy, waiting for ships promised from Frisia, ships that for months did not come.

According to Jacques de Vitry, who was then Bishop of Acre, there were few there apart from King John, the Knights Templar and the Knights of Saint John who welcomed the prospect of any renewal of war. On arriving in his see-city, he had found all those faults in the Christians of the Kingdom of Acre of which earlier writers had complained in those returning from the first crusade. The native Syrians, he wrote sadly, preferred Muslim to Christian rule. The Latin settlers lived lazy, luxurious, and immoral lives. And as for the clergy, they were worse even than any he had met in Italy: corrupt, avaricious, and continually involved in intrigue. In short, the Lebanon had exerted its age-old charm over everyone. The Syrians did not want liberators from the West. They already felt free.

However, King John of Jerusalem was determined that there should be a war. He began the fighting by sacking Beisan, only to see his army fall apart at the seams immediately the battle was over as bands of men went off in all directions to have a look at the Holy Land and pick up what booty they could find. The local relic-manufacturers did very well. Among the many parted easily from the booty of Beisan was King Andrew of Hungary, who bought a waterpot at Cana convinced that it was one of those used in the famous miracle there. Only a few weeks later, when attacks on Mount Tabor did not bring him instant glory, Andrew went home, clutching his waterpot and the alleged head of Saint Stephen, a present from Tripoli, north of Tyre, where he had been to the wedding of Bohemond IV of Antioch to Melissende, the half-sister of King Hugh of Cyprus.

Meanwhile, the Military Orders had built a castle at Athlit, south of Carmel, and Leopold of Austria had refortified Caesarea, though not very well, for it fell the following summer under the first assault of the late Sultan Saladin's nephew, al-Mu'azzam, Viceroy in Syria for the reigning Sultan, Saladin's brother, al-Adil. Not until April 1218 did the Frisians bring significant reinforcements, when the fateful decision was taken that the main Christian attack should be on the forces commanded in Egypt by al-Mu'azzam's brother, al-Malik al-Kamil, the first objective being Damietta, at the western edge of the Nile Delta.

If there was anyone in Egypt who wanted war less than al-Kamil, it was the three thousand or so European traders then living peacefully in Egypt under his protection, and their natural leader, the Ambassador of Venice. Nevertheless, al-Kamil was prepared to fight if attacked, although he forebore to destroy the miniscule force landed at Damietta on 29 May while the main Christian fleet lay becalmed somewhere off the Palestinian coast. He took the defensive measure of building a guard tower north of the city, to pin the Christians on the beaches. The tower was not attacked till 24 August; news of its fall the following day is said to have killed Sultan al-Adil, leaving his sons as sole masters in Egypt and Syria. Although the tower had fallen, al-Kamil still hoped to avoid all-out war. Leaving a garrison at Damietta, he withdrew the main body of his forces to al-Adilya, far enough south to make an accidental clash impossible.

All this time, the French volunteers for the pope's war had been waiting for ships at Brindisi. Fearing that if they were left there much longer, they might sack the city or go home in disgust, Honorius reluctantly equipped a fleet out of his own funds to sail for Egypt under the Spanish Cardinal Pelagio of Santa Lucia. For all the long-term good this move did his cause, it was 20,000 silver marks wasted.

Cardinal Pelagio was perhaps the worst choice as leader that Honorius could have made. He had been previously employed in the Latin Empire of Constantinople as arbitrator between the Greek and Latin churches. His blunt outspokenness and bad-tempered arrogance had made it absolutely certain that peace would not be achieved in that generation. Reaching Damietta in September 1218, he blundered from mistake to mistake, trampling on the tender feelings of the touchy knights as though they were slaves believed to have none. He counselled immediate action; King John was for caution. Before their conflict of opinions was resolved, al-Kamil at last attacked the camp, and was beaten off only with difficulty. From then on, troubles mounted day by day. Fever broke out, and many died. Not until 2 February 1219 could Pelagio coerce the Christians into a counter-attack upon al-Adilya. Their assault was thrown back, but three days later a patrol found the Muslim outposts deserted. Al-Kamil had withdrawn yet further south, to Fariskur. The sultans were unsure of themselves. In March, though mistrustful of their eastern neighbours, they appealed to the whole Muslim world for men and arms, while al-Mu'azzam took the panic measure of ordering the walls of Jerusalem and several forts to the north to Galilee to be razed, in order to deny them to the Christians should he be forced to surrender the Holy Land.

Cardinal Pelagio's reply to the Muslim moves was to mount an attack on the walls of Damietta on 20 July. The Muslims countered with Greek fire, and perhaps because the Christians lacked resolution and cohesion, they were thrown back, both that day, and when they attacked again on 6 August. It was at this stage, while the Christians were planning a third major assault, that Francis arrived in Egypt from Saint John of Acre.

What he had made of the moral squalor of Christian Syria is not known. But he can only have been heartened by the response to his preaching among those whom prevailing conditions had long disgusted. Brother Elias had done his work well. There was already a small community of Franciscans at Acre to welcome their founder, among them some who later became famous in the Order, pre-eminently Caesar of Speyer, an able German, who had preached the crusade so eloquently in the Empire, according to the *Little Flowers*, that finally he had had to take the cross himself to escape the wrath of the kin of the men he had persuaded to go adventuring.

No details are known of Francis's first brief stay at Acre. After so many years' dreaming of crusading, he wanted to go where men were actually fighting and dying for the cross. He reached the Christian camp in Egypt about the middle of August. 'The person who founded the Order of the lesser brothers', the author of the contemporary chronicle called the *Estoire de Eracles* wrote, 'by name, Brother Francis, came to the army at Damietta, and did a great deal of good there, and remained there until the city was captured.'*

Cardinal Pelagio's first reaction to the strange band of reinforcements under Francis's leadership is not recorded. Francis

---

* In *Historiens des Croisades*, vol. 2, bk. 32, c. 15.

obviously formed an unfavourable impression of the spirit he found among Pelagio's men, for on the morning of the third battle for Damietta he announced that he had a foreboding 'from the Lord' of a great defeat, but hesitated to warn the Christian leaders, because 'if I say anything, they will call me insane'. His companions urged him to pass the warning on. He did so, and was predictably called not only mad but also criminal. No commander wants his men demoralized by predictions of defeat immediately before a battle.

The date was 29 August. That day, the Christian casualties included more than four thousand men killed. The Spanish contingent was almost completely annihilated, and it was only the tireless courage and devotion of King John, and the staunchness of the Knights Hospitaller and Templar, that saved anything from the disaster. Perhaps al-Kamil held his troops back at the last. He still wanted peace. The Nile floods had failed that year, and famine threatened his people. Moreover, he was uneasily aware that his second brother, al-Ashruf, was intriguing against him and al-Mu'azzam with other Muslim leaders. Less than a week after the battle, a released Frankish prisoner entered the Christian camp with the offer of a truce from both sultans, and terms for a more permanent peace settlement, including the cession of Jerusalem to the Christians. Cardinal Pelagio accepted the truce, but rejected the peace terms, probably because he had heard of the Muslims' difficulties, and hoped for further concessions.

The truce lasted only about three weeks. During that time, many of the crusaders decided that they had done enough for the cause and made hasty arrangements to go home. Twelve shiploads left on 14 September. But reinforcements also arrived, and fearing the build-up of fresh Christian forces, al-Kamil attacked the camp on 26 September; his attack was turned, and he soon offered terms that look incredibly generous in exchange for peace in Egypt: all Central Palestine, including Bethlehem, all Galilee including Nazareth, Jerusalem with the Holy Sepulchre (left standing by Sultan al-Mu'azzam's decree, despite its fortifications), and the True Cross, one of Islam's greatest trophies since its capture at the Horns of Hattin.

Cardinal Pelagio incredibly argued against acceptance of even this offer. So too did the Patriarch of Jerusalem and the Knights

Templar and Hospitaller, together with the Italians who, having at first opposed war in Egypt, now wanted Damietta given to them as a trading post. Almost everyone else was in favour of accepting it. The debate grew so acrimonious that Jacques de Vitry, a distinguished visitor to the Christian forces in Egypt, wondered whether the Sultan had offered peace in the hope that it would spread dissent (Letter VI).

Either during the truce, or while al-Kamil's offer was being debated in the Christian camp, Francis decided that the moment had come for him personally to intervene in the war. 'Violent and brutal battles between the Christians and the pagans were a daily menace', the *First Life* says, exaggerating a little, 'nevertheless, taking a single companion, he went fearlessly to confront the Saracens' Sultan' (I Celano 1, 57). What he planned to demand from al-Kamil was not primarily an end to the fighting, but his conversion to Christianity. However, such a conversion would presumably have ended the war for a time, though political and territorial ambition would probably have led to its recommencement before long. People like the Venetian traders longing to gain control of the Delta were not deeply concerned about al-Kamil's soul.

According to the *Verba Fratris Illuminati*,* which purports to be an account of Francis's activities in Egypt by his companion on the mission to Fariskur, Brother Illuminato of Rieti, Francis had no doubts about the justice of the crusade. During their interviews, al-Kamil once asked him how he, a lover of peace, could justify the fighting, and he replied with a quotation from the New Testament: '"If your eye offend you, pluck it out". No one should be so dear to us that if he attempts to convert us from the faith and love of God we should not cut ourselves off from him, pluck him out, and totally eliminate him. For this reason, the Christians are right to invade you and the country you have occupied: you blaspheme Christ's name, and stop those you can from worshipping him.'

Despite Francis's clashes with the Christian leaders, he was not entirely friendless, and according to Bonaventure (9, 8–9), he made use of his connections to try and win a herald's status,

---

* Ed. Golubovich, in *Biblioteca bio-bibliographica della Terra Santa*, vol. 1, p. 37.

travelling to Fariskur under a flag of truce. The Christian high command saw no virtue in the plan. Cardinal Pelagio in particular was opposed to it, but Pelagio belonged to the war-party among the Christians, and was ready to read treachery into any dealings with the enemy. He had swallowed the Christian propaganda that anyone approaching the Muslim camp would be beheaded out-of-hand, and his assassin rewarded by al-Kamil in person with a gold bezant. Moreover, he was probably nursing dreams of a glorious military rather than religious victory. If he did not dismiss Francis as mad, he certainly deprecated him as a meddler, whose intervention could do no good, and might actually infuriate the enemy, so that anger strengthened his resistance.

However, Francis was determined. Denied the escort he had requested, he chose his own moment, and with only Illuminato as a companion, he set off on foot towards the enemy lines, singing Psalm 23 to keep his spirits up: 'Though I walk through the valley of the shadow of death, I will fear no evil.' He seems to have made no more preparation for this mission than he had for any other. His longing for martyrdom was very real. It would have set the seal on his imitation of Christ. It could truly be said of him that he did not care whether he lived or died. It seems that the only Arab word he had learned was 'Sultan!', and when the Muslim sentries tried to arrest him, he and Illuminato shouted it, until they were taken for messengers, perhaps bringing a reply to the terms carried to the Christian camp by the freed prisoner some days earlier. They were put into chains and ultimately, when Francis had explained in French what they wanted, were brought before al-Kamil.

Al-Kamil undoubtedly treated Francis well, but why he did so has never been adequately explained, unless it was by Jacques de Vitry, an eyewitness of the events he describes, in this passage from his *Eastern Chronicles*:

Not only Christ's faithful, but also the Saracens and their allies admire the humility and perfection of these people [the Franciscans]. For they go to them, and they, being granted the right spirit, receive them happily. We have seen the first founding master of their Order (and so he who is the first of all its priors, whom all the others obey), a simple and unlettered man, delightful to God and men, named Brother Francis: he was so inspired with exhilaration for heavenly things, and so caught up in the spirit of service, that when he came down to the Christian army at Damietta in Egypt, with a single companion he went fearlessly, armed with the shield of faith, to the Sultan of Egypt. And when they were in the Saracen lines, he said: I am a Christian. Take me to your master. And when they dragged him before him, the cruel beast seeing him, in aspect so much a man of God, gentle in manner, he listened to him, he and his people, most attentively over a period of days, preaching the faith of Christ. But at length, seeing that none from that army was actually converted to God by [Francis's] work, they crossed back to the Christian lines, being led back to our camp with all reverence and in all safety. And at the end of it all, he said, 'Pray for me, that God will be pleased to give me the laws and faith which so greatly delights you' (c. 32).

Though we may doubt whether the Sultan of Egypt actually spoke these words in Jacques de Vitry's hearing, it is obvious that Francis charmed and captivated him, at least temporarily. There may be some truth in the frequently repeated suggestion that he believed that Francis had been touched by the finger of God, and as a madman deserved the respect due to those who have been close to the divine. But granted that he may have reverenced insanity, would he actually have wanted to spend several days with a man out of his mind? It is more likely that the adviser who first interviewed Francis sensed the genuineness of his religious experience, and roused al-Kamil's interest in it. The Sultan is known to have been deeply interested in Sufic mysticism and to have had great reverence for the contemporary Arab mystical teacher Umar ibn al-Farid, whose chosen subject was Francis's own chief concern, intense love for an intensely personal God.

Yet again, there can be no doubt that under his outer covering of rags and dirt, Francis was a powerful and charming personality. The problem of charm is insoluble, but even those who are on perpetual guard against charmers are sometimes seduced into friendliness despite themselves by a voice, a face or a gesture. At this time, before blindness and dropsy marred his appearance,

Francis must have been still much as the *First Life* glowingly describes him:

> A most eloquent person, with a happy face and kindly look ... without a touch of obsequiousness, but not arrogant ... near average height, tending to shortness. His head was of average size, and round; his face rather long and drawn; his forehead unlined and narrow; his eyes of average size, black, and glowing with sincerity; he was dark-haired, his eyebrows were straight; his ears pointed but small; his temples smooth; his speech tactful but brilliant and to the point; his voice strong but pleasing, clear and musical; his teeth white, regular and even; his lips small and not thick. He had a dark, rather thin beard. His neck was thin, his shoulders square, his arms short, his hands fine, with long tapering fingers and nails. His legs were thin, his feet small; his skin was fine, and his flesh spare (I Celano 1, 83).

Whether any or all of these considerations influenced the Sultan is not known. When all the fanciful embroidery is stripped away from the story, the solid core of fact remaining about the interview at Fariskur is that when it ended al-Kamil had been converted to Francis, but not to Francis's religion. With his usual fanaticism, Francis offered to undergo an ordeal by fire to prove his God's omnipotence. The Sultan gently rejected the idea, and countered with the offer of gifts to Francis himself. Legend says that Francis refused everything except a horn which he later used to call congregations together to hear him preach.

On the face of it, nothing was gained, but at two other levels very important advances had been made. In the first place, something deep inside Francis was satisfied: he had at last crusaded, and preached the faith to the unbelievers. He had come one step closer to Christ and the Apostles. This gain is reflected in the fact that after his return from Egypt, he looked forward not to further missions and probable martyrdom, but to the perfect life of the hermit (so imitating Christ when he 'went into the wilderness to pray') and the perfect death of the Christian (saying 'not my will, but thine be done'). The mission to al-Kamil was crucial to Francis's interior development. All the sources recognize this, giving the incident a prominence which surely reflects the importance Francis himself attached to it. Until this moment, he had never known the limits of his courage: now he knew that he would dare anything for Christ. The *First Life* says 'he went fearlessly to confront the Saracens' Sultan', so echoing the earlier reference to this episode in Jacques de Vitry's letters: 'Brother Francis has not been afraid to leave the Christian army and go to the enemy camp, preaching the faith'. He had pushed himself to the limit, and in doing so won approbation both from himself, and from those around. Winning the accolade of their recognition was the second advance resulting from the mission to Fariskur. As a result, he was able, as the *Estoire de Eracles* says, 'to do a great deal of good' among the crusaders. To strike deep into the enemy camp and fight to disarm the enemy champion was a knightly action, a deed of valour commanding respect. That it failed was no disgrace. The attempt itself was enough. Had Cardinal Pelagio or King John stood face to face with al-Kamil?

There is a hint in Jordan's *Chronicle* that it was at Fariskur that Francis first felt the onset of the disease which was ultimately to kill him. 'When Francis was brought into the Sultan's presence', Jordan writes (c. 10), 'he was received well, and treated with kindness in his sickness'. This is the first datable indication of any physical illness since his conversion, and is significant because from this time onwards references to growing blindness, fever, and metabolic disturbance are frequent in all the sources. It may be that Francis contracted 'the fever' which racked both Christian and Muslim armies that year, and that weakened physically by his privations and mentally by his failure to convert al-Kamil, he never made a complete recovery. Jordan's very next sentence is indicative of his great underlying disappointment: 'But because he could bring forth no fruit among the Saracens, he decided to return to his own people.'

In the words of the *First Life*: 'So despite everything, the Lord did not fulfil Francis's desire', at least, not his superficial desire and declared purpose. He was given an honourable escort back to the Christian lines, and put himself to the consoling task of 'doing good' among the crusaders. It was a Sisyphean labour, but he did make noteworthy converts to his religion, either in the few remaining days before Damietta fell, or very shortly afterwards. Describing the Franciscans at this time, Jacques de Vitry wrote: 'The Order is spreading throughout the world. It imitates the nascent church and the apostles' life in everything. Colin the Englishman, our copyist, has joined its numbers, together with two others, *Messer* Michael, and *Dominus* Matthew into whose care I had given the district of Holy Cross [at Acre]. The *cantor*, and Henry, and others besides, I restrained only with difficulty.'

The fate of Damietta was a terrible blot on the record of crusading chivalry. Famine and fever finally compelled al-Kamil to withdraw all support from the city and abandon it to the crusaders' mercy. On the morning of 5 November 1219, Christian patrols were not fired upon from the walls, and found no evidence that they were still defended. An immediate attack was ordered. It met with no opposition. The whole garrison was dead or dying of fever, and the citizens' will to resist had gone. When the whole surviving population had been rounded up, there were less than three thousand men, women and children to suffer for the months the Christians had waited outside their walls. One in ten were kept as hostages; of the rest, the men were butchered, the women auctioned, and the youngest children baptized and given to the church as bondsmen. What treasures the soldiers could not steal were heaped up and later shared out on a sliding scale according to rank. Cardinal Pelagio claimed the city itself for the church, and a bitter quarrel broke out between him and the Italians, who had convinced themselves that it had been promised to them. Peace was temporarily restored on the basis of a compromise: Damietta was to be regarded as part of the Holy Roman Empire, and held by King John of Jerusalem for Frederick II of Germany, when he should arrive.

The army then moved on to the sack of Tanis, a second city of the Delta. Here, greed led to scenes worse than at Damietta. When the sack was over, the Italians demanded what was left, and being once more refused, rebelled against the Christian leadership. They tried to hold Damietta against King John, but were driven out by the Templars and Hospitallers, and left to die of fever or enemy action in the marshes of the Delta.

If these were the people among whom Francis had done 'much good' one wonders what they could have been like without his influence. No wonder that, in the words of the *Estoire de Eracles*, after the fall of Damietta, Francis 'saw sin and wickedness beginning to increase among the soldiers, and was troubled by it, and for this reason left there'.

He withdrew to Acre, taking the brothers with him. The work that he was able to do in Syria to drown the memory of his disappointments in Egypt is unfortunately not well enough documented for a full account of it to be possible. Elias seems to have established a permanent 'residence' in the city, and there is no evidence that Francis expressed misgivings about its foundation. His stay in Syria was brief, but it was long enough for him to wreak the havoc among the cathedral clergy gently complained of by Bishop Jacques de Vitry, to win the undying allegiance of Elias's convert subdeacon Caesar of Speyer, and, according to Angelo Coreno, to visit the holy places under a safe conduct granted by al-Kamil's brother, the Sultan al-Mu'azzam of Damascus. He must have been among the first pilgrims to visit the Holy Sepulchre after it had been specially spared from destruction by al-Mu'azzam's command.* It is unfortunate that he himself recorded no account of his reaction to imitating Christ physically by walking in his footsteps and praying where he had lain dead. A few decades earlier, Joachim of Flora's life had been totally changed by the experience of spending Lent on Tabor; Francis was probably less dramatically, but no less profoundly, affected by Jerusalem. We know that he was susceptible to the influence of places. It is impossible that a man of his sensitivity was left wholly unmoved. The visit *sepulcro Domini*, the supreme experience the medieval world offered the Christian pilgrim, and the proclaimed goal of all the crusaders' endeavours, must have played its part in shaping the perfect disciple who a few years later was – as he himself and his companions saw it – rewarded for his perfection with the *stigmata*, the divine seal of guarantee on his Christ-likeness.

Allowing reasonable time for these activities, and developments in Italy, leads to the conclusion that it was in January or February 1220 that the lay brother (named Stephen in John of Komerov's Chronicle) landed at Acre with his tale of the mismanagement of the Order's affairs under Cardinal Hugolin's kinsman Gregory of Naples. The story of how he broke the news is told by Jordan of Giano:

* In Golubovich, *op. cit.*, 1, 56.

Reaching Francis, he first . . . asked his forgiveness for having come to him without permission [from his guardian or the vicars]: he had been driven to come by the fact that the vicars left by Francis had added new injunctions to the Rule. . . . When Saint Francis had studied the Constitutions, and was afterwards sitting at table, where meat was set before them to eat, he said to Peter [of Catania]: *Messer* Peter, what shall we do? And he replied: Whatever pleases you, Father Francis. The authority is yours. . . . And when they had talked it over, Saint Francis said, Let us eat, as the gospel says, of the things that are set before us.

Though Jordan does not say no, he implies that the meal was illegal under the new laws: either the day was one of the new abstinence days when meat was forbidden, or the meat had not been freely offered, but had been begged from the faithful. By eating it, Francis repudiated his vicars and their activities, justifying himself by an appeal to the New Testament, and so condemning the new constitutions as foreign to the spirit of his religion. Eating this meal was a declaration of open warfare against the reforming party. 'So taking with him Elias, Peter of Catania, Caesar . . . and other friars, Saint Francis returned to Italy' where that war had to be fought out (*Chronicle* 14).

Death of a vision

It may be that later chroniclers were exaggerating for effect's sake when they described Gregory of Naples as persecuting the rebels against his revision of the Rule, and spoke of brothers going into hiding to escape his anger. It is, however, not impossible that there were excesses both of action and reaction. Because medieval law saw all authority as ultimately one, so that any rebellion threatened universal chaos, however remotely, it allowed extreme measures to be taken by legally appointed superiors against anyone who revolted. Moreover, many of Francis's converts were like himself hysterics and fanatics by nature: their reaction to anything that seemed to threaten them was naturally excessive. A Syrian woman with second sight reputedly told him that the Order was 'distressed . . . divided . . . and scattered'; it was certainly distressed and divided, though its scattering may have been only metaphorical. Unity, as Brother Stephen saw, could be restored only by Francis himself.

He landed at Venice, probably in the late spring of 1220, and after resting for a few days – he was still troubled by the sickness that had attacked him in Egypt – made his way to Bologna, where the minister was the former lawyer, Peter Staccia.

It was apparently only on arriving at Bologna that he began to realize how far the reformers had taken their movement against the spirit of his Rule, when he learned that Staccia had set up a house of studies at the University, which was famous for its commentaries on Roman civil law. Both the house itself and the books studied there were anathema to him. The story of his repudiation of them, and Staccia with them, is unfortunately preserved only in a late and overdramatic form. According to this version, he refused at first to set foot in the building, but summoned Staccia to him, asked him if he wanted to destroy 'my Order', cursed him, and finally entered the house only to drive out all the brothers resident in it. Staccia begged him at least to lift the curse, but he refused, maintaining that Christ himself had confirmed its justice. And very shortly afterwards Peter Staccia 'gave up his soul to the Devil, surrounded by a horrible stench'.

It is probably safe to ignore not only the curse and its consequences, but all the details of this story, saving only the bare fact that once again in 1220 Francis confirmed his rejection of both learning and property, the two prizes most sought after by the contemporary world. It is also noteworthy that in this crisis he ignored the legal rulers of the Order, the vicars he himself had appointed in due form. Not only did he clear the house of studies at Bologna without reference to them, he also made a point of snubbing them by by-passing Assisi and the Portiuncula after leaving Bologna, pressing straight on to Rome, to thrash out once more the whole question of the Order's existence with the pope.

Here again, the sources fail us at what should have been one of the most interesting points in their story. Anxious to show both Francis and Honorius in the best possible light, they ignore all the intrigue and preparatory work that must have gone on before Francis and the pope met. The earliest, and probably the best of them, Jordan of Giano's *Chronicle* (c. 14) presents the interview like something out of a folk story, with Francis waiting outside the palace for the pope to come out, because he would not 'make a disturbance' by knocking on the door, and refusing to ask anything except that Hugolin, 'Lord of Ostia' should be made the sole judge of causes within the Order, so becoming 'the pope' of 'the poor'. This petition was immediately granted. Hugolin received supreme authority over the Order, and used his powers first to expel John of Capella, who was trying to form an Order made up entirely of lepers, then to revoke letters apostolic granted to Philip, the Zealot for the Poor Ladies, under which anyone troubling them was automatically excommunicated.

No doubt Hugolin's recognition as 'the pope of the poor' was the principal outcome of Francis's visit to Rome, but it is incredible that this is how it came about. Remembering that he was

Gregory of Naples' kinsman, and already the legally appointed
protector of Francis's Order, it is impossible not to see him as the
key-figure in events from the beginning, and difficult to imagine
that he had no prior knowledge of the extraordinary title and
position Francis intended to seek for him. Exactly what com-
promises and secret agreements he made with whom in order to
achieve his ultimate position as 'pope' to the Order we cannot
know, but that they were made seems inescapable. Hugolin was
an ambitious man, and winning control of the continually growing Franciscan movement was an important step in the career that
was to end with him 'pope' over the whole church.* It is noteworthy that no action was taken against Gregory of Naples,
except that his vicariate was ended; an able man, despite his
tactlessness, within three years he had become minister in
France, a post he held for ten years, from 1223 until 1233, when
complaints about his overbearing officiousness and cruelty had
grown so vociferous that Hugolin, now Gregory IX, had to
promulgate a bull against him, ordaining his removal from office
and imprisonment.

Hugolin's assumption of juridical control over the Order was
quickly followed by other developments. On 22 September 1220,
Honorius signed a bull registered as *Cum secundum*, addressed
to 'Brother Francis and other priors or *custodes* of the lesser
brothers' commanding them 'not to admit anyone to profession
without a noviciate of one year' and forbidding friars 'to wander
from place to place, wearing the habit, without [letters of]
obedience'.

Though both these regulations were defensible, and indeed,
sensible, both went against the spirit of Francis's original concept, and forced the Order in the direction of monastic conform-
ism. That it was felt necessary to make them indicates both the
speed of the Order's growth and the magnitude of authority's
disquiet about it. John of Capella had obviously frightened the
curia, perhaps because he was not the only megalomaniac calling

---

* As Jordan nowhere explains precisely what he means when he calls
Hugolin the Order's 'pope', it is obviously impossible to say exactly what
new powers his status gave him. It seems that he acted as the final judge
and court of appeal in all cases concerned with aspects of Franciscan living
– its 'pope' in the sense that he 'bound and loosed' Franciscans.

himself a Franciscan at that time. In the very early days, when Francis had known every brother personally and all had been bound by intimate ties of affection and obedience to him, it had been practical to admit new brothers overnight (as Chiara had been admitted); the enthusiasms of the unbalanced and those of limited intelligence had been held in check by the founder's proximity and magnetism. Now, however, with residences from Paris to Syria, and the Order daily gaining in fame and respect, so that it had become advantageous in certain circumstances to call oneself a Franciscan, every 'Franciscan' was to be vetted and documented, so that there would be some measure of control both over the quality of recruits and the activities of the over-zealous, the ill-disciplined and the unbalanced. Europe was not yet preyed upon by an army of wandering friars, such as caused deep concern to civil and ecclesiastical authorities a century or so later, but the dangers inherent in the situation were already manifest.

The lesser brothers were actually paying the penalty of success, but what Francis himself – sick, tired, and tormented by an urge to withdraw into contemplation – thought of these enforced changes he made perfectly plain by refusing to resume day-to-day control of his Order after the dismissal of his vicars. In a surprise move, he nominated Peter of Catania as General of the Order at about the time when the bull *Cum secundum* was promulgated. Peter was Francis's man absolutely. It will be remembered that in Syria, when Francis had asked his advice, his reply had been, 'Whatever pleases you, Father Francis. The authority is yours'. Nevertheless, his appointment must have dismayed many who had been longing for Francis to take the reins again. Following Hugolin's advancement to the position of pope of the Order, it marked Francis's definitive abdication from power. Peter of Catania was known as a true Franciscan, the founder's chosen companion in many adventures since he had joined the Penitents of Assisi back in 1208, but while Francis lived, the brothers generally wanted him to rule them, and in the event, they usually had their way, by ignoring whatever other arrangements were made, and going straight to him with problems as they arose. Although he believed he wanted peace and quiet in retirement, he found it difficult to refuse direct appeals: he still thought of the movement as 'my' Order, and longed to determine the way that it should go, although he was not willing to make the necessary effort to lead it there.

Together with the news that Francis was no longer legal head of the Order, there also circulated a report that he was working on a revision of the Rule, aided by Caesar of Speyer. Recruited in Syria, Caesar was no more than a name to the majority of Franciscans, and there must have been many who wondered how powerful his influence was, and in what direction he would be seen to have wielded it when the revision was presented to the Whitsun Chapter of 1221.*

At mid-Lent, however, tragedy struck. Minister General Peter of Catania died at Portiuncula and was buried there on 15 March. His epitaph reads very simply: 'A.D. 1221, on the ides of March, Peter of Catania, whose body rests here, went to the Lord'.

All too quickly, Brother Elias was promoted minister general in his place. It is not known with certainty who proposed him, or by what formal process of election, if any, his appointment was confirmed. The probability is that his name was proposed by Hugolin and welcomed by a Francis more eager to avoid the burdens of office than concerned about the nature of the man willing to assume them.

At this stage, there was nothing undesirable about Elias as leader, except the fact, so obvious to hindsight but perhaps not so immediately apparent in 1221, that although a member of Francis's Order he was not by nature fundamentally a Franciscan. He had immense energy, unflagging devotion to Francis personally, a great pride in the Order, and (as even his enemies later admitted) profound learning, together with the ability to communicate his knowledge. His abilities had already been amply demonstrated by the smoothness with which he had established the residence in Syria and maintained good relations with those in authority there. He might have made a better pope than many who have actually ruled from Rome. But his obsession with power and glory for the Order made him an impossible minister general for the lesser brothers, if they were to remain truly lesser. Within the Order, he was the natural leader of the faction represented by Francis's vicars and the lawyer Peter Staccia; made head of the whole Order, he could only devote his energies

* Cf. Jordan's *Chronicle*, 15.

to changing it in the direction that Hugolin and Honorius III envisaged for it, that of more normal monasticism.

It is tempting to see his appointment as a development in Hugolin's 'plot' to subvert the Order, but it would probably be wrong to do so. There was no plot, in the strict sense of the word. Hugolin, Honorius, Elias, Peter Staccia, and probably even Gregory of Naples were all devoted to Francis, and believed themselves devoted to discovering the best way of expressing his vision in the real world. What they did, they thought they were doing for the best. But they tried to sell Francis and Franciscanism to the world, like advertising men with a new product, and like committed advertising men, they continually proposed changes in the product which they believed would help overcome consumer resistance to it.

Some of their proposed changes were not unacceptable to Francis himself, but as appears from the Rule that he and Caesar of Speyer drew up in 1221, they were very few indeed. His own personal and total obedience to lawfully constituted authority led him to write into the text provision for a year's novitiate (c. 3), and a prohibition of unauthorized tramping (c. 5), in the terms of the bull *Cum secundum*. But the other twenty-one chapters presented to the Whitsun Chapter were not so much a new rule as a gauntlet thrown down for any brother who dared to pick up.*

The chapter opened on Whitsunday 23 May, with a sermon by Francis on the text from *Psalms*: 'Blessed be the Lord, who teaches my hands to fight.' It was unfortunate that during the ensuing week, he became so ill that by the end he could not speak for himself, but had to use Elias as his spokesman, whispering to him whatever he wanted said to the assembled company.†
Hugolin had diplomatically absolved himself from his 'papal' duty of attending the chapter, and the ring was held by the more obscure Cardinal Rainerio Capocci. The sources maintain a tight-lipped silence about the kind of reception the revised Rule received, which suggests that it was a very mixed one. In unequivocal sentence after unequivocal sentence, it rejected all

---

* The Rule of 1221 is translated in Fahy and Hermann, *The Writings of Saint Francis of Assisi*, Franciscan Herald Press, 1963, pp. 27ff.
† Jordan of Giano, *Chronicle*, 17.

the reformers' main contentions. Quoting the Bible over a hundred times, it repeated and confirmed all that Francis had always said about the need for absolute poverty and humility if the quest for perfection was to be crowned with success. It forbade the brothers to attempt to maintain claims to ownership of anything whatsoever, ruling that although they might inhabit hermitages, they might not 'defend' them (c. 7). It warned them to value money 'less than pebbles' (c. 8). It commanded them to live – as it asserts that Christ and his Mother had lived – on the charity they were offered, making no distinction between foodstuffs (c. 3 and 9), carrying 'neither staff nor scrip, bread nor money' (c. 14), and using neither riding nor pack animals (c. 15). On the question of property, the only concession to years of expansion and development was the provision that brothers who were priests or deacons were to be permitted to use breviaries, so that they could discharge their prior commitment to recite the divine office. No other books whatsoever were to be allowed. Prayers for lay brothers were to consist of frequent repetition of the Lord's Prayer – a fact often offered as evidence that Francis was a Cathar, because the Albigenses used the Lord's Prayer and no others; in advocating its use, however, Francis was being not heretical, but strictly evangelical, demanding literal obedience to the injunction, 'When you pray, say: Our Father . . .'. In fact, the whole message of the revised Rule could be summed up in the slogan 'Back to the gospel', and it ends with two long chapters, one on suffering gladly, full of gospel texts and obvious references to the distress caused by the reformers, and the other part-prayer, part-sermon, thanking God for the creation on the one hand and calling on the whole world to pray for perseverance among the Franciscans on the other.

'Because our Lord Jesus Christ called a traitor "Friend"', Francis wrote, 'we must see as friends those from whom we have received pain and injustice, humiliation, torture, martyrdom and death.' This sentence could, of course, be taken as a reference to such enemies of the Franciscans as the unwelcoming Germans, Hungarians, and Moroccans, but there can have been few among the 'conservative' brothers who, hearing it for the first time, did not immediately think of Gregory of Naples and his supporters.

Almost at the end of the revised Rule there was a passage which is noteworthy although it has no direct bearing on the story of the controversy over the Order's future, because in it Francis attempts to express all that he felt at this crucial stage in his life about the incommunicable grandeur of God, and the duties that men owe to him. He wrote:

> Let us love, know, adore, serve, praise, bless, glorify, exalt, extol and thank . . . God unchanging, invisible, unutterable, ineffable, incomprehensible, unplumbable, blessed, praiseworthy, glorious, uplifted, great, sublime, merciful, loving, delightful, wholly and completely to be desired, for all eternity.

Francis's God was unknown and unknowable except through Christ and approachable only through perfect imitation of the poor Christ. Nothing and no one must be allowed to come between Francis's friars and gospel perfection.

Miraculous changes of heart among the reformers apart, this revision of the Rule could only be rejected by those who wanted to see significant changes in the Order and its approach to the world. Francis must have expected that it would be rejected. Perhaps he even hoped, albeit only half-consciously, to split the Order with it, purging his religion by provoking the mass defection from it of those who could not share his vision, and so would have been happier as Friars Preacher or even Benedictines. If that was his aim, he failed to achieve it. The reformers wanted to guide and shape the Order, not to divide it. After nine days of meetings, the only positive step that the chapter had taken was a decision to act on a proposal made by Francis himself for the renewal of the mission to Germany. The obvious man to lead it was Caesar of Speyer, but his appointment as Minister Provincial in Germany robbed '*the* Brother, Francis' of one of his most able supporters. While the mission to Germany was being prepared, the question of the new Rule was quietly referred to Cardinal Hugolin. If Francis made any protest before the vote was taken, Elias did not pass it on.*

The last scenes in this sad drama were played out over a period of two pain-filled years. Few echoes of the bitterness of those days have been permitted to survive in the chronicles and legends.

* Jordan of Giano, *Chronicle* 17–18.

The argument on both sides was probably fierce and uncompromising. The reformers under Elias were convinced that if the Order was to continue after Francis's death, it would have to have a legal framework capable of withstanding pressures both from within and without, pressures which were now for the most part being absorbed by Francis himself or his 'father and mother' Hugolin. Living in a capitalist world where property was king, and an outward display of wealth was counted essential to a man's dignity, they could only repudiate Francis's rejection of all tokens of material success. While accepting (more or less grudgingly) the general monastic rule that a monk should have nothing of his own, they found it not only incredible but also quite impractical that Francis should expect them to reject the common monastic compromise, under which a monk could enjoy the fruits of his monastery's wealth while technically and legally owning nothing himself. But that was precisely what Francis did expect of them. While money was secretly their king, poverty was overtly his queen. He demanded that his brothers should serve her with a devotion as total as his own. Very few of them were capable of doing so.

At the end of the 1221 chapter, the rule that Francis and Caesar of Speyer had composed was sent to the Cardinal-Protector for his comments and ruling. He rejected it outright, and threw his weight in with Elias to persuade Francis to rework the whole document. By the time his report reached Portiuncula, Caesar was in Germany. Francis had no one to fall back on but his former secretary and confessor, Leo of Assisi. The two old friends were not strong enough to withstand the pressures brought to bear on them. Taking with them a certain Brother Benizzo, who had trained as a lawyer before his conversion, they withdrew from the daily to-ing and fro-ing of life at Portiuncula to the calm of Fonte Colombo, a remote cave high in the hills above Rieti.

How long they worked on this second revision of the Rule is not known with any certainty, nor is the form of document they ultimately produced. For at this stage, the first hint of real malice against Francis showed itself among the reforming party. When the Rule was ready, Francis loyally submitted it to the Minister General Elias, who summoned a special chapter to discuss it. However, when the brothers had assembled, and the moment had come to read the rule, Elias refused to produce it, claiming that it was impossible for him to do so, because he had lost it. No copy had been made, and the loss of the original had been concealed until it was too late to do anything to repair the damage. Francis, who was by now too ill to do anything but what each succeeding moment demanded of him, made only the feeblest of protests, and resignedly took the weary road back to Fonte Colombo,* and began work anew.

The latest version of the Rule was an agony to prepare. Brother Leo later recalled that he took it down sentence by sentence at Francis's dictation, but the late thirteenth century *Legenda Antiqua* of Perugia credibly suggests often no work was done for days on end, while 'the Brother' told God how weak he felt, and how near to despair, and wondered aloud how he could satisfy the reformers while doing justice to himself. Between them, God and Brother Leo had to bear the burden of Francis's unhappiness. He realized that he could not satisfy everyone. His own thinking still centred on gospel perfection, while one of the conditions laid on him by the reformers was that in his new Rule he should try to avoid quoting from the gospels at all, and certainly should not use the three passages which had first inspired him. In the last resort, loyalty to himself – to the self that had invaded and now controlled him – drove him to ignore this condition. The three texts, literally interpreted, by which he and Brother Bernard had first lived were crucial to Franciscanism, and were what distinguished it from all other forms of the Christian life in the West.

The essential conflict between Francis and the reformers is brought sharply into focus by the story in the *Legenda antiqua*† relating that Francis did ultimately write into his Rule the gospel precept 'Take nothing for your journey', and that the conference of ministers vetting the draft before it was presented to the Whitsun chapter of 1223 struck it out, without telling him that it had decided to do so; warned what they had done by his intuition, however, Francis told the friars of his party: 'The ministers plan to cheat God and me, but so that all the friars may know

* Cf. *Mirror of Perfection* 1; Bonaventure IV, 11.
† *La 'Legenda Antiqua S.F.', texte du MS 1046 de Pérouse*, ed. F. M. Delorme, Paris, 1926.

that they must pursue evangelical perfection, it is my wish that these words should be written at the beginning and end of the Rule: friars are bound to follow the holy gospel of our Lord Jesus Christ'; a gospel which, as Francis taught it, was always a gospel of poverty, suffering and death. When the last revision of the Rule was read to the friars, it did in fact begin with the words: 'The following is the Rule and religion of the friars minor: to follow the holy gospel of our Lord Jesus Christ, living in obedience.'

This story is probably not literally true. It reads too much like an edifying folk story: an aetiological tale, explaining how the Rule came to begin as it does. Nevertheless, there is a good deal of truth in it. Francis was fighting for 'the holy gospel'. It was a losing battle. Despite the remoteness of his mountain retreat, the reformers maintained continual pressure on him throughout that autumn and winter. The details of the three-way negotiations on each chapter of the Rule in turn – three-way, because Hugolin was certainly involved in them – have unfortunately been suppressed, in the interests of Franciscan unity. The burden on Francis was very great, but so was the strain on the ministers, whichever faction they followed. At least one of them felt it was too much, and planned to resign, till Francis wrote to him, encouraging him with the promise that when they all met at Whitsun, he would find that all the problems had been amicably resolved. This end was finally achieved, but only by Francis's surrender on every major point at issue.

In the bull *Quo elongati*, dated 8 September 1230, Hugolin, by then Gregory IX, declared that he had personally collaborated in the compilation of the Franciscan Rule seven years earlier. One is left asking: collaborated with whom? and against whom? The answers to these questions are all too obvious. If Hugolin had fought with Francis, the Rule would surely have contained just one at least of the three fundamental Franciscan texts. But they have all disappeared: the passage from Matthew 10 which had inspired Francis to begin preaching with 'neither gold nor silver nor money . . . nor two coats, nor shoes, nor a staff', and those he added to form the primeval Rule for Brother Bernard's sake: 'If thou wilt be perfect, go and sell all . . . and give to the poor', and, 'If any man will come after me, let him deny himself, and take up his cross, and follow me'. The prohibition against books has also disappeared, and although the declaration survives 'the brothers shall possess nothing, not a house, nor a place, nor any thing' (c. 6), the Order resolutely ignored it, or took it to apply only to individuals. But in the early days, many were still troubled by the problem of property, and continued to be so, till the Franciscan Pope Nicholas III (1277-80) ingeniously resolved it by proposing that any property offered to the friars should be accepted in the name of the Holy See, which would then grant the friars actual use of it (what Roman Law called *simplex usus facti*) in perpetuity, so that it would not belong to them, but no one could deprive them of it. The complications and abuses to which this legal fiction led were so scandalous that the Order barely survived them. A story has persisted, and still sometimes appears in modern studies of early Franciscanism, that it was first suggested by Hugolin himself in 1223, and that among the first properties 'loaned' to the Order in this way was the residence at Bologna from where Francis had driven Peter Staccia only three years earlier. Certainly, by the end of that year the school there had reopened under the learned Anthony of Padua, and soon schools 'owned' by the Franciscans were to be found in every Province of the Order. It would not be unfair to say that when this stage was reached, the intellectuals and budding capitalists had taken over the Franciscan movement.

And beside them stood the authoritarians, the moral police-men, justifying their condemnations by referring to the provisions of the new Rule, under which the emphasis was to be no longer on freedom, but on law. In 1223, a clause in Francis's rejected draft of 1221 permitting the brothers to follow their own insights rather than commands from superiors seemingly in conflict with their personal concept of perfection ceased to be a part of Franciscan orthodoxy. The new Rule did, it is true, enjoin obedience (in chapter 10) only to commands 'not contrary to conscience and the rule', but the same chapter reminded brothers that they had 'discarded their own wills' on entering the Order, and chapter 8 ordered strict obedience in all things to the minister general.

With this new and definitive Rule, the ministers and the cardinal-protector did in fact succeed in 'cheating God and Francis', substituting their own view of what the Franciscan Order should be for Francis's vision of it.

The Rule was formally adopted by the Whitsun chapter of 1223, and imposed on the whole Order by the authority of Pope Honorius III in the bull *Solet annuere* of 29 November that same year. It is a clear and legally unquestionable statement of creditable aims, but the aims it proposes are not those of Francis the visionary and the fanatics who in the early years had abandoned the world in order to follow him. He knew it, and they knew it. They no doubt called on him to save them and their way of life, but neither at Portiuncula in May, nor at Rome later in the year, did he take any effectual action. He did, however, react against the self-betrayal that rewriting the Rule had forced upon him, in what the *Legenda antiqua* 21 calls 'the great temptation'.

Although the 'great temptation' is nowhere systematically described, it is obvious that what threatened Francis was total despair. In a very real sense he had betrayed himself, attempted to rebel against the self controlling him, denying the anthropos-vision and turning aside from the quest for gospel perfection, in order to please and satisfy those he, albeit unconsciously, identified as lesser men. Believing that he had denied and destroyed his own handiwork, he momentarily felt that he had nothing left to live for, and probably believed that he was no longer fit to live. As his anxiety deepened, he was precipitated into an interior conflict so profound and far-reaching that for months he did little but wander about in desolate places, questioning himself and God. He stopped visiting even the Poor Ladies. He accused himself of disloyalty to Hugolin. He wondered what his reaction would be if the brothers decided to expel him from his own Order for contumacy. Celano's *Second Life* describes him, a lost and pathetic figure, sitting up in bed and crying out: 'Who are these men, who have torn from my hands my own Order, the Order of my friars?' (c. 188).

Some of his more fanatical early supporters reacted even more violently against their founder's surrender to the forces of medieval normality. They rebelled outright, and had to be driven not only out of the Order, but also out of society by excommunication. On 18 December 1223, only three weeks after the promulgation of *Solet annuere*, Honorius sealed a new bull, registered as *Fratrum minorum*, ordering prelates to treat as excommunicate any lesser brother refusing obedience to the new Rule.

Francis himself never resolved the problem of the duty he owed to obedience. Realizing somewhere within himself that it was insoluble, he evaded it, as he had to do if he was to go on living. One of the brief *Admonitions* in his *Opuscula* offers the unworkable compromise: 'If a superior should order something contrary to spiritual good, though the friars ought not to obey him, let them at no time separate themselves from him.' Brothers unhappy with the orders they received were to find a way of disobeying without rebelling; very few of them can ever have succeeded. Francis himself was one of the few. He finally did what he had so often longed to do, withdrew all but completely from the world and into himself, to live as a hermit.

The wounds of Christ

Dismayed, confused, saddened, even sickened by events though Francis himself was, the Order he had created went from strength to strength, growing daily bigger, richer and more influential. After Whitsun 1223, the reformers found that they had succeeded in eliminating him all but totally from its organization, so that from then on only his name and fame, and no longer his dangerous, demanding devotion to an idea, influenced its daily life.

None of them ever said so, perhaps none of them ever allowed himself consciously to think so, but in their secret opinion, Francis's work was done, and it was time that he died. Once dead, he could be canonized, and his name could be used as a cover for almost any development that the minister general and provincials might want to force on the Order, while his tomb would inevitably become one of the most lucratively holy places in Christendom. But while he lived, he was always potentially dangerous. His *religio* had originally grown out of a rebellion. His charm had once persuaded those now opposed to him to change their lives and follow him in the imitation of the poor Christ. People still flocked to him: 'Crowds of people... collected daily with the deepest devotion to see him, and listen to him', the *First Life* says (I Celano 91). Faith in him was so general that no one openly denied that he frequently performed miracles. Were he to revolt against his erstwhile followers, and his 'pope' Hugolin, the result could only be disastrous.

One at least of the many brothers who still came to him for help whenever they sensed conflict between the Order's new Rule and its old ideals did urge him to change the minister general and his assistants 'who have so long misused their liberty', but though obviously troubled and angered by those leading the brothers away from 'my precepts' in the direction of 'the example of those of old times' – the founding fathers of the traditional monastic orders – Francis would go no further in condemning them than a contemptuous '*Vivant pro libitu*: Let them live as they like. The damnation of a few is a smaller loss than the damnation of the many'.* The meaning of this somewhat obscure saying would appear to be that the ministers would damn themselves by the changes they were imposing on the Order, but that brothers could only damn themselves by disobedience; and so it is yet another reflection of the influence exercised by the concept of conformity to the law and established authority over the medieval mind, even a mind as unconventional as Francis's.

Thus the reformers' worst fears were never realized. That quirk of character which impelled Francis simultaneously both to command and to obey ensured that he lacked the single-mindedness to raise a rebellion within the Order against the cardinal whom he had accepted as its 'Governor, Protector and Corrector'. Instead, he shrank further and further from all action except the barest fulfilment of his own personal rule of life. Immediately after he had made public his surrender of his principles by allowing to pass without protest the publication of *Solet annuere*, he once more tried to become a hermit by accepting an offer from Cardinal Brancaleone to go and live in a tower standing in his garden, making the condition that no one should visit him there except Brother Angelo Tancredi, who was then earning his keep as the cardinal's servant. It is difficult not to see significant symbolism in this withdrawal to an 'ivory tower' from where he could look down on the passing world. But his restlessness would not let him stay there. During his first night there 'the devil' came to him, as Celano's *Second Life* (c. 119) puts it; he was tormented by the thought that God did not want him to be there. He had no idea what he ought to be doing, but knew that he was certainly wrong to be 'living at his ease' in a cardinal's household while his brothers shivered

* II Celano 188.

and starved in their hermitages. He left the following morning, saying that devils had driven him out of the house.

Quitting Rome, he made his way back to the cave of Fonte Colombo near Rieti, perhaps deliberately seeking to relive, and so exorcise, the bitter experiences of the two previous winters spent working on the Rule. By this time, the worst of his depression was behind him; he seems to have already begun to plan his first positive action in rebuilding his life, the never-forgotten Christmas mass in a little wood on a hillside at Greccio. Before leaving Rome he had, it is said, asked Pope Honorius's consent for a scheme to re-enact the scene at Bethlehem. Strictly speaking, the pope's permission was hardly necessary. Probably Francis asked it merely to show his loyalty, either because he did not want it said that he was 'running away' from Rome; or, less credibly, because what he planned might be construed as a revival of the 'theatrical games' forbidden by Innocent III at feasts as recently as 1207, though the prohibition had in fact been directed rather at processions with masked figures and tableaux vivants, such as those commonly held in honour of Saint Nicholas, than against the dramatic representation of the mysteries.

The Christmas crib at Greccio was not the first ever seen. Similar representations had long been customary in many places, including Santa Maria Maggiore at Rome. Nor, despite a story still current, did Francis actually prepare the Greccio crib himself. He planned it, but wanted it to be a surprise nonetheless. The work was done by John Velita, former Lord of Greccio, now a friar: 'A man of good reputation', Celano says, 'and even better life'. Francis told him: 'As far as I am able, I want to see with my physical eyes how he suffered for lack of all that a child needs; how he was laid in a manger and rested on straw, with an ox and an ass nearby.'

The event was well-publicized. Many friars came long distances to be with their founder for the feast. Francis himself did not appear until everything was ready and the people assembled, carrying candles and torches to light the scene. Then 'he saw . . . and was glad'. Wearing the deacon's vestment to which he was entitled (though when he had been ordained is not recorded), he sang the gospel of the mass and preached a sermon, talking, naturally, about poverty and humility in imitation of the Christchild. Now that he had survived the critical period of the Rule's promulgation, he seems to have forgotten his various ailments and disabilities. But if the brothers who had shown their loyalty by walking to Greccio in order to be with him at the first major feast after the publication of *Solet annuere* expected revolutionary fervour from him, they were disappointed.

At the end of that long winter's night, the people of Greccio knew that they had been in touch with that *mana* which they called sanctity. One man claimed to have seen a vision of Francis breathing life into a dead child lying in the manger, so reviving Christ himself, as his followers claimed that his Order was revivifying Christ in his church. Others claimed that they had been cured of their various sicknesses. The straw from the manger was carefully collected up and used as a magic medicine for sick horses and cattle, and as a charm laid across the bodies of women whose labour was dangerously overlong.*

Francis passed the whole of that winter in the neighbourhood of Greccio, not returning to Portiuncula until the time arrived for the General Chapter in June. Nothing has been recorded of his activities during those five months, apart from a few pious tales relating how he tried by his example to keep the spirit of true poverty alive among the handful of his chosen companions.

At the Chapter, it was decided to send a mission to England. Francis himself may have inspired this further extension of the Order's work, as the previous year he had proposed the second mission to Germany. The opening words of Thomas of Eccleston's 'The Coming of the Friars to England' are: '1224: it was this year that the rule of the Blessed Francis was approved by (Honorius)...the Friars Minor arrived for the first time in England....Its clerks were: first, Brother Agnellus Pisanus, aged about thirty, in deacon's orders, who was designated minister provincial in England at the time of the last general chapter by Blessed Francis....' This may, of course, imply no more than that Francis approved the nomination, but it suggests much more.

There is, however, no record of Francis's having taken part in the discussions over discipline and the new Rule, or having interfered in the direction of the Order, though much that he

---

* I Celano 1, 85–7; students of mythology cannot fail to be struck by the many echoes of the Tammuz-Adonis cycle in this tale.

saw and heard must have troubled him. Inveighing against the ministers, he had said, apparently during the period immediately before this chapter assembled:* 'If I go to the General Chapter, I will show them what my will is.' But when the moment came, he was already too remote from the day-to-day life of the Order actively to combat Minister General Elias' determination with his own.

There is still a school of thought among Franciscans that ascribes Francis's silence on this and similar occasions to his general agreement with what was happening to his Order and in his name, and to his absolute loyalty to the papacy and hierarchy. He was certainly loyal, but unless one is willing to discard in favour of generalized statements all the circumstantial stories related by his biographers, it is impossible to escape the conclusion sustained here: that Francis was acutely aware of the fact that Elias, with at least the connivance of Hugolin if not his active collaboration, was grossly changing the spirit of the Order and its attitude to the world in general, but felt powerless to do anything about it except suffer it and by his example inspire a few of his closest companions to keep his old religion alive. There is no proof that he ever distrusted the motives of even Brother Elias, but plenty of proof that he distrusted Elias's actions. Perhaps he sometimes saw the inevitability of changes, but he nevertheless suffered because they had to be.

It is very unlikely that his total inactivity in the face of these later changes – he had fought earlier ones, very vigorously – was entirely due to his physical incapacity. Much more significant was his psychological state and spiritual condition. Twenty years earlier he had longed to fight for God, and die a martyr to him. In 1219, he had achieved a crusade in Egypt, but by his own exacting standards his crusade had failed, because he had neither converted the infidel nor died at his hands. Since then, he had come close to losing the brothers God had given him. So if he was not to end a complete failure in his own eyes, he had to die fittingly, in perfect imitation of Christ. Obviously, he could not achieve crucifixion at the hands of the imperial authorities. He

* Though this cannot be proved, as the part of Celano's *Second Life* in which the story is preserved it is, like most of the rest, without any indication of date.

was not a criminal, and in any case crucifixion as a means of execution had been banned nine hundred years earlier by the Emperor Constantine. Nor could he persuade Christ's enemies to kill him; his first and last chance of doing so had been missed at Fariskur. He was too weak to undertake another crusade, so the only form of death for Christ open to him was what must be called psychological martyrdom. This is the only reasonable explanation of the next development in his quest for perfection, the appearance in his flesh of 'wounds' analogous to those he believed to have scarred Christ's body after the crucifixion, the *stigmata*.

Thomas of Celano carefully sets the scene in the opening chapters of the second part of his *First Life* (c. 91–3), chapters often ignored by Francis's later biographers, perhaps because they seem to parallel too closely the paragraphs describing his first vocation to poverty and preaching.

Celano says that Francis now withdrew totally from the world 'wanting to pass his time with God and to shake off from himself any dust that might be clinging to him from his association with mankind'. He retired to 'a quiet and secret place', Fonte Colombo, and after a period spent 'in continual prayer and frequent contemplation' found himself 'longing to know what with regard to himself might be made yet more acceptable to the Eternal King and what was likely to happen next'. So one day 'he put himself before the Holy Altar ... then lay prostrate in prayer to God ... and ... asked ... that the Great God ... would condescend to make his will known to him ... at the first opening of the book [of the gospels, lying on the altar].'

He had gone through a similar procedure before, at the moment when he and Brother Bernard had been agonizing over the direction that they should take to find perfection. It is easy to laugh at it: equally easy to argue that the text to be discovered had been prearranged. The texts found were apt ones, but it is impossible to be sure that Francis would not have followed as literally whatever precept his divinations had disclosed. It is equally impossible to disprove by rational means that the texts were miraculously revealed.

On the first occasion when he had used the gospels as an oracle, he had 'found' the three chapters of the primitive Rule. On this second occasion, the book fell open at 'the passion of the

Lord Jesus Christ, at the part where it says that he would suffer tribulation'. The text is not immediately identifiable from this insufficient description, but several passages in the gospels would fit. Then, Celano adds, 'so that there could be no suspicion of coincidence' he repeated the experiment 'a second and a third time, and found the same text or a similar one each time'. So he accepted the fact that 'he was to enter the Kingdom of God through many tribulations' and (as this is precisely what his urge for martyrdom was driving him towards) 'remained blithe, and sang happy songs in his heart'. This preliminary scene-setting is essential to what follows.

Two years before Francis returned his soul to heaven, while he was living at an hermitage called Alverna ... he saw in a divine vision a man standing over him, like a six-winged seraph, his hands spread, and his feet joined, and fixed to a cross. Of the wings, two were stretched over his head, two were extended as though to fly, and two wrapped round the whole body. Seeing these things, the blessed servant of the Most High was filled with the greatest amazement, but could not understand what the vision might mean. . . . Alternately he was filled with joy and sorrow. . . . And while he was not able to attain any comprehension of the vision, and its strangeness filled his heart, the marks of nails started to appear on his hands and feet, just as he had seen them shortly before on the crucified man above him. His hands and feet appeared to be pierced through the centre with nails, with the heads of the nails visible on the inner sides of the hands and the upper sides of the feet, and the points on the other sides. In the hands, the marks were round on the palms, but elongated on the outside, and small pieces of flesh assumed the likeness of nails, bent, driven back, and rising above the other flesh. Similarly upon the feet, the nail marks were impressed and raised in a like manner above the other flesh. In addition, his right side was as though pierced with a lance and bore a wound which often bled so that his tunic and drawers were very frequently drenched in his sacred blood (94–5).

This is not the earliest version of the story of Francis's stigmatization, but is a typical example of what might be called the 'received' version, as it was current throughout the later middle ages. There have been many stigmatizations* since Francis's, but it is important to realize that his was the first ever recorded. Why he, or his immediate followers chose to call the phenomenon 'stigmatization' is not known, though the source of the word was probably the New Testament passage in which St Paul says that he 'bears in his body the marks of the Lord Jesus', where the Greek word translated 'marks' as 'stigmata'. To Francis himself, and those most intimate with him, the meaning of the impression of the stigmata on him was too obvious to need discussion. It showed that he had brought his imitation of Christ to such a pitch of perfection that he was given physical resemblance to the God-man, the crucified, as he envisaged him. In our jargon, the invasion of his ego from the undifferentiated self was complete; Francis had become the embodiment of the anthropos archetype.

Like all visions, Francis's of the seraph was essentially indescribable. The seraph, a man-beast peculiar to Jewish mythology, though not without near parallels in Persian legends, has only been reported as seen three or four times in history. It was a seraph that guarded the gate of the Garden of Eden after Adam's expulsion from paradise, and seraphim were seen guarding the throne of God in the Temple at Jerusalem by the prophet Isaiah. The seraph was part man, part angel, and part serpent. In the Garden of Eden, it carried a sharp sword to protect what was holy to God and banned to man. In the Temple, it proclaimed the otherness, the holiness, of God, singing 'holy is the Lord of Armies'. On Mount Alverna, its task was to imprint that holiness on Francis, making him what the serpent-tempter promised Adam and Eve that they would be once they had tasted the fruit of the tree of the knowledge of good and evil, 'like God'. The seraph is, of course, a manifestation of God himself, or in this case, of the God-man, the Cosmic Man, Christ almost as Stephen, the first Christian martyr, saw him, 'as it were crucified . . . and lifted up'.

The immediate effect upon Francis of this very biblical vision

---

* The literature is vast, and much of it very technical. Other stigmatics are discussed in: Siwek, *The Riddle of Konnersreuth,* Brown and Nolan; Schmoger, *Anna Catherina Emmerick,* Britons Publishing Company; J. Clarke, *Padre Pio*; Scott (trans.), *The Riddle of the Stigmata*; cf. also Dinit (ed.), *Stigmatization and Social Reaction.*

was to please and excite, but also to depress him. In other words, it confused him; just as the vision of the cross is said to have confused the Emperor Constantine before the Battle of Mulvian Bridge in A.D. 312, until it was explained to him by an angel; and as Joseph the Carpenter is said to have been confused by his visionary dream of the birth of Christ, until told what it meant. It seems to be characteristic of visions that those receiving them do not immediately connect them with their current anxieties, though once the connection is explained, it seems quite obvious. Francis's earlier visions (that at Foligno, for example) were often explained to him by 'heavenly' voices. The vision of the seraph remained unexplained except by the 'signs' that followed it.

Celano says that the marks in the hands and feet were actually shaped like nails, with heads and points modelled in flesh and set in the middle of the organ stigmatized. The earliest record of their appearance, as they looked two years after their first manifestation, on 3 October 1226, the day Francis died, locates them in the same places, but describes them differently. It was written by Brother Elias, at that time still Minister General of the Order, and forms part of the letter announcing Francis's death which he addressed to 'Gregory (of Naples), the minister of the friars in France, and to his brethren and ours'. He wrote:

> What I had been fearing has overtaken me and you . . . the man who used to carry us like lambs on his shoulders has set out for a far country . . . we are fatherless orphans. . . . But now I have told you that, I must announce a great joy to you, a new miracle: a sign unheard of since time began, except in the Lord Christ, the Son of God. A short time before his death, our Brother and Father was seen to be like the Crucified, having in his body the five wounds that are Christ's marks. His hands and feet bore the scars of nails, being pierced on each side, carrying the marks and colour of nails. His side looked as though it had been laid open with a lance, and bled frequently.

There is some ambiguity in the Latin of 'the marks and colour of nails' which could be translated in the sense of the shape of nailheads, as in fact Celano and, following him, Bonaventure (neither of whom actually saw the body) have translated it. But its plain meaning is that there were blackened holes in the hands and feet, which at least appeared to run right through, and could have been made by nails. According to Bonaventure's *Life*, more than fifty people actually saw the wounds, including Brothers Leo and Rufino, and Chiara and some of her sisters, and Reginald Conti, Count of Segni, yet another of the family from Anagni who won supreme power in the church after serving as Cardinal-Bishop of Ostia, being elected as pope Alexander IV in 1254.

It would, of course, be more comfortable to be able to reject the story of the stigmata outright in all its forms, and it would no doubt have been all but universally rejected were it not for the fact that since Francis died the phenomenon has been recorded several hundred times. When I asked a British psychiatrist his professional reaction to the story, he admitted that he wanted at first to say, 'It did not happen', but faced with the evidence, which seems undeniable despite the disagreement about the appearance of the wounds, drew my attention to Jung's discussion of the anthropos archetype, and asked pertinently, 'Assuming the injuries were not self-inflicted, where exactly were they?'

The implications of this question are obvious. Hysterics often inflict wounds on themselves which they afterwards attempt so clumsily to conceal that others cannot fail to see them. Technically, Francis was a hysterical type. Whether the wounds were self-inflicted or not, they were in the centre of the hands and feet, in the position where popular representations of the crucifixion had always placed them since 'realistic' portrayals of the crucifixion had become acceptable to Western Christians, some time in the eighth century. By that date, however, the anatomical details of execution by crucifixion in first-century Judaea had long been forgotten. Recent archaeological discoveries in Israel have established that in crucifixions by nailing a single nail was driven through the heel bones of both feet placed together side by side with the knees swung sideways, so that it was the heel and not the instep that was asked to carry the weight. Hence, whether Francis's wounds were self-inflicted, self-induced, or imposed from without by a divine or other agency, the new Christ their manifestation physically produced belonged to the thirteenth century and Christian mythology, and not to the era of the gospels. Just as Francis's concept of the poverty of the poor Christ belonged to his own time, and not to Christ's, so also did his concept of Christ's wounds. As a symbol and example, it was, of course, all the more powerful for that: we all understand best when things are explained to us in terms of our own world and times.

Francis's attempts to conceal his wounds were, if anything, even less efficient than the average failed suicide's. With great insight, Celano claims that 'the divine providence' did not want the secret successfully kept, although Francis's conscious wish was to hide the facts. The relevant passage in the *Second Life* might be translated:

But divine providence did not want them always hidden, unrevealed to those dear to him. And the very fact that his limbs were exposed [parts of the body] did not permit their concealment. But when once one of his companions saw the stigmata in his feet, he said to him: Good brother, what is this? And he replied: Mind your own business. Another time, a brother took his tunic to wash it, and seeing the bloodstains said to the Blessed when he gave it back to him: What was that blood spotting your tunic? And putting his fingers to his eye, the Blessed said: Knowing that this is an eye, do you ask what it is? And he rarely washed the whole of his hands, rather rinsing his fingers, so that those around should not know. His feet he washed very seldom, and as secretly as rarely. When anyone asked for his hand to kiss, he would give only enough of his fingers for a kiss to be possible and sometimes offered only his sleeve. He wrapped his feet in woollen footcloths, so that they would not be seen, putting skins over the wool to lessen the pain of it. And although it was impossible for the holy father to hide the stigmata in his hands and feet completely from his companions, if anyone did see them, he was nonetheless bitter about it (c. 135).

The *First Life* makes the same point, though more briefly: 'He hid these marks from strangers most assiduously, and concealed them with the utmost care from those close to him, so that even the friars nearest to him, his most devoted followers, long remained ignorant of them.'

Brother Rufino, who was with him constantly during his last years, learned of them only accidentally, when he brushed against Francis's side, and caused him 'no little pain'. Others came to know of them in various similar ways.

However, Francis himself must have told someone the story of his vision – unless we assume that it was a later invention – and according to Bonaventure, he himself did take action to speed the brothers' realization that something very unusual had happened to him, asking them 'in veiled words' if 'certain extraordinary graces' ought to be revealed or concealed. Brother Illuminato said that it would be wrong to conceal anything that might be instructive to the whole community, and after that Francis spoke more openly about the stigmata, but still refused to display his wounds. Once the brothers had been alerted to the fact of their existence, however, curiosity must have sharpened their observation.

The suggestion that Francis was an hysterical subject, totally absorbed to the point of indifference towards others by his vision of perfection, and identified so completely with the popular Christ, the poor Christ, the humble Christ, that ultimately his body in some way reproduced the wounds that he believed Christ had suffered, in no way reduces the value of the challenge his life threw down to his own and succeeding generations. The steadfastness of his purpose and the strength of his will allowed him to present the people of his own times with an image of Christ-likeness that shocked or delighted, or moved, or pursued them, but left very few totally indifferent. The validity of his testimony to the ideal of Christ was demonstrated close to his own times by the phenomenal growth of his Order of lesser brothers (together with the accretion to his name of a large body of miracle and folk stories), and is shown still today by the esteem and even reverence in which his memory is held by many who do not share his confidence in the divine origin of the papacy and Roman hierarchy. The brother who dreamed not long after Francis's death that Francis was Christ and Christ Francis was not far from the truth; as Thomas of Celano comments: 'He who cleaves to God is made one spirit with him.'* To Christians, both Christ and Francis have symbolized the perfect man, the anthropos, coming as close as any human being can to the Christian concept of God. So 'Christ and Francis were one person', often

* II Celano 219.

in Francis's own mind, and even more frequently in the minds of his companions. It is not surprising that popular Christianity averred that Francis performed Christ's miracles, especially miracles of healing, and bore the marks of Christ's wounds.

In this connection, it is revealing that many of Francis's miracles resembled more closely those of the 'popular' Christ of the apocryphal gospels, banned centuries before Francis's time by the fathers of the church, than they did those of the Jesus of the orthodox gospels of the New Testament. Like the young Dionysos, the Christ-child of the apocryphal gospels was the master of the animals and callous Lord of life and death. He created clay birds from river mud and breathed life into them. He tamed animals that threatened him, and even killed a bullying and annoying boy by ill-wishing him. This early, non-orthodox Christ is, in his gentler aspects, the Christ of many modern children's stories and is often depicted on Christmas cards. He is not the Jesus of history, even gospel history, but the anthropos of popular semi-Christianized imagination, and as such is completely identifiable with the popular wonder-working Francis, now the gentle saint, talking to wolves and birds, or persuading a *tinca*-fish in the Lake of Rieti to say a prayer with him (I Celano 1, 61), and now the magician who curses Peter Staccia to death or, when 'a son of Belial', having begged a piece of chicken from the saint's plate on a fast-day, tries to use it to discredit him, persuades a crowd at Alessandria that it is seeing not a piece of forbidden chicken but a piece of legitimate fish (II Celano 78–9).

Among the 'blasphemous doctrines' that the *Alcoran of the Barefoote Friers* alleges was taught by the friars of the sixteenth century was, naturally, the story of the stigmata. The following three paragraphs from the *Alcoran* are of special importance, because echoing as they do ideas then current about Francis's stigmatization, they show how Franciscan preaching had embroidered upon the original relatively stark story:

In the handes and feete of Frances were nailes as it were of sinowes and fleshe, the whiche nailes were on the heades hard and grosse, they were long and stretched farre bothe thorow his handes and fete, and turned again as it were clinched, so that a finger myghte have bene laied betweene the clinching:

as the righte worshipful Bonaventure bishop of Allonence and Cardinall of Rome in the third parte of his Legend dothe affirme by the credible report of them whiche sawe them, felte them and by their own othe confirmed it so to be. Therefore it came neither by nature nor yet be imaginatiō, neither could nature presens it in such mannere without putrifaction, if by any arte it had bene devised, for by the space of ii yeares out of those wondes issued blod (folio 2).

But:

S. Frances used all wayes to put a certeyn thyng in his woundes to kepe them from bledyng, but upon Maundy thursdaye nyght and all good Friday he would put nothyng in them, but suffred theim to blede, for the love of Christ (folio 49).

The soul of every Franciscan bears the imprint of the five wounds of Saint Francis, or so suggests an obviously popular story about the struggle a somewhat disreputable friar had to persuade the porter at the gate of heaven to let him in, related on folio 120. The dead friar appealed to Francis, and the saint come down to the gate of heaven with all his brethren:

When S. Frances with all his brethrē sawe (him), he sayd to the porter, let him in, for he is one of my brethrē. And truly the prynt of the wondes of S. Frāces shone as bryght as v. of the fayrest sterres in the element.

In 1303, Pope Benedict XI, himself formerly the General of Saint Dominic's Order of Friars Preacher, granted the Franciscans the right to celebrate annually the Feast of the Stigmatization of Saint Francis, and early in the seventeenth century Pope Paul V (1605–21) decreed that it should be celebrated universally throughout the western church. At the beginning of the modern reform movement within the Roman church, however, in 1960, during the reign of Pope Pius XII, the feast was reduced to a simple commemoration.

13

Francis's teaching

There is no doubt whatsoever that Francis's influence on his own and succeeding centuries in the West has been seminal. Yet there is little if anything in his teaching that was uniquely new, not even his insistence on the role of poverty in the quest for perfection – as the single instance of the priest who quoted the verse from the gospel 'Sell all, and give to the poor' to Peter Waldo a generation before Francis's birth is itself enough to show.

In his teaching, he laid emphasis on the significant name of Jesus – but so had preachers since Saint Paul, both orthodox and heretical. He enthusiastically embraced the teaching of the Fourth Lateran Council about the reality of the substantial presence of Christ in the bread and wine of the Eucharist, calling again and again for due reverence in handling the sacrament, and the use of fitting furnishings in church – but so were modern preachers everywhere at that time. He had great reverence for the bible (even going so far as to use it for divining the will of God for himself), for the relics of the saints, and for the persons of bishops and priests – but so also did many in his century. He called for an all but absolute obedience to superiors, and at least acquiesced, towards the end of his life, in the severe disciplining of any who would not obey – but in this he was only following the legalistic and authoritarian trend of his times. So wherein lay his originality? Only, it would seem, in his personality, and his approach to religion, in his way of expressing it and himself, the second Christ, the new covenant.

Thomas of Spalato, who had heard Francis preach, said that the key to his appeal was his unceasing emphasis on the importance of peace 'for indeed, everything he said was directed towards the extinction of enmity, and re-establishing the brotherhood of peace'. In preaching peace, he was speaking for, as well as to, the poor, to whom the constant wars and threats of war of the times meant nothing but additional burdens in a life already all but intolerably hard.

Would Francis have the same appeal today? Probably not, even in his native Umbria, unless he changed his life-style considerably. He was – let it be repeated – a man of his time. If he were to appear in modern Europe or America, he might attract the lunatic fringe of the middle-class, as in the thirteenth century he attracted so many merchants' sons and law students, but he would surely find it difficult to catch the attention of the pope and secular rulers, and to win the favour of a considerable number among the cardinals. He belonged to his century, at least in his mode of self-expression, in his manner of expressing those elements of the self which had invaded his consciousness. Yet his appeal has proved wider than that century, simply because, of course, it was certain aspects of the self which he expressed. It is informative to look at a collection of 'portraits' of him (no genuine likeness exists, apart from Thomas of Cclano's pen-picture, quoted on page 131).

Over the centuries, his public image has changed from ascetic and gaunt near-skeleton to plump and jolly friar, the smiling friend of children. He was never Everyman – he was always too much of a personality for that – but he has frequently assumed the appearance of the ideal Christian, changing as the ideal itself has changed.

The process of hiding the man under the image actually began in Francis's own mind, with his identification of himself with Christ and the new covenant. But it was carried on with vigour by those who took that image over from him on his death. While he was still alive, and able to protest (however feebly) at the gross distortion of his personality and message, 'reformers' like Elias and Hugolin were already at work normalizing the image of the Franciscan movement and its founder, and in the process already undermining the memory of the man behind the image. The success of their takeover makes circumspection necessary even in using the writings ascribed to Francis himself to discover how he thought and what he taught. They have all been edited to a greater or lesser degree. Nevertheless, dangerous as they are, some account of them is necessary, for the sake of the few lines that do reveal something of the quality of the man himself.

Before looking at them, however, it may be valuable to quote a passage from Cardinal Jacques de Vitry's *Historia Occidentalis* which describes the position of the Franciscan Order in the western church only a few years after Francis's death, and sets out those elements in the way of life of the Order which seemed significant to an intelligent partisan of Francis and Franciscanism at that time. The cardinal wrote:

To the three religions already mentioned, Hermits, Monks, and Canons, the Lord has added in our own days a fourth religious institution, with a fitting order and holy rule. . . . If we had paid proper heed to the standing and order of the primitive church, He would not have given a new rule, but rather would have renewed the old, improving what was falling down, and restoring what was so nearly dead, in these last hours of the evening of the world, when the times of the Son of Perdition are at hand. However, in these dangerous times, he has trained new athletes against antichrist, and strengthened the church with a fortification. This is the *religio* of the Poor Men of the Crucified and the Order of preachers that we call the friars minor. They are truly lesser man (*minores*) and humble people, patterns to all their age in dress, and destitution, and contempt for this world. And they have one chief prior, whose commands and rules the lesser priors reverentially obey and transmit to the other brothers dispersed throughout the various provinces of the world to preach and to care for souls. And they do try diligently to recreate among themselves the religion of the primitive church by their poverty and humility . . . expressly imitating the life of the Apostles. . . . And their rule was confirmed by the Lord Pope, and they were authorized to preach in whatever churches they came to; but for respect's sake, they ask the consent of the prelates of these places. And they were sent out two by two to preach before the face of the Lord and in preparation for his coming. And these same Poor Men of Christ do not take either purses or pouches with them, nor bread, nor any sort of money in their belts, they have neither gold nor silver, nor sandals on their feet; they have neither monasteries nor churches, nor fields nor vineyards, nor animals, nor houses, nor other real estate property, nor anywhere to lay their heads. They have no cloaks or hoods, nor indeed any other clothes to wrap round themselves. And if anyone invites them to eat, they eat and drink what is before them. And if anyone offers them anything for pity's sake, they do not save it up for later. Once or twice a year, they come together to keep a General Chapter at a certain place and a fixed time, except for those cut off by very long distances, or by interposing seas. And after the chapter, they are sent out again by their superiors, two or more together, to the various districts, provinces, and cities.

The life reflected in this passage is that of the earliest rule known and that envisaged by Francis's abortive rule of 1221. In part, it records the Franciscan life as Cardinal de Vitry had himself seen it in Italy and Syria between 1216 and 1220; in part, it is an idealization. The ideal is, however, based not on the Rule approved by Honorius III's bull of December 1223, but on Francis's original vision. It is further proof, if any were needed, of both the rigour of the demands Francis made in poverty's name, and the degree to which those demands were mitigated by later Franciscans. The life it presupposes is so harsh that only a powerful and dedicated individual could survive it for long. All the soft holy pictures, and even softer holy stories and plays, of the centuries since 1220 have blinded Europe to the reality of the Franciscan challenge to Christian comfort.

Most of the writings traditionally ascribed to Francis are usually said to date from the last five years of his life, and the greatest of them, the *Canticle of Brother Sun*, almost certainly belongs to the period of his stigmatization. But the full tally of the compositions at some time or other said to have been written by him is improbably long and variable in quality, ranging as it does over some twenty-four pieces, from a short blessing for Brother Leo, through admonitions and instructions to friars and others, to a complete Office of the passion in five different forms for use at various seasons of the church's year. And all this allegedly the work of a man who, as Eccleston says, was capable only of 'bad' Latin.

The fact is that like many before and since, Francis himself

did not actually write very much, but used a secretary, not only
to write down his words, but also to express his thoughts in an
acceptable form. So Caesar of Speyer helped him to write the Rule
of 1221, and Brother Leo is frequently referred to as his secretary,
although Francis himself regarded him primarily as his confessor
– Leo was in priest's orders – and confidant.

It is generally conceded that nothing has survived in Francis's
own handwriting except, probably, the *Blessing* for Brother Leo
now kept at Assisi, and a brief letter to the same brother now
preserved in the Cathedral at Spoleto.

The *Blessing* for Brother Leo is the conventional blessing of
Aaron the High Priest, with a brief addition:

> May God bless and keep you,
> May God smile upon you, and have mercy upon you.
> May God turn his face towards you,
> And give you peace
> May God bless, Leo, you.

Through the last line, the blessing of Leo himself, and below it,
is a carefully drawn Greek cross, growing out of what has usually
been described as a sketch of a human head. The *Blessing* is
accompanied by a note in another hand which (if as is usually
maintained, Leo himself wrote it) may be an even earlier record
of the stigmata than that in Minister General Elias's encyclical
letter announcing Francis's death:

> At the place called Alverna, where two years before his death
> Blessed Francis kept Lent in honour of the Blessed Virgin
> Mary, the Lord's Mother, and the Blessed Archangel Michael,
> from the Feast of the Assumption of the Holy Virgin Mary
> until the Feast of Saint Michael in September (i.e. 15 August-
> 29 September). And the Lord's hand was laid upon him.
> Following a vision of, and conversation with, a seraph, and the
> impression on his body of Christ's stigmata, he wrote with his
> own hand the praises on the other side of this sheet, so giving
> thanks to the Lord for the blessings bestowed upon him.

Under the *Blessing* are the words: 'Blessed Francis wrote this
blessing with his own hand for me, Brother Leo'; and finally:

'Similarly in his own hand he made this sign T, together with the head.'

According to Thomas of Celano, the occasion of the blessing of Brother Leo was the composition of the *Praises* of God on the other side of the sheet. Brother Leo, it seems, wanted to ask Francis to write something for him, to encourage him during bouts of an attack of 'a temptation not of the flesh' (II Celano 49), a temptation that may well have been to despair at the thought of the perilous times through which the Order was passing. While he was hesitating over making his request, Francis himself proposed the composition in writing of 'the Lord's words and praises which I have been considering in my heart'. The handwriting of the *Praises* is very rubbed and faint now, but part of the text does appear to be in the same handwriting as the *Blessing* of Brother Leo: Celano's story would account for the wear also. He says that after writing the *Blessing*, Francis told Leo to keep it safely, carrying it with him wherever he went 'till the day of your death'. So for nearly fifty years, it travelled with Leo wherever he went, and consequently became badly worn. Early copies of the *Praises* were made, however, and from them it is possible to reconstruct the original text. It has no obvious lyrical merit, but consists largely of a long series of titles and attributes of God. Its opening lines are:

> Lord, you are Holy: the Sole God
> and your acts are wonderful.
> You are strong, you are great
> You are the Most High
> You are almighty.

Thus, the concept behind this composition is very close to that of the long prayer at the end of the Rule of 1221.

The only other scrap of writing apparently in Francis's own hand, that preserved at the Cathedral of Spoleto, is a brief note written, like the *Praises* and the *Blessing* in Latin, the bad Latin of which Eccleston complained. It cannot be accurately dated, but would seem to belong to a period before Francis was chronically sick and Leo remained constantly with him. Preserved for centuries at the Franciscan convent in Spoleto, it disappeared for several decades during the nineteenth century, but in 1902 was bought by Pope Leo XIII from a Spoletan priest and presented to the city's cathedral.

The problems of its translation and interpretation begin in the first lines, the salutation: *F. Leo f. frācissco tuo salutē et pacē*. Should this be read as 'Brother Leo: to your brother Francis (send) health and peace' or 'Brother Leo, from your brother Francis, health and peace'?

The note continues:

Yes – I tell you, my son! – and like a mother! Everything we talked about along the road I (can) sum up briefly in this one short piece of advice. And if after this you need to come to me for advice, my advice is this: whatever way you believe you will best please the Lord God, and follow in his footsteps, and his poverty, take you that way, with the Lord's blessing, and in obedience to me. And if it is necessary for your soul's peace or other consolation, and you wish to come to me, then come.

The inner tension impelling the writer of this note is more obvious than his meaning. It shows in the jagged, uneven hand-writing as well as in the composition. It is a pity, of course, that no one can more than guess what Francis and Leo had talked about 'along the road', and even more disconcerting that the grammar of the opening lines is so confused that it is impossible to tell which of its clauses embodies the piece of advice summariz-ing 'all we talked about'. Nevertheless, brief and nearly incom-prehensible as this letter is, it is important because the contrast between it and the other compositions attributed to Francis is so great. Generally speaking, his amanuenses may have accurately transcribed his thought, but they have preserved very little of his way of expressing himself, the manner of a man all but illiterate. The only exception to this is in the *Canticle of Brother Sun*, where ambiguity persists, even though the language is not Latin, but his native Umbrian dialect.

Generally speaking still, it is reasonable to suppose that the shorter documents are the least distant from Francis's original thought, if only because there is less room for error in the trans-mission of a short text, and less for 'improvement' of the mes-sage. Two very brief messages to Chiara fall into this category. They may, in fact, be only first- or second-hand copies from the original, for they were discovered in 1893 in a copy of the Rule of Saint Clare, wrapped together with the original bull of Innocent IV, dated 1255, confirming that Rule, in an ancient habit alleged to have belonged to Chiara herself, long preserved in a reliquary at her convent in Assisi. The first of them is a promise from Francis to all the sisters that he himself will always regard them as the equals of his brothers:

Because it was God who inspired you to become daughters and maidservants of the highest and Supreme King, I personally promise you, speaking also for my friars, that I will for ever have the same loving care and special concern for you as for them.

This appears to be the promise on which Chiara based her own acceptance of Francis's *religio* and which she called her *forma vivendi*, her way of life, saying that Francis wrote it for the sisters when he saw that they did in truth 'fear no poverty, toil, misery, humiliation, or contempt from the world'. It may also be the *formula vitae* that Gregory IX writes of as Blessed Francis's gift to 'Chiara and certain other devout women in the Lord' who had 'chosen to serve the Lord in religion' in a letter that he wrote to Agnes on 11 May 1238, after he had spent years trying to destroy that way of life, years surely reflected in the other message from Francis also preserved with Chiara's Rule, which she calls his 'Last Testament', adding in a note that he wrote 'shortly before his death ... so that we might never fall away from the highest poverty':

I, the little brother, Francis, wish to live according to the life and poverty of our most exalted Lord, Jesus Christ, and of his most holy Mother, and to continue in this until the end. And, my ladies, I beg and exhort you always to live in this most holy life and poverty. Keep careful watch over yourselves, so that you never abandon it as a result of the teaching or advice of anyone.

Only a little less probably the work of Francis himself are a series of twenty-eight undated 'Words of Admonition of our

Holy Father Francis'.* They belong to no special period of Francis's life and were probably collected together in their present form only after his death. They resemble the *Sentences* used as handy collections of proof-texts and summaries by the lawyers; it will be remembered that Peter Waldo's followers also used collections of *Sentences,* drawn from the scriptures and the saints, to prove the validity of their doctrine. Francis's *Admonitions* are the proof-texts by which later Franciscans could judge themselves and their actions by the standards of their master's quest for perfection. Their style, as they have been preserved, is not Francis's, but that of the clerk who formalized them, yet they may fairly be taken as examples of the 'admonitions, corrections and precepts' which *The Chronicle of the Three Companions* says it was Francis's custom to give to the friars at General Chapters. There is nothing in them that would not fit this assertion. Most of them are unexceptionable statements of the Franciscan's duty to love and follow God, keep the Franciscan Rule, and welcome the teachings of the church, showing special reverence to the eucharist. The most original of them is the ruling already quoted that it is wrong to obey when conscience forbids obedience (*Admonition 5*). Also noteworthy is the somewhat startling near-Cathar rejection of the body in the sentence 'our lower nature is opposed to every good' (*Admonition 12*). Apart from these two, what makes the *Admonitions* important is not what is said in them, but who said them; because they were Francis's, they have been deemed significant by Franciscans. The truth is that Francis was not an intellectual, and it is a disservice to him to try and represent him as one.†

* Often called the *Opuscula*; they are preserved in the thirteenth-century Ognissanti Manuscript at Assisi (Assisi 338).

† The *Admonitions* are translated in Fahy and Hermann, *The Writings of Saint Francis of Assisi*, Franciscan Herald Press, Chicago, 1964; here all the compositions sometimes ascribed to Francis are to be found: cf. also H. Boemer (ed.) *Analekten zur Geschichte des Frankiskus von Assisi*, Tuebingen, 1961; and *Opuscula Sancti Patris Francisci Assisiensis*, Quarrachi, Rome, 1949. Of the writings sometimes claimed as Francis's not discussed here – a note on the religious life in hermitages, a letter to all the faithful, another to the clergy, a letter to a General Chapter of the Order, a letter to an unnamed minister general, another to all superiors, an open letter to 'the rulers of the people', a note to Anthony of Padua, the office of the passion, and two prayers – little can be said that would

Controversy has raged around the most literary, as well as the most spiritual of all Francis's writings, the *Canticle of Brother Sun*, which is undeniably the most important of all his compositions, and will remain so, unless someone discovers a copy of the original Rule of 1210. It is especially powerful because in it Francis ordered his thoughts in his own Umbrian dialect; existing Latin versions of it are undeniably translations from an original which has survived the centuries to come down to us in a form at least substantially unchanged.

The *Mirror of Perfection* tells the story of the composition of this hymn 'For My Lord Brother Sun', credibly claiming that Francis composed it 'because he believed the sun to be the most beautiful of created things, as it is that most closely resembling our Lord, whom the scriptures call the sun of righteousness, therefore he gave its name to the praises he wrote about God's creatures when God promised him his kingdom, naming them the *Canticle of Brother Sun*'. What this not does not record is that when Francis wrote these verses, he could enjoy the beauty of the sun and the other creatures only in memory, for he was in constant pain and almost blind, 'promised the kingdom' by an early death.

The *Canticle* now exists only in late copies. Indeed, if the traditions of its composition are to be trusted, it may not have been written down during Francis's lifetime. They represent it as a true troubadour's song which he used to sing to a tune of his own composition, inviting his companions to join in, repeating the verses after him, as psalms were usually sung by the illiterate congregations of the early church. The first twenty-two lines, which are concerned wholly with the majesty of God and the beauty of the world, strongly recall the nature poems of the troubadours, only baptizing them, as it were. They were composed, it is usually said, some time in 1225, although whether at

---

not immediately be gainsaid by some protagonist either of the view that the document in question was not in any sense authentic, or of the opinion that it belonged to some other period in Francis's life than that to which we assigned it. In other words, all is darkness, a darkness made impenetrable by the fact that all the documents have been so frequently polished and repolished by editors and copyists (themselves often protagonists of some particular view of Franciscan origins) that little or nothing remains in them of their alleged author's work.

Saint Damian's at Assisi, or forty miles south from there at Rieti, is a matter of sometimes acrimonious dispute, unimportant though the point is.

Not surprisingly, there are minor differences between the manuscripts.* Unfortunately, none of them suggests the correct answer to the one great problem posed by the poem, that of the correct translation of the word *per* in such a line as *Laudato si, mi Signore, per sora luna e le stelle.* Should it be translated as though the Lord were to be praised 'by', 'through', 'on behalf of' or 'on account of' sister moon and the stars? Thomas of Celano once likened Francis to the three young men in the *Book of Daniel* who called on all things natural and supernatural to praise God in the hymn often known as the *Benedicite* (I Celano 80); if this was Francis's habit – and those stories about him in which he preaches to birds and animals, reminding them to praise their creator are the best-remembered tales about him – it is not unlikely that in his *Canticle* he reminded all creation of the duty of praise it owed to God, and 'by' is the correct translation. However, recent opinion, based on what is becoming known about the development of the Italian language, has favoured the translation 'through' and 'on account of', a view supported by the *Mirror of Perfection* (c. 120) which says that the *Canticle* was written about 'the things the Lord has created, which we use every day, without which we cannot live, yet with which humanity gives great offence to its creator [by abusing them]'. The *Canticle* is then an act of reparation, praising God 'through' or even 'for' his creatures.

Is it possible that Francis himself was being deliberately ambiguous, using a word with many overtones and undercurrents of meaning? With this possibility in mind, I offer this nearly literal translation of this famous poem:

Most high, omnipotent [and] good Lord
To you alone: praise, glory, and honour, and all benediction.

To you alone, O Highest, do they belong
And no man is worthy to name you.

* Cf. V. Branca, 'Il Cantico di Frate Sole', article in *Archivum Franciscanum Historicum* 41, 1948, pp. 37ff.

Praise be, my Lord, through all your creatures
Especially my Lord Brother Sun
Who is the day, and through whom we have light.

Beautiful is he, and shining with great splendour
Of you, O Most High, he bears the likeness.

Praise be, my Lord, through Sister Moon and the Stars
In heaven you have made them, bright, and precious, and
    beautiful.

Praise be, my Lord, through Brother Wind
And through breezy and cloudy, and serene, and every
    weather.

Praise be, my Lord, through Sister Water
Who is so useful, and humble, and precious, and chaste.

Praise be, my Lord, through Brother Fire
Through whom the night is made bright
He is fine and joyful, and powerful and strong.

Praise be, my Lord, through our Sister Mother Earth
Who sustains and brings forth different fruits,
With coloured flowers and herbs.

The poem is complete as it stands, but all the manuscripts continue it with two additional sections of unequal length, traditionally said to have been composed in special circumstances which called for them. The first, of four lines concerned with penance and peace, are much more specifically Christian (and medieval Christian, at that) than the more generally religious opening verses. The *Mirror of Perfection* says that what inspired Francis to add these four lines was an unedifying quarrel between Bishop Guy of Assisi and the *podestà* for the year 1225, one Oportale. The original cause of the quarrel appears to have been forgotten. By the time that Francis decided that it was his duty to intervene and make peace, matters had reached a stage where the bishop had excommunicated the mayor, and the mayor had countered by promoting a law forbidding anyone in

Assisi to sell anything to the bishop or his household. Francis, who had long ago made his own peace with the contentious bishop, and is said to have stayed twice at the episcopal palace during periods of illness, sent a summons to the *podestà* to go to the bishop's house and there listen to the brothers sing the *Canticle* antiphonally under the leadership of Brother Pacifico, the former King of Verses. The mayor obeyed, and he and the bishop were instantly reconciled when the singing concluded with the lines:

> Praise be, my Lord, through those who forgive for love of
>   you
> and endure weakness and tribulation.

> Blessed are those who continue in peace
> for by you, O Most High, they shall be crowned.

The final lines of the poem in all the manuscripts were added later still, when Francis had been told that there was nothing more that medicine could do for him. They are the intensely personal, and hence, universal:

> Praise be, my Lord, through our Sister Bodily Death
> From whom no man living can escape.

> Woe to those who die in mortal sin!
> Blessed those whom she finds doing you most holy will
> For the second death will do them no ill.

> Praise and bless my Lord
> And render thanks, and serve him, with great humility.

Only one composition of Francis's may conceivably be later than these lines, the *Testament* that Gregory IX declared was written *circum ultimae vitae suae,* 'around the end of his life'. It is a long document – unlike the brief *Last Testament* he wrote for Chiara – and cannot possibly have been written by the blind and dying Francis personally, but although it itself claims that 'this is not another Rule' it is so strikingly at variance with the Rule of 1223 that Franciscan scholars have been hard put to it to demon-

strate that it is not a final attempt by the dying founder to make
the Order face up to the fact that it had turned its back on his
original vision. The whole text runs to something just short of
fifteen hundred words. It opens with a brief account of Francis's
conversion:

> This is the way God inspired me, Brother Francis, to begin
> on a penitential life: while I was still in my sins, the sight of
> lepers used to sicken me immeasurably, but then the Lord him-
> self led me among them, and I felt pity for them. . . . (Soon) I
> left the world.

Francis speaks then of the devotion that churches inspired in
him, and the confidence he felt in the office and powers of priests
'living in accordance with the laws of the holy Roman church',
confidence such that 'if they persecuted me' (as some had in the
early days of the Order) 'I should nevertheless be prepared to turn
to them for help'. He saw all priests as superior to himself, because 'in them I see the Son of God'.

Next, he discusses the eucharist, to which he had such devotion: 'I want this most holy sacrament honoured and venerated,
and reserved in richly ornamented places': and the respect due
to the gospels: 'Whenever I see his holy name or writings with
his words in an unsuitable place, I make it my business to pick
them up, and I ask that they should be picked up.'

Following this brief discussion of his own religious views and
habits, he returns to the subject of his Order and its Rule:

> When the Lord gave me some brothers, no one told me what
> I ought to do, but the Most High showed me that I must live
> the gospel life. And I had it written down in a few simple
> words, and the Lord Pope confirmed it. . . . The brothers gave
> everything to the poor, satisfying themselves with a tunic, a
> cord and drawers. . . . Clerics said the office . . . laymen, *Our
> Father*. . . . I used to work with my own hands. . . . And those
> who do not know how to work, should learn. When we are
> not paid for our work . . . we may beg alms. The Lord
> revealed to me . . . the greeting . . . 'God give you peace!'

He had finally compromised on the question of property: the

brothers 'should not accept churches, houses' or other buildings 'unless they are in keeping with the Rule of poverty' and can be temporarily occupied 'as strangers and pilgrims'. But there was not even this degree of compromise on the constant medieval temptation to seek special privileges and protection 'from the Roman curia': 'If the brothers are not welcome anywhere, they should flee to some other country', rather than seek papal, military, and diplomatic protection. Francis then declares that he himself is 'determined to obey' the minister general – a phrase suggesting that it was not always easy: 'I want to be a prisoner in his hands'; and he enjoins strict discipline on the brothers, ruling that the contumacious should be brought before the *custos,* then before the minister, and ultimately before 'the master, protector and corrector of the whole Order', the Lord Bishop Hugolin of Ostia.

Finally the brothers are warned that this is not a new rule, but 'a reminder, admonition, exhortation and testament'. On the other hand, the minister general 'and all other ministers and *custodes*' are forbidden 'to add anything, or subtract', and to ensure that 'these words are also read' whenever the Rule itself is read. Moreover, no one is to make glosses on, or 'interpret' the Rule: 'God inspired me to write both it and these words simply and plainly, so you should understand them simply and plainly, and so live by them, doing good until the End'. The testament then ends with Francis's own blessing upon the brothers.

It is impossible not to be distressed by this document, or at least to be aware of the distress of the man who, lying on his deathbed, felt obliged to dictate it in order to try and remind the friars of who their founder had been and what he had tried to do.

Typically, as soon as Francis was dead and his glory had been recognized by his canonization as a saint, the reformers set to work to have these last wishes annulled. Typically, as they were negotiating with Hugolin, they were successful. In 1230, four years after Francis's death and only two after his canonization, Gregory IX was asked whether the *Testament* and the rigorist elements still remaining in the Rule were binding on consciences. He replied in the negative in the bull *Quo elongati*: 'By that command [the testament] you need not be influenced; what is not held by the consensus of all the brothers, and especially of the ministers, cannot bind; nor could he bind his successor in any way whatsoever.' Francis could write the Rule, but could not bind with it: here again, he is reduced to a holy figurehead, a leader to be honoured, but not obeyed.

There is one early Franciscan text which, although no one claims that it was written by Francis himself, has always seemed more perfectly than any other to capture the spirit of his teaching about poverty. This is *The Holy Espousals of Blessed Francis with Lady Poverty.** Its author is unknown, though one of the thirteen ancient manuscripts known attributes it to John of Parma, who was minister general from 1247 to 1257, and this attribution has been widely accepted. This allegory seeks to tell the story of 'Why blessed Francis, at the beginning of his conversion, threw himself...into the quest for holy poverty'...'her whom my heart loves'. Before Francis's day, the writer alleges, the Lady poverty was an object of general loathing, and when he began to talk about her in terms usually reserved by gallant knights for the ladies of their choice, his fellow townsmen claimed that they did not know whom he was talking about, or even what language he was speaking. But two high-minded old men told him that he would find her 'at the peak of a lofty mountain', 'for God loves her'. She could be reached only by those who had stripped themselves naked of earthly pleasures and of sin, and few if any could reach her alone: 'Woe to the man alone in travelling, for falling he has no one to help him up again.'

Following their advice, Francis collected companions to climb with him to Lady poverty's mountain retreat. At the prospect of the precipitous slopes, their hearts failed them, but he told them: 'Marriage to poverty is a wonderful experience, yet we shall easily enjoy her embraces, for at this moment she is a widow... and all her former friends have become her enemies.'

Much of the rest of the 15,000 word text is taken up with illustration of this axiom that poverty's former lovers now loathe her. Poverty herself says that in the beginning she used to live in God's Paradise 'where man was naked': 'I was in man, and of his essence... and I thought to remain with him for ever.' Thus, poverty was man's original wife 'bone of his bone' as Eve

---

* *Sacrum commercium beati Francisci cum Domina Paupertate*, Quarrachi, 1929; trans. M. Carmichael, *The Lady Poverty*, London, 1901.

was at the beginning. In fact, as the text continues it becomes clear that the Lady poverty and mother Eve are one and the same, poverty is Eve in all but name, and the reader is left to draw the obvious conclusion that for Francis and his companions, the chosen bride can never be a woman: the true Franciscan loves poverty not only spiritually and intellectually, but also imaginatively and sexually.

Only once in the history of the world, the writer tells us, has poverty truly come into her own since 'the poor man' was reduced by sin to 'owning only sin itself, and a few figleaves'. This was during the time of Christ and his Apostles and for a short while afterwards 'while the blood of the crucified poor man was still fresh' in the memories of Christians. Since then avarice has consistently defeated poverty until the coming of the Franciscans 'the Poor in Spirit' lacking earthly goods and abounding in holiness of life. But now even they are in danger because 'some have broken away from their superiors and secretly twisted the Rule', under the impulse of avarice.

When, towards the end of the text, it becomes obvious that Francis and his companions are willing to undergo any trial for love of Lady poverty, she consents to leave the mountain, and go to live with them. They ask her to share their meal and she says: 'After you have shown me your oratory, chapterhouse, cloister, dormitory, refectory, kitchen, stables, upholstered chairs, carved tables, and great houses.' They say they are tired; they will show her enough to content her after they have eaten. She asks if she may wash her hands: they bring her water in an earthenware pot, and offer her the hem of a tunic to dry herself on. Supper consists of a few crusts of stale bread dipped in cold water, and bitter herbs gathered from the woods. The only knives are the companions' teeth, they tell their Queen when she asks for cutlery, and as for wine, 'We have no wine. . . . It is not good for the spouse of Christ to drink wine.' When the meal was over, they thanked God and showed the Lady to the place where she was to sleep 'and she threw herself down naked upon the naked earth . . . and a stone was put under her head for a pillow'. When she awoke, the brothers took her to the top of a little hill to show her their cloister: it was, they said, all the world she could see spread around them. The allegory ends with solemn warnings from the Lady poverty against the spirit of despair that lies in wait for the companions. Constancy is always the mark of true love.

The Sacred Espousals is an attempt, on the whole a successful attempt, to discuss the quest for poverty in the language of a *chanson du geste*. Although the comparison between the friars seeking perfection and the knight seeking to fulfil the tasks laid on him to win his lady is only doubtfully valid, it is in keeping with Francis's own ideas about the way of life offered to him. He saw his quest, as this allegory sees it, in chivalrous terms.

By his title, the *Sacrum Commercium*, the 'sacred marriage', the author goes back beyond chivalry to the sacred marriage which was a feature of so many of the mysteries of classical and post-classical times. Over and over again, this element of universality re-emerges in Francis's life and in the thinking of others about his life. In other people individuality so often masks the elements of universality, but with Francis in a very real sense the essence of his personality is his universality, modified though this is by the demands of institutional and historical Christianity.

14

September 1224–October 1226

The exact date of Francis's stigmatization is not known, though it is traditionally said to have been 14 September, the Feast of the Exultation of the Holy Cross in the medieval Christian calendar, the anniversary of the day on which the Emperor Heraclius restored the True Cross to the Basilica of the Holy Sepulchre in Jerusalem after recovering it from the Persians in A.D. 628, and thus a great feast at the time of the crusades.

Francis is said to have fasted a further fortnight after his vision, until the feast of Saint Michael the Archangel, 29 September. He left Alverna the following day. His sad leave-taking of the mountain, the subject of so many moving hagiographical pages, may or may not be a fact; it is first described in two spurious chronicles, the earlier of them written four hundred years after the event. Both accounts make him foretell that he would never see the mountain again, so suggesting that he already knew that he would not live long enough, or be fit enough, to return there. In fact the tradition that the time of his death was foretold more or less precisely at the time of his stigmatization does go back to the thirteenth century. According to Thomas of Celano's *First Life* it was not Francis himself who fixed upon the date; it was the Minister General Elias, when he and 'the blessed father' were once staying at Foligno. Elias claimed that 'a priest' of 'very advanced age and very venerable' appeared to him in a dream and told him that 'eighteen years had now been completed' since Francis had turned his back on the world, and that he could expect to 'stay in this life only for two more years: then the Lord will call him to himself'. Celano says that Elias related his dream to Francis at that time, and that from then on Francis treated it as 'a revelation from God' and firmly convinced himself that he would die when the term promised expired,* which, granted his suggestibility, may not be unconnected with the fact that he did die two years later.

Leaving Alverna, Francis turned south, towards his main centre of activities, Saint Mary of Jehosophat. By the time he reached there, he was seriously ill with what appears to have been dysentery, but he refused medical attention, and insisted on making a preaching tour through Umbria, no longer walking as in the old days, but riding on a donkey,† so that he should be strong enough to be able to preach in three or four villages every day. In addition to his other troubles, his eyes began to pain him and it soon became only too apparent that unless something was done he would go blind. The argument between Francis and his chosen 'mother' Elias (as the texts call him) as to whether or not physicians should be called in was finally won by Elias, who seems to have put out a general call for help from anyone who thought he might have a remedy sovereign against Francis's disabilities. 'Many came', Celano says, 'intending to help Francis with their medicines, but no remedy was found'. It must have been a horrible winter for all those who held Francis in high regard, especially perhaps his 'mother' Elias, whose personal devotion to him can no more be doubted than can his professional opposition to the primitive Franciscan Rule. His ambivalence may appear paradoxical, but it was typically human.

At some stage in their travels, Elias heard that there was a noted physician staying at Rieti, and determined to take Francis to him. This man was probably a member of the papal retinue, for Honorius III and his *curia* were at Rieti from 23 June 1225 to 31 January 1226, having been driven out of Rome by riots stirred up by a certain senator Parenzi and kept alive by faction fighting between the followers of Innocent III's brother, Richard Count of Sura, and the adherents of Honorius's nephews. Honorius had lived too long to please the Romans, and Hugolin – now generally recognized as bound to be the next pope – found himself with the unenviable task of making the peace.

* I Celano 2, 108–9.
† I Celano 2, 98.

Despite this crisis, however, 'the Lord Pope' and 'the whole *curia*' found time to receive Francis 'with kindness and reverence'. Francis, it appears, was still resisting attempts to make him take his cure seriously, for Hugolin 'found it necessary to admonish the Holy Father to take care of himself'. Neglect of the needs of the body, he pointed out, was not praiseworthy, but smacked of sinfulness. Francis took this rebuke 'humbly', and 'henceforth was more cautious, and less fearful with regard to what was necessary for his cure'.

His fear of the treatment prescribed for him is easily understandable. It included cauterizing his head 'in several places' with red-hot irons, bleeding, and the application of ointment to his eyes. Not surprisingly, under this regime 'he grew no better, but seemed only to get worse continually'.*

The most painful of these treatments were carried out not at Rieti itself, but up in the hills, at Francis's favourite retreat at Fonte Colombo. He was accompanied, and no doubt comforted, by four brothers left nameless by Celano 'to spare their modesty', though named by later sources as Angelo Tancredi, Brother Rufino, Brother Leo, and Brother John of Lodi.

When it became obvious that the treatment was not succeeding, and probably when the physician who had prescribed it moved back to Rome in Honorius's wake, it was decided to move Francis more than a hundred miles north to Siena, where better doctors were said to be performing more skilful cures. By this time, the news that the founder of the Franciscan Order appeared to be dying had spread throughout central Italy. Already at Rieti there had been scenes so enthusiastic as to appear ugly. Tales are told of Francis's hair and nail clippings being fought over, and his clothes stolen, as holy relics. The water he once washed his hands in was used by a farmer to cure his sick sheep. When the Emperor Vespasian was dying, he made a macabre joke of it, saying, 'I think I am becoming a god': Francis was turning into a saint. It was not an easy process to endure. The story is told that he once asked to hear some music because 'it would help Brother Body such a lot to have his mind taken off his sufferings', but was told firmly that it would not be fitting: people would be scandalized. He had to die with dignity, as became a saint. It is

* I Celano 2, 100–2.

probable that the move from Rieti to Fonte Colombo was made for the sake of peace and quiet. At Siena, things were even worse than they had been at Rieti. The demands of curiosity and piety combined to make life all but intolerable; the sources naturally record only the more spiritually enlightening of the fun and games that went on, but these were unpleasant enough to suggest that a lot went unrecorded, and is probably best forgotten.

The story of the stigmata was obviously spreading, and awakening a good deal of interest. A brother from Brescia was so anxious to see the wounds for himself that he importuned Brother Pacifico to arrange it for him. There is something very distasteful about the story as it is related in Celano's *Second Life*. The plan Pacifico proposed was that as he left Francis's room, he would ask to be allowed to kiss his hands. 'And when he offers them to me, I'll give you a wink, and you come and look.' Because Francis was all but blind, the trick worked up to a point. The Brescian brother saw the wounds in both Francis's hands, but then Francis realized that something was going on, and called Pacifico back from the door: 'Brother, one time and another, you really do cause me a lot of pain.' Pacifico was too pusillanimous to apologize. He prevaricated with, 'How have I hurt you, dearest Mother?' Francis did not reply.

The tale is sickening, especially with its disclosure that Pacifico used the most secret and intimate name used by the brothers for their founder to turn the edge of his expected anger. However, those becoming saints in the Middle Ages had to expect this sort of thing, as public figures have to expect television coverage of their every activity today.

While the doctors at Siena were piercing Francis's ears to improve his sight – the superstition that short-sightedness can be cured by piercing one ear, and a squint by piercing both is probably not even yet quite dead – the people of Assisi were beginning to worry in case death should rob them of their new saint. As the *Legenda Antiqua* (c. 24) points out, they had just lost the body of their former patron, a certain Saint Crispaldo, who had been allegedly a disciple of Saint Peter's, and had guarded Assisi through the centuries since, until stolen by raiders from Bettona. Neither prestige nor devotion (nor yet profit) would allow them to face with equanimity the prospect of losing their home-bred Francis to the alien Siennese. Messages were sent from Portiuncula to Brother Elias, who was travelling somewhere – no one seems quite sure where – warning him of what seemed about to happen, and he hurried to Siena, to drag Francis back home to die.

He arrived almost too late. The pain of the treatment, and the unending hubbub, had reduced Francis's reserves of strength to a dangerously low level. At the end of April, or early in May, 1226, he suffered a massive haemorrhage from the stomach, and the doctors announced that the 'infection' had spread to his liver. However, as so often seems to happen, he rallied temporarily after this set-back, and was soon well enough to travel with Elias to Le Celle, a hermitage belonging to the friars lying some two miles outside Cortona, and so almost exactly midway between Siena and Assisi. But moving him nearly proved fatal. His feet and legs began to swell, and the limbs that had been so desiccated were soon obscenely puffed out by dropsy. In this extremity, Francis begged that the party should press on to Assisi, and no doubt urged to it by frantic messages from Portiuncula, Elias reluctantly agreed. Travelling slowly, they reached Blessed Mary of Jehosophat – the place, as Francis said, frequently visited by celestial spirits – early in June.

Now that everyone was satisfied – the native son was going to become a saint within reach of home – there was time to be concerned for his comfort. The fierce heat of summer troubled him, and the oedema climbed up into his abdomen. He was moved yet again, this time to the hermitage of Bagnara, just outside Nocera, fourteen miles east of Assisi; and a good deal higher in the mountains.* How long he was allowed to rest there is not known. It was probably only long enough for the townspeople of Assisi to realize that his condition was not improving, and that he might well die where he lay. They sent an escort, almost a prisoner's escort, but a royal prisoner's, with swordsmen and cavalry, to bring him back. War was brewing between the Lombard cities, the pope, and the Germans, and the Assisians were determined not to be cut off from their saint: 'The people of Assisi', Celano's *Second Life* records, 'sent messengers to that place, demanding to have him back, lest they should lose to other

---

* *Legenda Antiqua* 59; II Celano 77.

people the glory that would be theirs in having the body of the Man of God' (c. 77).

Now quite blind, and in agony from the pressure on all his organs, Francis was loaded on to a horse to be dragged back over the country roads to Assisi. It is not surprising that soon 'as his disease increased, the strength of his body failed, and stripped of all his powers, he was not able to move himself at all'.* Suddenly, the oedema was reversed, and he became dehydrated to such an extent that his body seemed to be reduced to a skeleton, wrapped in tight-fitting, darkening skin. No wonder that when a brother, no doubt long cognizant of his longing for martyrdom, asked him which was worse, what he was now enduring 'or a hard martyrdom at the hands of an executioner', he replied that 'three days of this is harder to bear than any martyrdom could be'. The journey to Portiuncula was made more difficult than it need have been by the suspicion and fear of the people of the country-side in the critical political situation confronting them. They refused to have any dealings at all with the knights of Francis's escort, not wanting to sell food that they might not be able to replace should war break out, and the soldiers being unable to buy supplies, the friars in the party had to beg them. In these circumstances, the fourteen-mile journey probably took two or even more days to complete.

Francis himself asked that once again his destination should be the Portiuncula, and his request was granted. He obviously expected to die there almost immediately upon arrival, but he did not die, and once again the Assisians grew afraid of losing him. It was true that the Portiuncula was only two miles from Assisi, but if an army was suddenly to camp in that two miles, their saint-to-be might just as well have stayed in Siena. 'The whole city rejoiced', Thomas of Celano says, 'at the coming of the Holy Father ... for the whole multitude of the people hoped that the Holy One would soon die there.'

To ensure that he was within Assisi's grasp when he did finally die, Elias had him moved yet again, carrying him inside the walls, safe from both enemy soldiers and relic-hunters from other cities. He was lodged at the palace of his old antagonist, Bishop Guy, who happened to be away from the city, making a

* I Celano 2, 107.

pilgrimage to the shrine of Saint Michael in Monte Gargano. According to the *Mirror of Perfection*, a guard was set around the palace, to make sure that he was not spirited away (c. 109).

It was a cruel, but in medieval eyes absolutely necessary, precaution. Even Francis himself 'though he believed that the grace of God could be given to the chosen at any place' nevertheless felt that the site of the Church of Saint Mary at Portiuncula was endowed with 'extra fruitful graces'*; lesser men carried this belief one stage further, and saw actual physical possession of a saint's corpse as in some mysterious way guaranteeing his favourable attention. The danger that Francis might be snatched away while still living so that some other city than Assisi might call on him as its patron when dead was very real indeed. Moreover, the financial aspect of holdings in relics was not to be overlooked; pilgrims spent money in shops, markets and inns, as well as in churches.

All this concern for Francis's whereabouts did not lead to total neglect of his physical welfare. The townspeople hoped that he would die 'soon', but the brothers, including Elias, were genuinely fond of him as a person, and were not without human feelings. It was just that the needs of religious and political economy had to be put before the individual's agony of body and mind. At the palace, everything was done to make Francis's last days as comfortable as possible. Among those called to his bedside while he rested under the bishop's roof was the physician who was to confirm the death sentence under which he already knew that he lay, a certain Buongiovanni of Arezzo, whom Francis called Bembegnati, well-blessed, or well-beloved. The time was probably late in August, for directly challenged by Francis not to prevaricate, Buongiovanni told him: 'Medically speaking, your disease is mortal, and in my opinion you will die either at the end of September or the beginning of October.' Perhaps not surprisingly, Francis's reply, according to the *Legenda Antiqua*, was: 'Welcome, Sister Death!' It was now that he added to the *Canticle of Brother Sun* the strophes beginning, 'Praise be, my Lord, through our Sister Bodily Death', and from that day onwards the whole *Canticle* was sung several times

---

* I Celano 2, 106.

daily, and sometimes also during the night 'to comfort him . . . and please and edify the guard'.*

Naturally, there were those who found such levity shocking in one who was in the process of becoming a saint. Among them was Minister General Elias. 'For my own part, I am delighted to see you so happy', he said, 'but here in this city where people are thinking of you as a saint, I am afraid it may well scandalize them to see you preparing for death in this fashion'. However, at this stage, Francis would not be deprived of his music, whatever anyone thought.

By this time, his skin had become very dark and hard, as the skin does in extreme dehydration, and his body seemed a mere shell packed with pain. Within a few days he began to fret for the Portiuncula; he was determined to die there, whatever the danger to Assisian plans. He argued his case with all his strength, but before he could bring Elias to agree, his condition worsened to such a degree that it was believed that he must die where he lay. All who could crowded into his room, pressing close to the bed, and he blessed those he could reach, beginning with Minister General Elias, who happened to be on his left, so that, as Celano is careful to record, he had to cross his arm over his body in order to bless him by laying his right hand on his head: 'I bless you, my son, above all, and in all.'† Later sources, including Celano's *Second Life*, speak of another special blessing to Brother Bernard before the general blessing on all the brothers.

It would seem that not only the brothers in attendance, but also Francis himself, believed that he was on the point of death. However, he rallied that day, at least sufficiently for Minister General Elias to realize that to lie dying in the palace was too distressing for him; he wanted, as he said, 'to restore his soul to God from the place where he first came to perfect knowledge of the way of truth'.

After what was undoubtedly an acrimonious conference with the city fathers, Elias won his point. They gave their permission for Francis to be moved back to the Portiuncula, as long as the litter was accompanied by an armed escort, which would mount

* *Legenda Antiqua* 65.
† I Celano 2, 108.

guard on the chapel of Saint Mary and its hermitages until the time came to accompany the Holy Relics back to Assisi.

The sources later than Celano's *First Life* maintain that on the way from Assisi to the Portiuncula, Francis had himself set on the ground near the lazar-house of San Salvatore, where some of his earliest work had been done. Lying there, he solemnly blessed the city. Like many of the stories describing aspects of Francis's protracted agony, this story is too neat to be acceptable, especially as all the chroniclers disagree as to the form the blessing took. The difficulty in evaluating the historical worth of the various accounts of Francis's death is that his biographers were so intent on showing that he died a perfect death, parallelling as nearly as possible the passion and death of Christ, and offering a good example to all, that their accounts become incredible. Christ prayed over Jerusalem before he died: Francis had to pray over Assisi. Christ instituted the eucharist before he was crucified: Francis had to offer his brothers bread. The accounts become too circumstantial, and rejecting part of what they tell us as fiction, we are left not knowing whether we can accept anything at all except the bare statement that Francis died on the evening of Saturday 3 October 1226. This date is given in the best of all the available authorities, the encyclical letter that Elias sent to all the ministers of the Franciscans, written immediately after the funeral. Even here there is some room for confusion, because Elias, following the tradition of medieval Umbria, where the day was held to begin not at dawn but at sunset, called the time of his death not the evening of Saturday 3 October, but 'the first hour of the night before' Sunday 4 October.

In considering the historical value of all the other texts relating to Francis's death, it is worth recalling that Elias in that letter states categorically that before Francis died 'not one part of his body was free from excessive suffering, and because of the tightening of his sinews all his limbs were stiff, exactly like those of a dead man', a condition which passed off immediately after death. If only for this reason, it would seem that the simple narrative offered by Celano's *First Life* is to be preferred to later more complicated, more edifying, but less readily credible stories.

Celano says that at Portiuncula 'after resting a few days', Francis realized that although he was perhaps a little stronger, he was nevertheless likely to die at any time, so he asked the brothers to sing 'the Song of Praise to the Lord concerned with his approaching death' while he himself 'recited as best he could' Psalm 141, with the verse 'I cry unto the Lord with a loud voice'. Asked to give a final blessing to the Order, he said: 'I am being called to God. I forgive all my friars all their faults. Bless them all for me.' Then at his own request he was covered with sackcloth and sprinkled with ashes, and the story of Christ's passion and death was read from the Gospel of Saint John. Probably before the reading ended, he died.

Those days at Portiuncula before Francis died were no more restful and quiet than the weeks at Rieti and Siena had been. As well as the natural confusion and restlessness among the brothers, and the extra noise generated by the presence of an armed guard around the place, no one thought it necessary to discourage visitors. In his brief *Treatise on the Miracles of Saint Francis*, Celano tells the story of one of them, Jacoba of Settisole, a noble Roman woman, the widow of Graziani Frangipani. She, it seems, was a 'brother' of the Order, though not one of Chiara's Poor Ladies.* She had somehow 'earned the privilege of special love' from Francis, and when he realized that he could not live much longer, he sent for her. She immediately set out for the Portiuncula (so suddenly, in fact, that Celano maintains that she had received a special revelation of Francis's need for her, and had actually set out before the messenger from the friars reached her home). She took with her all that was necessary for Francis's burial: a cloth the colour of ashes to cover his body, candles, a cloth to cover his face, and 'a small pillow for his head'. She also took his favourite candy – as he had asked that she should. She arrived while he was still alive, and her coming 'with her children and her servants' revived Francis, and he told her that he

---

* Was Jacoba of Settisole one of the first members of the so-called third Order (the brothers being the first, and the Poor Ladies the second)? Members of the third Order are lay people, prevented by some circumstance in their lives from entering the first or second Orders, but following a simplified form of the Rule 'in the world'. According to Brother Mariano of Florence, writing about 1537, it was Francis himself who enrolled the first recruits to a deliberately-constructed third Order, on 20 May 1221, after discussing the practicality of the scheme with Hugolin, following his return from Syria. But there is no mention of a third Order, regularly constituted, in the Rule of 1221, and it is probable that it was of later formation.

would live until the end of the week. It is a pity that we know no more of Francis's relationship with the lady Jacoba 'who was not bound by the decree against women' entering the friars' hermitages at the Portiuncula, a rule apparently otherwise rigorously enforced.

After Francis's death, Elias told her: 'He whom you loved living, you shall hold in your arms dead.' She accepted the offer, and 'wept hot tears, sighing deeply ... holding ... and kissing him' and 'loosening the shroud, so that she might see him'.

Celano, or whoever wrote the *Treatise,* represents the lady Jacoba as a witness to the reality of the stigmata, and as the person on whose advice the fact of Francis's stigmatization was no longer hidden: 'Her advice was that the ineffable miracle ... ought to be unveiled before everyone's eyes. So they all ran eagerly to see the miracle.' Francis was no longer in any way a private person: he had entered the public domain as a saint. As the news spread, people ran to the Portiuncula to see whatever there was to see. There were cries of rejoicing, the bells rang, tears of joy and sorrow ran down in streams,* while 'one of his brothers, a person of no little fame ... saw the soul of the most holy father go straight up to heaven over many waters'.

The scene is medieval, Christian and Italian. It is also classical, pagan, and Roman. Once again, there is an echo of the Emperor Vespasian's 'I feel that I am becoming a god'. Not for nothing is the traditional word used by the Roman church to classify a saint 'divus', 'the divine one', precisely that used of the emperors who were deified on their deaths.

Is the story of the lady Jacoba true? She herself was no invention of the author of the *Treatise.* She lived on at Assisi until 1239, when she was buried in the lower Basilica of Saint Francis. But it is difficult to escape the feeling that the story of her role at Francis's deathbed hovers between fact and fiction. There had to be a lady at Francis's dying, to take his corpse into her arms, so that the parallel with the death of Christ might be more exact. There is nothing more moving in Christian art than the *pietà.*

The lady Jacoba does not appear in the *First Life,* but Celano did quite well without her in drawing the parallel between Francis and Christ:

* *Treatise on the Miracles,* 38–9.

The whole city of Assisi . . . rushed to see the wonders of God . . . everyone sang a hymn of joy. . . . And blessed the Saviour's omnipotence that their desire [to have a saint of their own] was fulfilled. But Francis's sons were filled with sorrow . . . until . . . their mourning was turned to song [at the sight of the stigmata].

For there really was in him the appearance of the cross and passion of the Lamb unspotted, who washed away the sins of the world: for he looked like one recently taken down from the Cross, with his hands and feet pierced by nails, and his right side as though pierced by a lance. And finally they saw his flesh, which before had been blackened, shining with unmatched brightness, and by its beauty promising the rewards of the blessed resurrection.

The *Second Life* and other sources maintain that before Francis became totally moribund, he had himself stretched naked on the floor 'so that he might wrestle naked with a naked enemy', the devil attacking him on the point of death.* It is even said that he covered the wound in his side with his hand so that no one should see it, as well as calling for bread, blessing and breaking it as Christ did in instituting the Eucharist,† before having the story of the death of Christ read to him. All these things were done, it is said, several days before he died, in a kind of macabre rehearsal of death, so that the brothers should know what was expected of them when the time came. These and other even more unlikely tales abundant in the narratives must be dismissed as pious fiction interesting only in so far that they show the lengths to which determined Franciscan chroniclers were willing to go to prove Francis's Christ-likeness, a concern which is to be found in Francis's earlier actions, but with which he can hardly be credited at the time of his death, when he was allegedly all but unable to move or even to speak.

Whether or not the lady Jacoba stripped Francis of his shroud so that everyone might see the stigmata, the brothers and the townspeople were all convinced that they had their saint at last. The *Second Life* records that Francis had asked that after he was

* II Celano 214.
† II Celano 217.

dead his body should be left lying untouched 'for as long as it would take an unhurried man to walk a mile'. If that simple request was granted, it was all the decency that was shown to the corpse. From the time the crowd from Assisi arrived onwards, the turmoil was unceasing.

Even Bishop Guy of Assisi, still away on his pilgrimage in the south, later claimed not to have been unaffected by Francis's death. He had, the story runs, spent Saturday 3 October at the shrine of the archangel, and was returning to Benevento 'where he was staying' when Francis appeared to him and told him, 'I am leaving the world'. He said nothing of his vision to anyone that night, but the next morning he sent for a lawyer and swore an affidavit, in which the time and content of the vision were noted. Unfortunately, this document has not survived.

Simultaneously, we are told, two other men also saw Francis. One was Brother Augustine, Minister of the Order in the Terra di Lavoro on the west coast of Central Italy. He was himself on the point of death when Francis died, and telling the brothers attending him, 'Can't you see father Francis going to heaven?' he cried out, 'Wait for me, father!' and died forthwith.* The other was an unnamed brother who, in his meditation, saw Francis standing in a crowd, some of whom asked him, 'Isn't that Christ, brother?' and when he said, 'Yes', asked him, 'Isn't it Francis?' And he said 'Yes' again. The two were indistinguishable. How far, one wonders, has the western Christian view of Christ since 1226 been coloured by Francis's presentation of him?

The natural place to have buried Francis would have been at the Portiuncula, but the idea was apparently never even considered. He belonged to the people of Assisi. The funeral procession formed up on the Sunday morning as soon as it was light. Tree branches and torches were carried, and a band played, as though to celebrate a victory. The body was taken first to Saint Damian's, where it was shown through the grille to Chiara and the other Poor Ladies, who were permitted to kiss its hands.† The procession was then reformed, and made its way into the city, to the church of Saint George, where Francis had first preached, and was buried there that same day.

---

* II Celano 218.
† I Celano 117. Gone were the days of Chiara's freedom!

15

Saint Francis

With Francis safely buried in Assisi, the city felt proud and secure. The cult of Francis the Saint began to be observed immediately, indeed, it had begun before his death, in a very unofficial way, with such excesses as the medication of a flock of sheep with the water in which he had washed his hands.

Nowadays in the Roman church the cult of the recently dead is officially discouraged, but there is no evidence that in the thirteenth century anyone spoke out against the worship of the father of the Franciscans. Assisi's senate and shopkeepers needed a home-grown saint as much as did its clergy and its common people. The shrine was good for trade and morale. A city needed a pleader at the court of heaven as much as it needed an advocate at the bar of the pope or the emperor.

Moreover, at that moment the pope himself needed fresh support in central Italy, and had rarely in his long life felt that he needed it more urgently. And what more practical help could there be than a new central Italian saint – a man the pope had known personally – to unite the people, symbolize the victory of religion, and draw divine attention to the needs of the church on earth?

Innocent's former ward, and Honorius III's former pupil, Frederick II of Sicily, declared adult in 1210 at the age of fourteen, had proved his manhood in the succeeding sixteen years by not only uniting the Sicilian kingdom under himself, but also securing his election as emperor of Germany and imposing his authority on all the German princes. In 1215, the year of the Fourth Lateran Council, he had promised to undertake the crusade that Innocent longed to see, and in recognition of his promise had been crowned as King of the Romans. In 1220, still promising to join King John of Jerusalem on crusade when the time was right, he had received the imperial crown from Honorius at Rome. But he had no intention of actually fighting in the East at any time if he could avoid it, and certainly not before he had united his western possessions by winning control of all Italy, which meant crushing the Lombard cities, capturing papal Tuscany and driving the rectors from the duchy of Spoleto and the March of Ancona. The Lombard cities he believed that he could deal with piecemeal. The papacy was a more knotty problem. He did not want to destroy it – even if he could have done – but was prepared to work unceasingly to undermine its political power. The pope, meanwhile, fought on to make him keep his promises to go on the crusade. On 25 July 1225 he took an oath before two papal legates at San Germano, promising to set out for the East within two years, and backing his oath with a large deposit of gold, to be forfeit to the papal treasury if he should be foresworn. But he spent the time when he should have been arming soldiers and finding ships intriguing to pierce the papal block between Apulia and Calabria in the south and his German-based armies in the north. He may or may not have had a hand in the troubles at Rome in 1225 which drove Honorius temporarily out of the city; certainly, by 1226 he and the Lombards stood on the brink of war. The Lombard League was revived against him. From Foggia, on 26 September, he stirred old memories by naming Rainald, the son of Conrad of Urslingen, as Rector of Tuscany and Duke of Spoleto, so that when the dying Francis was being carried from Bagnara to Assisi, the fear of war was genuine. A few weeks later, the heat went temporarily out of the conflict. Honorius offered to mediate between the emperor and the Lombards and, surprisingly, Frederick accepted. The Lombards, however, would not agree to the proposed terms. During the winter of 1226–27 disaster struck at Rome. The city had always been vulnerable to food shortages, and in February 1227 famine held her tightly in its grip. It was only from Sicily that Honorius could obtain food quickly enough to save his people, and he found himself forced to appeal to Frederick for help, so losing face though saving lives. A month later, in March, he died; a very old and tired man.

He was succeeded – at last, many felt – by Innocent III's cousin Hugolin, who took the regnal name of Gregory IX. Hugolin, well known in the Lombard lands through his many years as a legate there, succeeded where Honorius had failed in persuading their representatives to sign the peace with Frederick, so that the emperor would leave Italy for the crusade. But the two-year term of Frederick's oath passed with no sign of the emperor's departure. The new pope brought pressure on him. So too, many thought, did God. During the late summer, an epidemic of malaria severely weakened his army in Apulia, and at last, ten years after the first crusaders had set out for Acre, he embarked on 8 September, only to put back into Otranto within hours because a close friend had developed symptoms of the fever.

Once on land again, Frederick himself fell diplomatically sick. Gregory IX refused to believe the reports of his disability, and from his family home at Anagni formally excommunicated the emperor, repeating the excommunication from Rome in November, and declaring forfeit the massive surety in gold that Frederick had deposited as a guarantee of good faith in July 1225.

The tensions in Italy throughout this period, and especially from September 1227 onwards, are easily understandable.* An explosion somewhere was inevitable. It occurred at Rome in March 1228. On the Holy Thursday 29 March, Gregory excommunicated Frederick for the third time, putting every place sheltering him under an interdict, and thus in effect calling for the election of a counter-claimant to the imperial throne. Frederick countered by provoking the anti-papal party at Rome to riot against the pope. The first trouble occurred on Easter Monday,† when Gregory was saying mass. It took the form of a riot inside Saint John Lateran itself. The pope held out in Rome for almost a month. Describing this time, Thomas of Celano is scathing on the subject of the Romans: 'The Romans, a rebellious and savage

---

* The naming of Rainald as Rector of Tuscany and Duke of Spoleto seemed to many a declaration of war; cf. Boehmer *Regesta imperii, 5*; in 1242 a chronicler remembered 'what a great stir' it provoked.

† *Ann. Zurifaltenses*, x, 59. 'At the emperor's command, the Romans attacked Pope Gregory, a severe setback for the pope'; cf. also Conrad of Ursberg, *Chronicle*, 115.

race, rose up against their neighbours, as their habit was, and overboldly stretched forth their hands against the holy place. . . . Pope Gregory . . . at first protected Christ's church, but then, on weighing the situation, felt compelled to abandon the city'.* That was in April 1228. Five days after leaving the city, heading north towards papal Tuscany, he arrived at Rieti, where he and his *curia* stayed for nearly three weeks before taking the road north again, to Spoleto 'where all honoured him with great reverence'. Just outside the city walls, he visited the Poor Ladies of Saint Paul, a daughter house of Saint Damian's at Assisi.

Obviously, the plan to canonize Francis, the Lombard saint of the loyal poor, was already well advanced, and had become a major part of papal strategy. The pope was fleeing. But he had to flee with dignity, and for a purpose. However, it is not surprising that in his difficult and tiring circumstances 'he was moved by the glorious way of life of the Poor Ladies' and felt 'kindled within him' a longing for 'a life of retirement'.

From Spoleto 'he hurried to Assisi, where a treasure of glory' – Francis's corpse – 'awaited him'. He arrived there on 26 May, and stayed for seventeen days. 'The Poor Brothers went out to meet him, and when Christ's vicar arrived, he went first to the grave of blessed Francis, and saluted it with reverence and eagerness. While he stayed there, a formal discussion was held concerning the saint's canonization, and several special meetings of their lordships the cardinals were held on the subject. From all around came people who had been freed from their afflictions by God's holy man. A vast number of miracles shone forth. They were proved, verified, pondered upon – and accepted.'

But now the political crisis worsened. The former King John of Jerusalem, who had surrendered that title to the Emperor Frederick on his daughter's marriage to the emperor, joined the pope. His daughter, Yolande, had died on 25 April, leaving a six-day old son, Conrad, as heir to the Kingdom of Sicily, and ultimately Jerusalem; and, if Frederick could arrange it, to the elective Holy Roman Empire. Still no one knew whether Frederick would finally decide to move north, through Italy, pursuing the fleeing pope, or east from Brindisi, to claim his kingdom of Acre at last. Exasperated, the pope had sent him a

* I Celano 3, 122.

message to say that being excommunicated, if he sailed for the East he would go not as a crusader but as an outlaw, bent on aggression. Frederick's reply was to march his army northwards, and name Duke Rainald of Spoleto as his legate in the papal March of Ancona. Rainald invaded Ancona, and his agents became active among the people of Spoleto and the patrimony of Peter itself. Gregory excommunicated him, but prudently removed the *curia* beyond the Tiber, into the protection of traditionally-papal Perugia, and named John of Brienne as joint commander with Cardinal John Colonna of a papal army charged with the destruction of Rainald's forces.

All Italy waited to see what Frederick would do. In fact, he had already decided that the time was not right for him to mount a full-scale war against the pope. Legally, as a consequence of the oaths he had taken, it could be argued that he was no longer king in Jerusalem but only regent for his son, if the barons should choose so to name him; he believed, however, that he might claim rights both there and in Cyprus, if he could reach the East before it was realized that Yolande, the queen through whom he made his claims, was dead. So on 28 June, he sailed from Brindisi, leaving Rainald to contain the pope in Italy.*

Meanwhile, at Perugia, in the midst of all the diplomatic activity of these weeks, or rather, as a significant part of that diplomatic activity, Gregory collected proofs of Francis's sanctity in preparation for his canonization: 'A further meeting was convened at Perugia: a sacred assembly of cardinals was held about the matter in the Lord Pope's rooms.' At this meeting, the pope told the cardinals that 'there is no need of miracles to attest to this most holy man's most holy life'.† Yet the certificates attesting the miracles were read – including, one suspects, evidence sent from France, where Francis's pillow had been doing the work of the pope's ambassador at the court of the fourteen-year-old King Louis IX.‡ According to a note in one copy of the abridged *First Life* 'arranged to be read in choir', the first two books of the *First Life*, telling the story up to Francis's death, were among the documents made available to the cardinals; the note reads: 'At

* *Historia diplomatica Friderici Secundi*, vol. 3; and *Estoire de Eracles*, II.

† I Celano 3, 124.

‡ I Celano 3, 120.

Perugia, the happy Lord Pope Gregory, in the second year of his pontificate, on the fifth day of the kalends of March (February 25) accepted, and confirmed this *legenda*, decreeing that it should be held fast. Thanks be to almighty God and our Saviour for all his gifts now and through all ages. Amen.'*

At the Perugian consistory, it was decided to proceed immediately to the ceremonies of canonization themselves, without further formalities. The news provoked an outburst of joy and loyalty to Francis's friend, the pope, throughout Tuscany and Umbria, as it had been calculated to do. The date was set for 16 July 1228, and no effort was spared in the brief time available to put on the grandest possible show. The move from Perugia to Assisi on that Sunday morning was to be the first stage in the pope's journey back to Rome. Cardinals, bishops, and abbots, together with ex-King John (now named Rector in Tuscany) and 'a noble concourse of counts and bishops' all accompanied 'the Lord of the World' to Assisi. The procession was intended to be a great display of papal glory, though ostensibly mounted in honour of God and the Little Poor Man. Gregory 'the Spouse of Christ's Church', 'the Lord', 'the Anointed of the Lord', wore the papal crown and vestments of cloth-of-gold adorned with jewels. 'The cardinals and the bishops surrounded him, decked out in splendiferous necklaces, and wearing white robes, and all the people stood there, full of expectation'.

'The day was bright', Celano says;† 'there were green olive branches, and branches fresh-cut from other trees. All the people were dressed in bright shining clothes.' Gregory was determined that the ceremonies should be spectacular, and succeeded in making them so, with the full consent and co-operation of the whole countryside.

The ceremony of canonization itself took place, as was customary, within the framework of a pontifical high mass. Gregory himself preached the sermon on the text from the book of Ecclesiasticus; 'He shone in his days as the morning star in the midst of a cloud, and as the moon when it is full. And as the

---

* National Library, Paris, MS. 3817; but note that the Pope was at Rome in February.

† I Celano 3, 126. Celano appears to have been an eyewitness of the ceremonies.

sun when it shineth, so shone he in the temple of God.' He was so carried away by his eulogy that he broke down in tears.

When the sermon was at last finished, 'one of the Lord Pope's subdeacons, Octavian by name' – Octavian Ubaldini de Mugello, who was made a Cardinal by the first Franciscan pope, Innocent IV, in 1244 – read the depositions concerning the miracles which had been accepted by the cardinals as authetic, and a commentary on them was given by Cardinal-Deacon Raynerius Capocci of Viterbo, a Cistercian monk who had been associated with the Franciscans since at least the general chapter of 1221, over which he had presided, and later, with Gregory, was to write part of the office for the Feast of Saint Francis. While this recital was proceeding, 'the Shepherd of the Church... breathed deep sighs... and shed a torrent of tears, while all the other prelates ... poured forth a flood... and all the people began to weep... and grew tired from being on edge with expectancy'. Nerves were overwrought that day, but as an exercise in propaganda and public relations, Francis's canonization was an unqualified success.

Now the moment had come for the actual proclamation of Francis's sanctity, and the pope himself declaimed the essential lines from the bull of Canonization:

To the praise and glory of almighty God, the Father, and of the Son, and of the Holy Spirit, and of the glorious Virgin Mary, and to the honour of the glorious Roman Church: the most glorious father Francis, whom God has glorified in heaven, we venerate on earth, and by the counsel of our brothers here present and other prelates, we decree that he shall be numbered in the catalogue of the saints, and that his feast shall be observed upon the day of his death.

The *Te Deum* was sung. The people shouted, cheered and wept. Newly composed hymns were sung to new tunes played on organs, the singing being led by specially trained choirs. When the noise abated a little, 'the Lord Pope Gregory came down from his high throne' and 'went to kiss the grave', which, it seems, had not been opened, and the mass moved on to its solemn conclusion.

For two more years after the crowds had dispersed that day,

the body of Saint Francis rested in Saint George's, while miracles multiplied around it. Meanwhile Frederick II won Jerusalem and Bethlehem, with a corridor to the sea at Lydda for the Kingdom of Jerusalem by a treaty that all Christendom (except the Teutonic Knights) denounced, and returned to Italy leaving civil war behind him in the East, to face the threat of a papal army that had struck south under John of Brienne early in 1229, and make his peace with the pope at San Germano on 23 July 1230 in a treaty that restored to the pope recognition of his authority over the church in the two Sicilies, but left Frederick in actual control.

Concurrently, Brother Elias, after 1227 freed from the burden of ruling the Order, as he had been free since 1226 of the restraint of Francis's presence and personality, allowed his imagination to soar in a grandiose building programme, the first-fruits of which were the great twin basilicas of Saint Francis *inferiore* and *superiore* at the southern edge of Assisi's plateau. The work had actually begun before the canonization, and by the day after it the foundations had been marked out clearly enough for the pope to lay the foundation stone. In the bull announcing the foundation, registered as *Recolentes qualiter*, the legal fiction by which the holy see owned the property while the Franciscans used it, appeared for the first time.

Father Leo spoke out strongly against the ostentation of building a permanent church for Francis, whom he was sure would have held the idea in abomination, but was overruled, as he and his party were to be many times in the years that followed. The work of construction went ahead so fast that the lower church was ready to receive Francis's remains by spring 1230.

With so many miracles already attributed to Francis, there was reckoned to be a very real danger that Assisi would lose him the moment that he was disinterred. But Brother Elias, in whose hands, it seems, the work of planning the translation was left, had everything worked out to the last detail.

The pope himself, busy with the Emperor Frederick and the affairs of the south, did not attend these latest ceremonies, but three papal legates were present to ensure that proper reverence was shown, and that there was no deceit. Almost all the Franciscan Order is said to have attended, together with many bishops, and enough soldiers to line the whole route and guard the outer walls of the city. The carriage was drawn by oxen. Everybody wept, cheered, and prayed.

Elias received the body at the doors of the lower church and had those doors locked even in the faces of the pope's legates as soon as the body was inside, so that only a handful of Franciscans sworn to secrecy should know where Francis finally rested: in an oak coffin, bound with iron, set in the thickness of a pillar in the vaults of the church.

The secret of the burial place was so well kept that when in the early nineteenth century it was finally decided that all danger of Francis's body being stolen was passed, no one knew where to find it. A papal commission of historians and antiquaries had to be set up and empowered to make any necessary excavations, and if it found anything, to write a report for the pope which would make impossible any argument over whether what it had found was indeed Francis. The commission found the iron-bound oak coffin now venerated at Assisi; its report was published with papal authority in Rome in 1819, with the title 'On the discovery of the Body of the Divine Francis'.*

* J. M. de Bonis, *De inventu corpore Divi Francisci.*

BIBLIOGRAPHICAL NOTES

SOURCES

Saint Bonaventure, *Legenda B. Francisci Ass.*, Quarrachi, Rome, 1898. Eng. versions: B. Fahy, *The Greater Life of S Francis*, Chicago, 1965.

Lockhard, *The Legend of St Francis by St Bonaventure*, London, 1898.

E. G. Salter, *The Legend of St Francis*, London, 1904.

Thomas of Celano, *Legenda Prima* and *Legenda Secunda* (1227–1230 and 1247), many edns., notably d'Alençon, Rome, 1906. Eng. versions: A. G. Ferrars Howell, *The Lives of St Francis by Thomas of Celano*, London, 1908.

P. Hermann, *The First and Second Life of S. Francis*, Chicago, 1963.

The Three Companions, *S. Francisci Legendum Trium Sociorum*, ed. Faloci-Pulignani, Foligno, 1898.

G. Abate, *Legenda.... Redactio antiquior iuxta Cod. Sarnanensem*, in *Miscellanea francescana* 39, pp. 375ff.

(*The Chronicle of the Three Companions*, which claims to have been the work of three men of Assisi, and has sometimes been dated as early as 1270, contains interesting material, the value of which will be judged by the date ascribed to the work.) Eng. version: N. de Robeck, *The Legend of the Three Companions*, Chicago, 1964.

E. G. Salter, *The Legend of St Francis by the Three Companions*, London, 1905.

Thomas of Eccleston, *Fratris Thomae vulgo dicti de Eccleston Tractatus de Adventu Fratrum Minorum in Angliam*, ed. Little and Moorman, Manchester, 1951.

Jordan of Giano, *Chronica Fratris Jordani*, ed. H. Boehmer, Paris, 1908. Eng. version in Anon., *Early Franciscan Classics*, Paterson, N.J., 1962.

Blessed Giles, *Legenda B. Aegidii*, ed. Lemmens, Quarrachi, Rome, 1901.

'Legenda Antiqua', *Extractiones de legenda antiqua b.F.A.*, ed.
Lemmens, Quarrachi, Rome, 1902.
Little Flowers of St Francis, *Actus Beati Francisci et Sociorum
Ejus*, ed. Sabatier, Paris, 1902. Eng. versions: T. Okey,
The Little Flowers of Saint Francis, London, 1912.
R. Brown, *The Little Flowers of Saint Francis, First Complete
Edition, etc.*, New York, 1958.
The Mirror of Perfection, *Speculum Perfectionis S. Francisci*,
ed. Sabatier, Paris, 1898.
Speculum perfectionis, etc., ed. L. Lemmens, Quarrachi, Rome,
1901. Eng. versions: de la Warr, *Saint Francis of Assisi,
the Mirror of Perfection*, London, 1902.
R. Steele, *The Mirror of Perfection*, New York, 1963.
Papal Documents, C. Eubel, *Bullarii Franciscani Epitome*,
Quarrachi, 1908.

MODERN STUDIES

E. Brem, *Papst Gregor IX bis zum Beginn seines Pontificats.*
Heidelberg, 1911.
R. Brooke, *Early Franciscan Government.* Cambridge, 1959.
E. J. Coulton, *Two Saints: St Bernard and St Francis.* London,
1932.
Cuthbert of Brighton, *The Life of Saint Francis of Assisi.* London, 1912.
O. Engelbert, *Saint Francis of Assisi*, trans. by E. M. Cooper,
research by R. Brown. Franciscan Herald Press, Chicago,
1965.
A. Fortini, *Nova Vita di S Francesco.* Assisi, 1959.
J. Jörgensen, *Saint Francis of Assisi*, trans. by T. O'Conor Sloane.
London, 1912.
D. Knowles, *The Religious Orders in England.* Cambridge,
1948.
M. D. Lambert, *Franciscan Poverty, the Doctrine of the Absolute
Poverty of Christ and the Apostles in the Franciscan
Order, 1210–1323.* London, 1961.
J. R. H. Moorman, *The Sources for the Life of Saint Francis of
Assisi*, Manchester, 1940.
P. Sabatier, *The Life of Saint Francis of Assisi*, trans. by L.
Seymour. 2nd edn., London, 1942.

D. Waley, *The Papal State in the Thirteenth Century*. London, 1961.

F. Wiegand, *Analekten zur Geschichte des Franciscus von Assisi*. 1930.

Index